AF395138

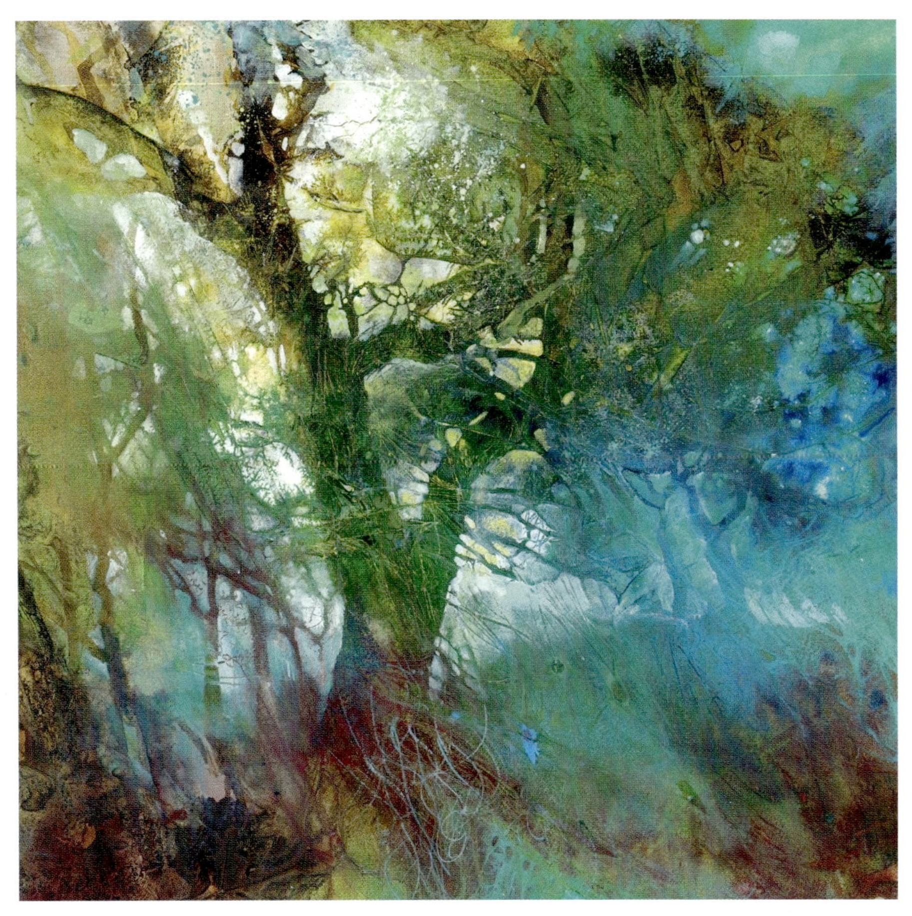

Poetic Woods

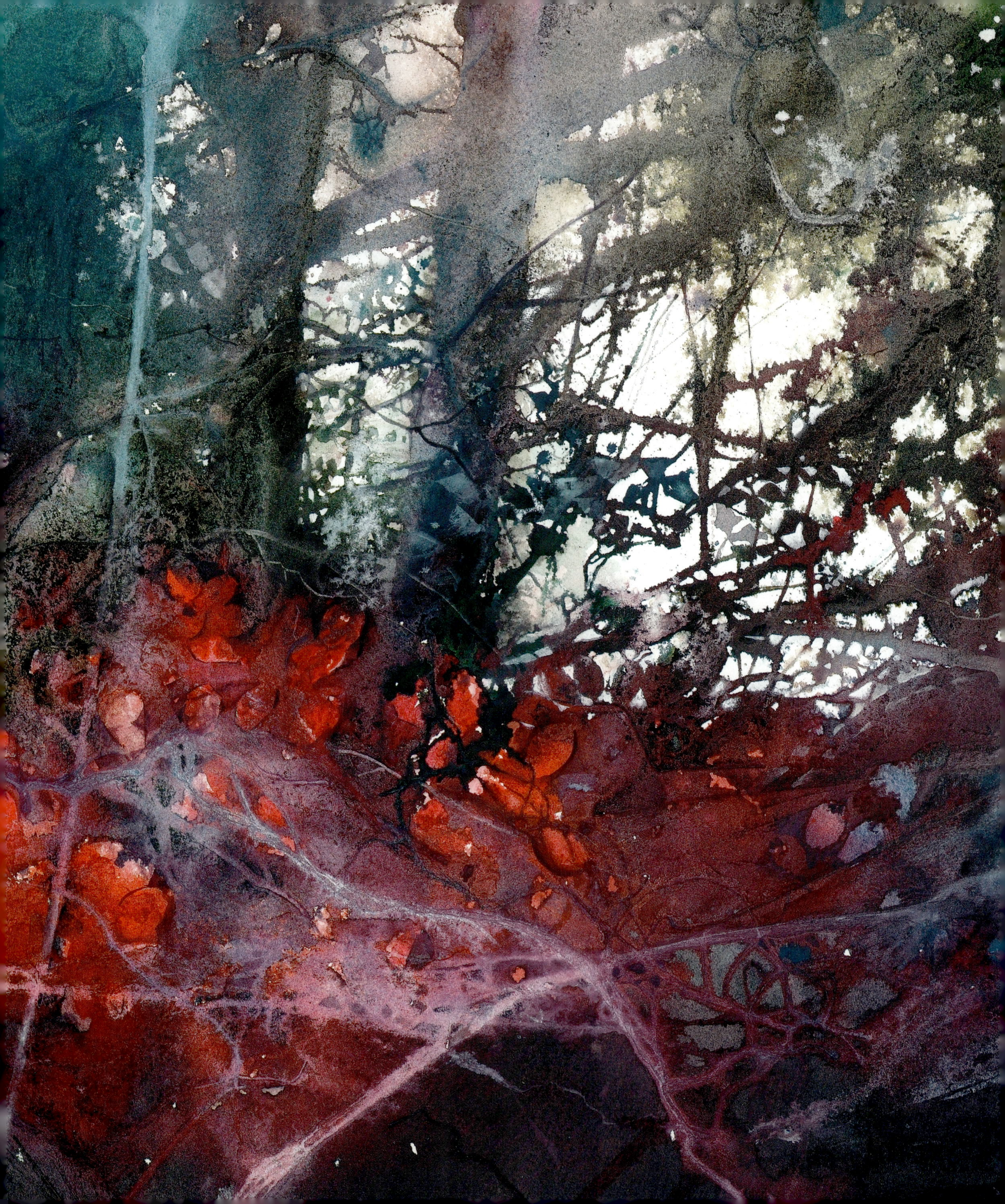

Poetic Woods

Experimental Watercolour and Collage

Ann Blockley

BATSFORD

First published in the United Kingdom in 2023 by
Batsford
43 Great Ormond Street
London WC1N 3HZ

An imprint of B.T. Batsford Holdings Ltd

Copyright © B.T. Batsford, 2023
Text and paintings © Ann Blockley, 2023

All rights reserved. No part of this publication may be reproduced,
stored in a retrieval system, or transmitted in any form or by any means,
electronic, mechanical, photocopying, recording or otherwise,
without the prior written permission of the copyright owner.

ISBN: 9781849948081

A CIP catalogue record for this book is available from the British Library.

30 29 28 27 26 25
10 9 8 7 6 5 4 3

Reproduction by Rival Colour Ltd
Printed by Leo Paper Products, China

This book can be ordered direct from the publisher at the website
www.batsfordbooks.com, or try your local bookshop.

Distributed throughout the UK and Europe by Abrams & Chronicle Books,
1 West Smithfield, London EC1A 9JU and 57 rue Gaston Tessier, 75166
Paris, France

www.abramsandchronicle.co.uk
info@abramsandchronicle.co.uk

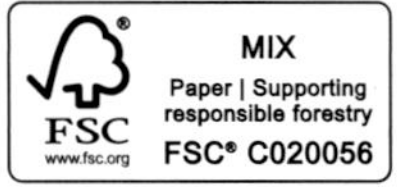

Contents

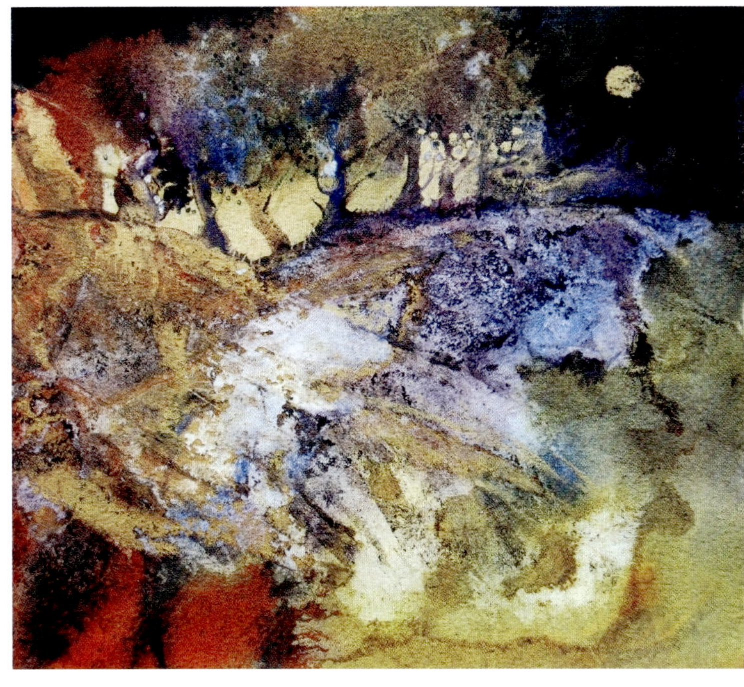

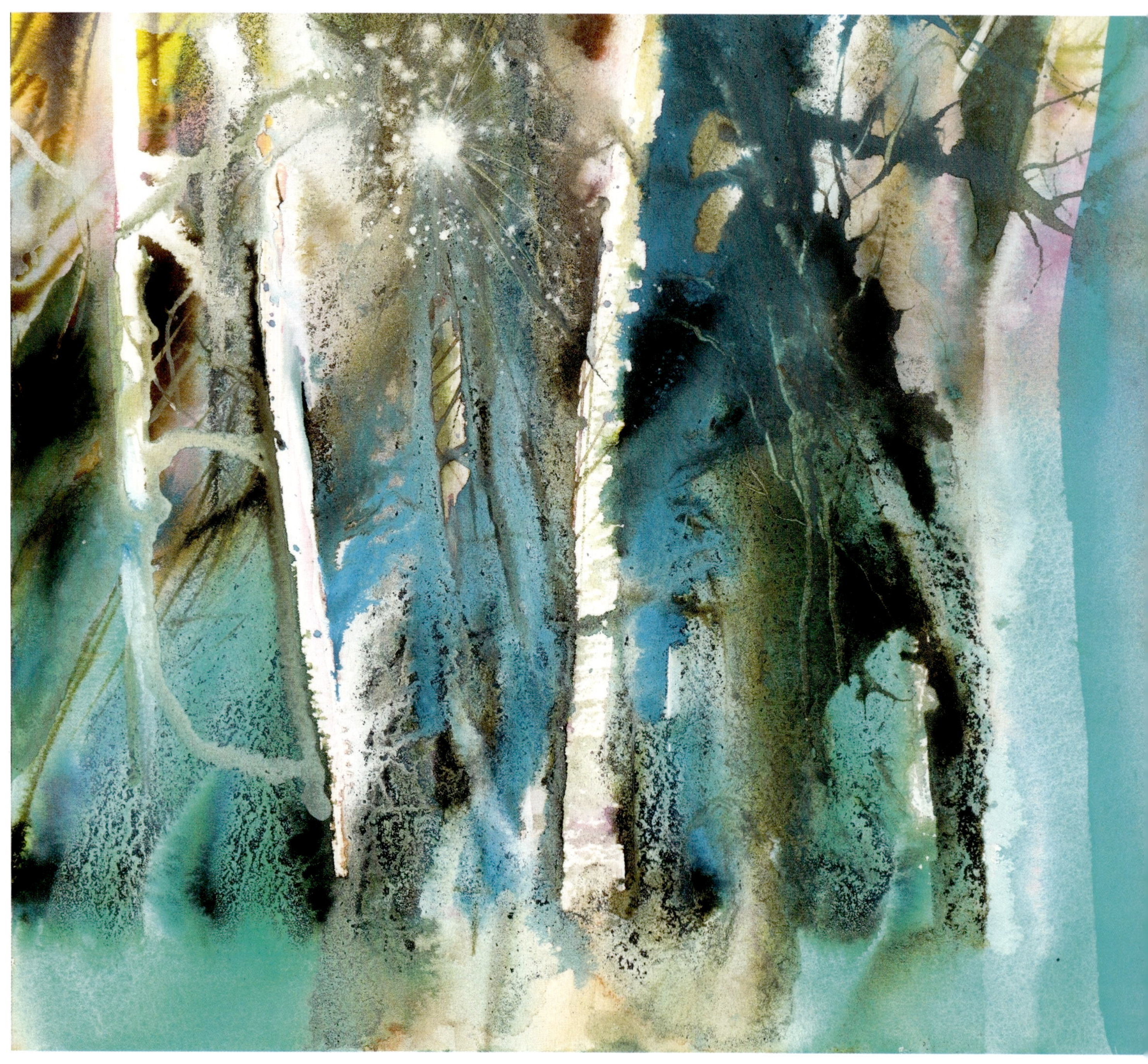

Above: By the Light of the Silvery Birch

Introduction

In *Poetic Woods* I explore ways of using watercolour and collage to create lyrical and atmospheric interpretations of our woodlands. I start with practical information about making marks that seem especially appropriate for capturing aspects of woods and trees. These tools and tips are there to help you pursue your own versions of these subjects, together with examples of my own in the section called Poetic Interpretations (see page 69), to inspire you and give further advice. The final chapter, Through the Seasons: A Personal Project, is based on my own woodland garden and is intended to stimulate you to recognize and develop your unique interests and voice.

I strongly feel that true learning is best achieved through personal experimentation, trial and error, failure and success. A guiding hand from someone with experience is useful in terms of tried-and-tested techniques and tips, but how you apply these and develop them into creative expression only progresses through practice and play. This book sets about encouraging you to do this using examples and ideas to kindle and spark your imagination. This is not a book about how to paint a tree. It is more of a woodland celebration inviting you to enter an alternate reality and paint in a poetic way or write in a painterly way. Let us turn the world upside down and stand the pond trees on their heads. Let us slip into a leafy dreamworld and join Puck, Cobweb and Titania. Let us be green outlaws, defying rules and flouting convention like Robin Hood. Let us shake off our comfortable spaces and joust with thorns and nettles. Life is not always well in the woods and the challenges of being creative echo the different faces of nature, both cruel and kind. Let's enter with an open mind to forage for ideas.

Creativity through trees

My painting life constantly evolves, and it has been a natural and instinctive progression for me to move towards tree subjects, as if I am going back to my roots. When I was born, my father had a house built at the edge of a wood on Beechwood Lane. My childhood was spent playing among the beech, oak, rhododendrons and horse chestnut trees. I now have a house with a magical, wild-wooded garden. It feels like living within a folkloric fairy tale and that I am still breathing my childish dreams. I would love to think that by sharing them with you it might inspire you to express your own fantastical ideas. Woodlands are inspirational places and I think most of us feel a strong connection with these primeval sites. Underground, in the hidden mystical world of the forest, roots and fungi connect and spread, helping each other in ways that we can only begin to understand. Earth is full of wonder, so let us celebrate it through art in the kaleidoscope kingdom of the trees.

In my book *Creativity Through Nature*, I explored how reconnecting with the natural world might help negotiate a way out of artist's block. During this nature pilgrimage, I had fun with re-wilding experiments, including how to use more sustainably sourced art materials. Refreshed and stimulated by these explorations, I assessed the findings. My conclusion was to reduce

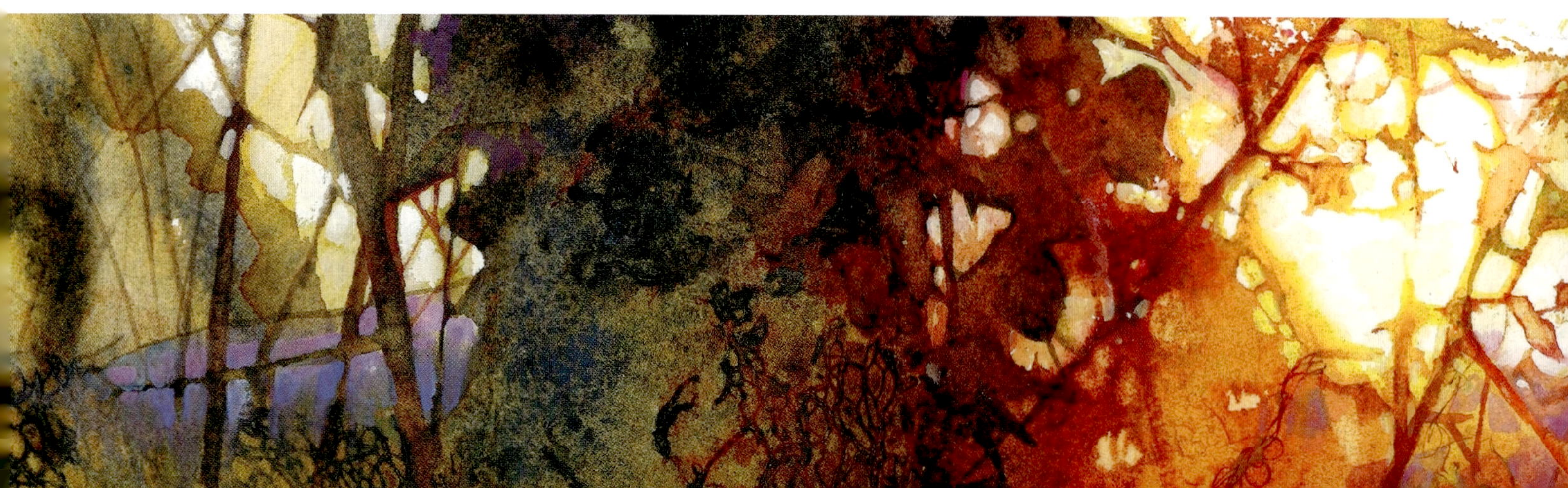

what I purchase where possible and only use fancy 'products' when deemed
necessary to their creative purpose. I continue to use water-based mediums,
such as watercolour, ink and gouache, which feel like they have a close affinity
with trees and nature. I also concluded that collage is a useful way forward
from an ecological perspective. The only essential bought product is glue
– almost everything else can be gleaned from recycled materials, including
elements from discarded paintings. It is a satisfying way to create new-style,
contemporary watercolours, where further layering and improvements are
easily possible.

Collages are visual poems where you can superimpose veils of surface and
image. Snippets that remind you of an elusive reality are woven together in
ensembles that can be childish, quirky, romantic or even nightmarish. They
are like dreams in which messages dissolve and fuse in extraordinary ways.
When I visit woods to paint, I often find it hard to settle in front of a single
view and trap it in a rectangle. All the surrounding sights, sounds, smells and
previous memories build a bigger picture. Using collage is a poetic way to
mirror this amalgamation of experiences. It can blur and fragment images
just as atmospheric watercolour can be enigmatic, with its melting edges and
expressive textures. Both artforms use mark-making as simile to represent
subject and this book explores these two genres.

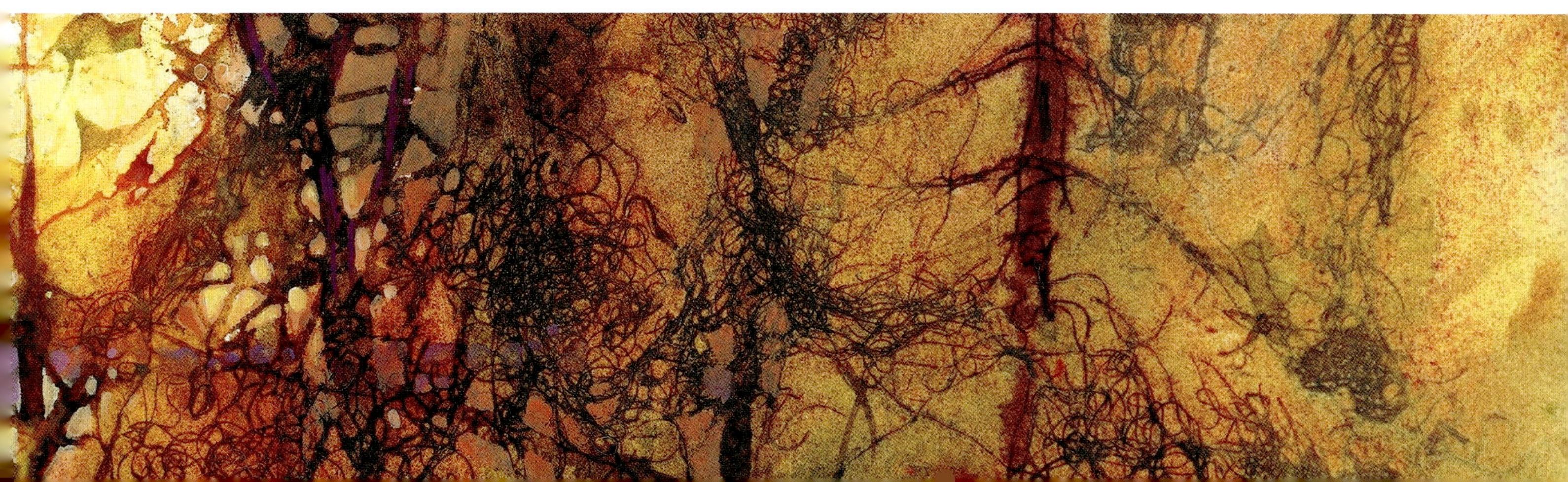

Poetic painting

Finding a title for a book to summarize its unique emphasis is something I always consider carefully. This time, I looked for a word that I felt described my style of artwork and came up with 'poetic'. This led me to question what gives a painting that particular quality. What kind of marks and interpretations might we choose to create a visual poem? In the context of writing I have mainly confined myself to prose, which seems more ordinary, using everyday language with conventional grammar – like these sentences and paragraphs. I think of poems as being symbolic, imaginative, emotional forms of expression. I compared this to the way that paintings range from detailed representation (a kind of visual prose), to spontaneous abstract expressionism and every variation in between. I realized that the boundaries between all mediums and genres are blurred. Writing can flow between prose and poem, and veer from formal structures to more abstract. It was time to explore how both my writing and painting could become more poetic by letting go of limiting beliefs.

'The heaventree of stars hung with humid nightblue fruit.'
James Joyce, Ulysses *(1922)*

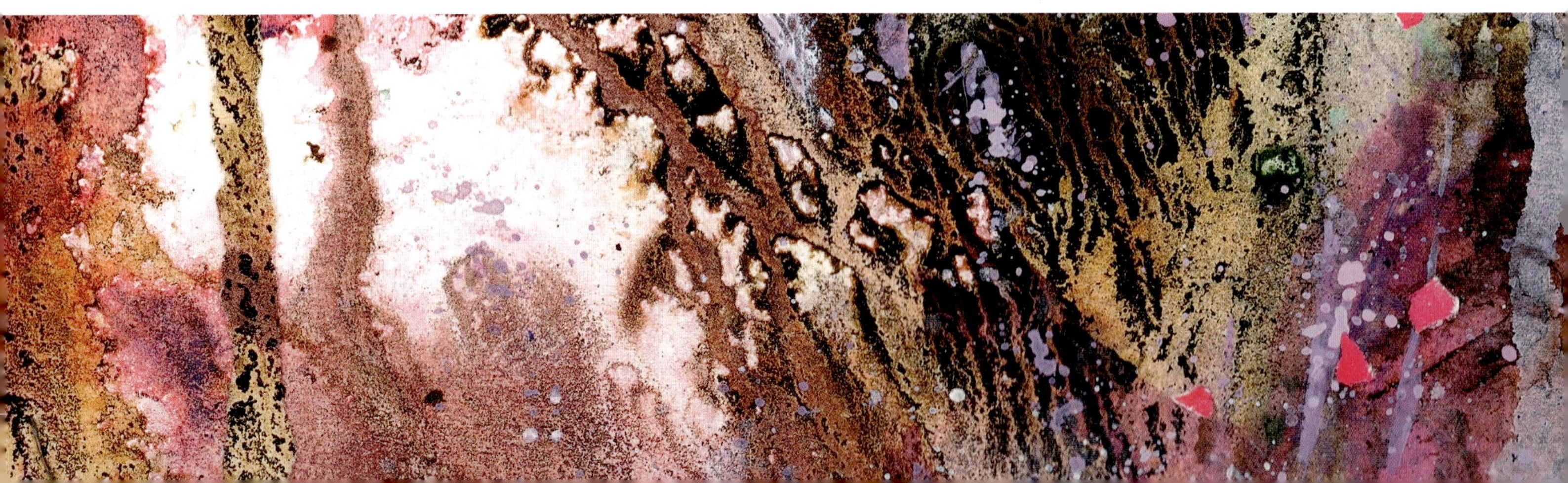

My dream is to write poems, although I am terrified of appearing silly or banal. If I am afraid of being judged, it may not seem logical to include fledgling poetry here! My reason for doing so is clear – I want to set an example about 'having a go', taking risks, doing something new that may be difficult. As I progress through the dwindling time we have, I want to continue taking on challenges, not with the sole aim of being 'good', but to enjoy the pleasure of trying. Once I had got over the self-doubt that I felt on reading 'proper' poets – Dylan Thomas, Ted Hughes, James Joyce – I reminded myself to just enjoy it. On this basis, I have scattered my own verses throughout the book, to echo the sense of childlike wonder in the magic of nature that I aim for in my paintings. I hope that this example and my practical tips for using poetic licence will help you to create your own lyrical interpretations of the woods and all that lies within.

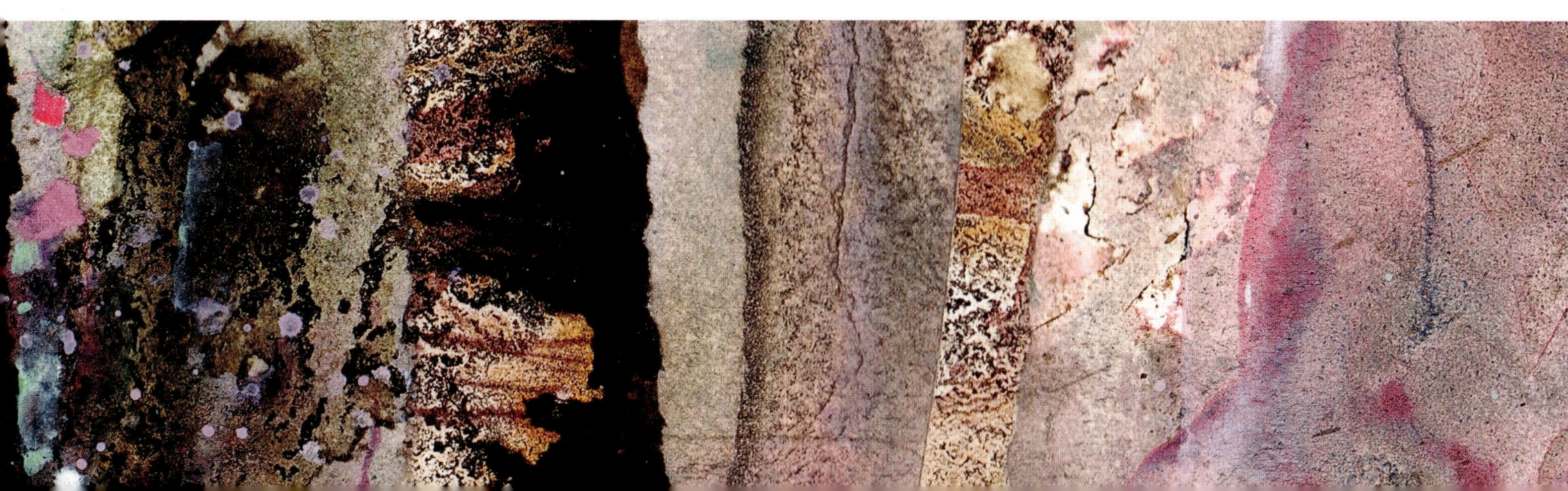

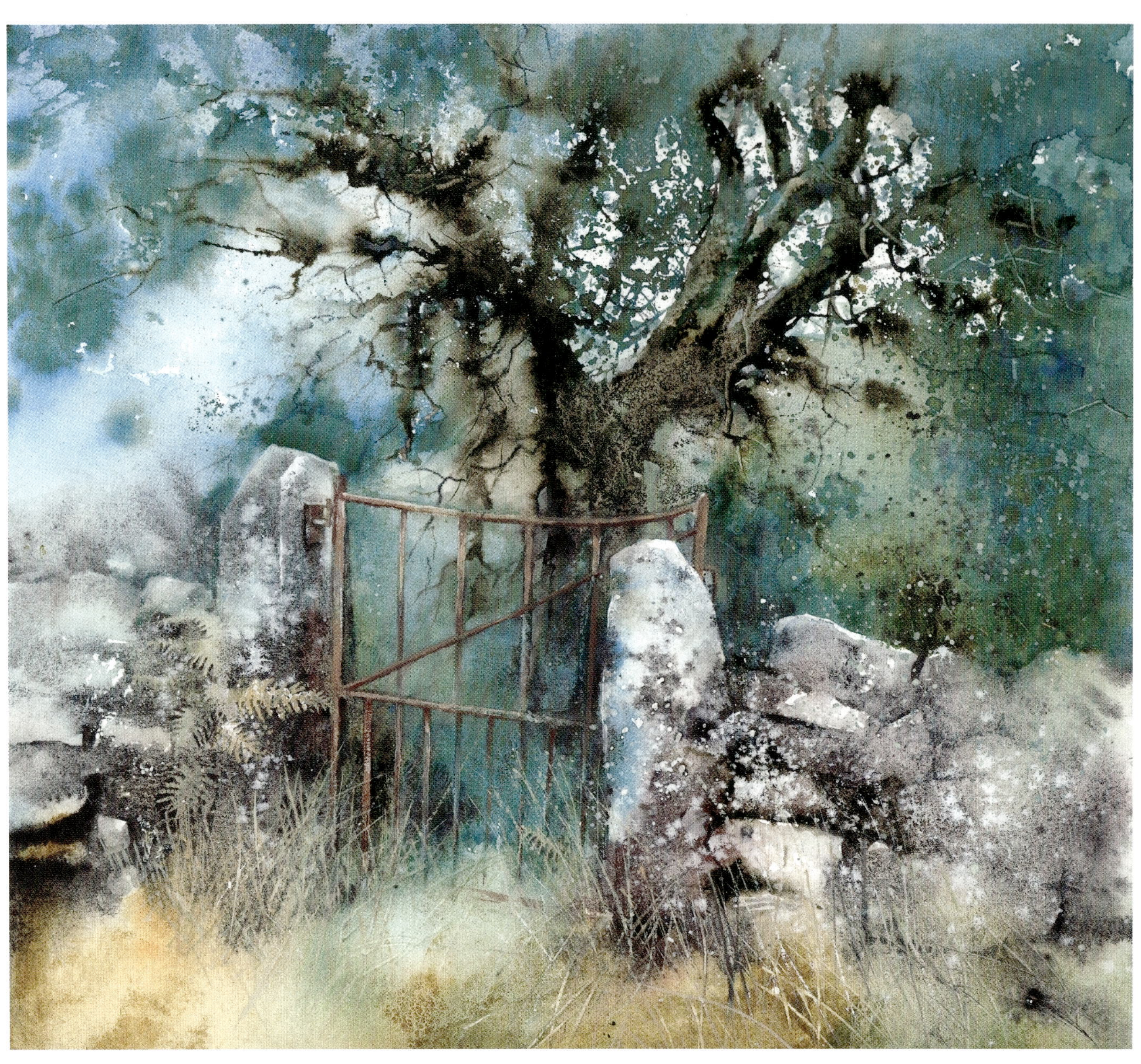

Above: Beyond the Old Iron Gate

Watercolour and ink on paper.

Welcome to the Forest

Welcome to the forest,
but only enter if you dare
to face your childish fears,
and play without a care.

There will be threat and danger
within these wildwood tangles,
where all the brambles scratch,
and the woven ivy strangles.

Creative paths do wane and wax.
Doubt hides behind each tree.
But as each cycle starts again,
hope lies in bud and bee.

So make your brush a magic wand.
Let ink become a mystic spell,
to paint each leaf and verdant frond,
and capture sounds and smell.

Enter this tinted paper glade.
Push aside the rustic gate.
Walk into your woodland dream –
See what wonders lie in wait.

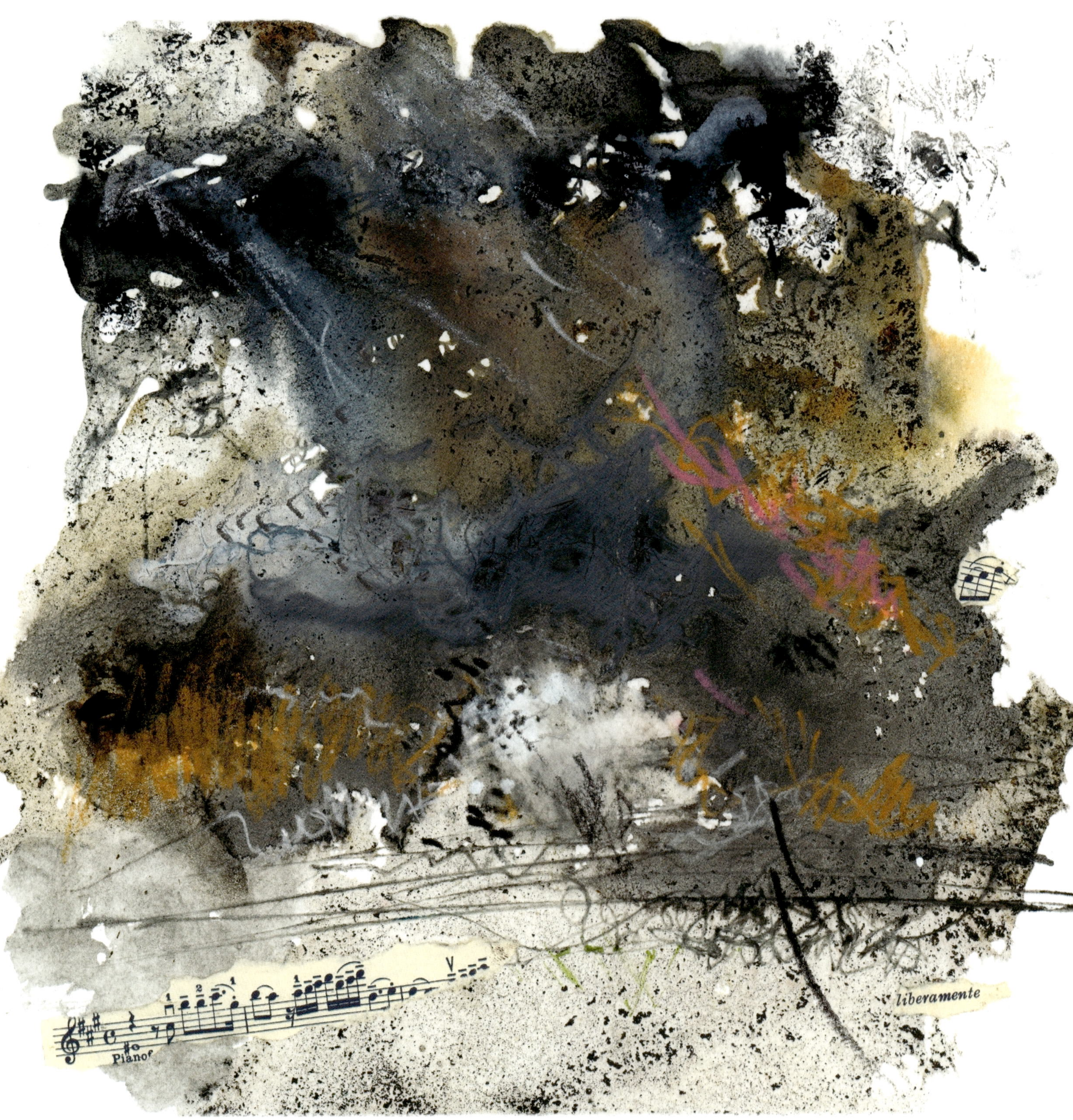

14

Woodland mark-making

Poetic Woods is a book about making woodland-inspired marks, textures, patterns and shapes. Watercolour and water-based mediums or collage are used in ways that evoke a mood or atmosphere to remind you of something seen in the woods, or perhaps dreamed or imagined. These are marks that suggest and celebrate in a poetic way the potent tangible sights, as well as the less easily defined emotions created or discovered through an immersion in the forest environment or a connection with trees. Through scrape and dribble, blotting and distressing, we will let paint reflect the flow of nature. We shall explore and experiment with ways that connect to the life force of trees, the variety and relentless cycle of decay and regeneration. Peeling back and building up the layers of our imagination, we use collage to encompass ideas that tell stories and visual poems in an organic, tactile, inventive style that can juxtapose and superimpose different dialects.

From a practical point of view, we will look at ideas for painterly, impressionistic methods to represent branches, twigs, leaves, bark, groups of trees, distant wooded landscapes, forest floor, foliage colour and other abundant delights. The watercolour techniques can be used to create complete paintings or pieces for inclusion in collage work. We will sketch using different tactics and a variety of tools, including photography.

Left: The Distant Woods Are Singing

Watercolour, gouache, liquid charcoal, crayon and collage.

Messy beginnings

Woods are messy places with wild scrambles and tangles of colour and
texture. Neat paint application is inappropriate here. Nature creates a joyous
cornucopia of shape and colour that is broken and blended by shadows and
dappled light. This can be echoed in the way you paint – especially with
water-based mediums where colour flows, following gravity and reacting to
the underlying surface textures. Wet paint explores paths through the surface
of different papers from smooth to rough, like a stream through a forest
that meanders around rocks and roots. Play with this idea in mind. Work on
different watercolour papers or create your own unique irregular surfaces.

You could either layer scraps of different paper types together with glue or roughen up the surface with applications of gesso. Whatever you choose, let your paint play. It has the best ideas. Learn by enjoying it. Nudge the paint, tilt it, add watery washes to thick, creamy mixtures, splash and blot. Let paint flood into back runs. See how the possibilities can mimic the shapes of the clouds above the canopy, the cumuli of distant summer trees, the earth, peat or rock of the forest floor. Try not to be too controlling. Let the paint speak its enigmatic poetry. But just as nature, if left to its own devices, can turn to chaos, let's learn how we can work alongside it, gently managing our unkempt artworks, developing and enhancing these beginnings. Try painting different versions on dry or damp paper, either wetting one area or the whole sheet. Draw into some of them with crayons or pastels. It is an opportunity to experiment and loosen up.

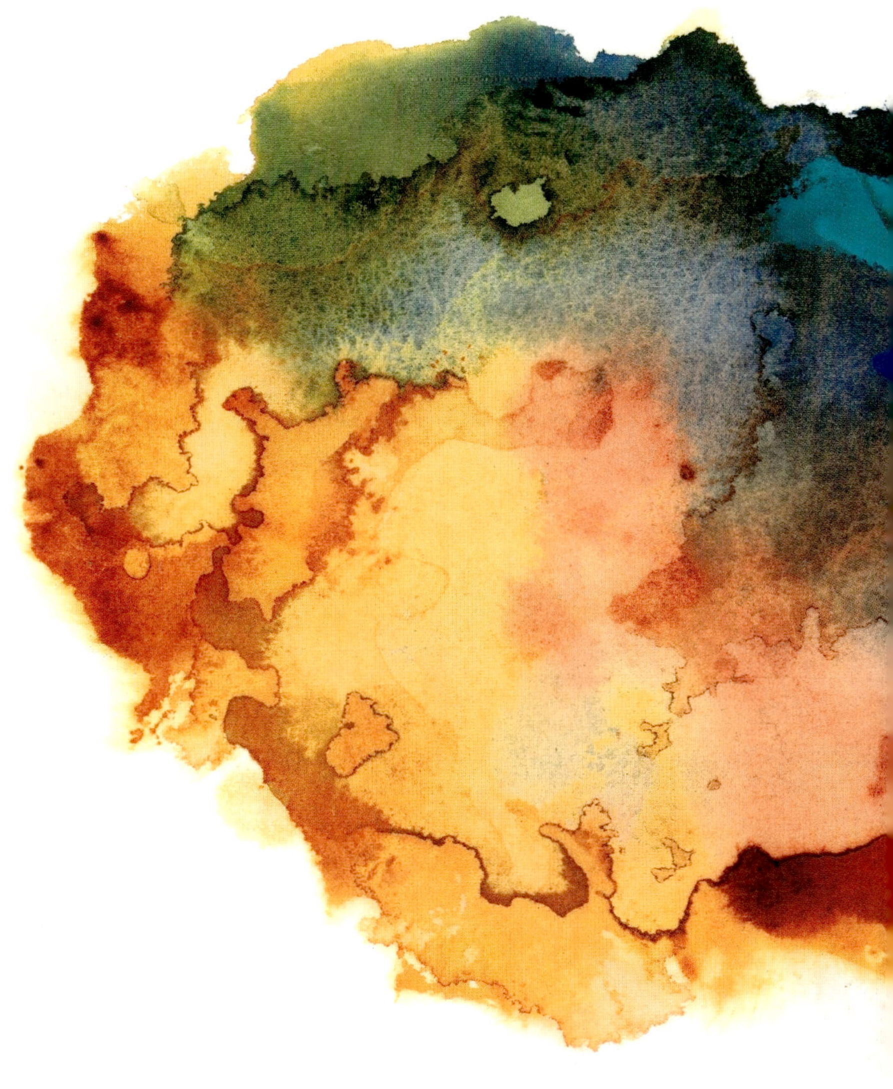

Left: Messy watercolour washes.

A wet-into-wet wash made with diluted translucent watercolour contrasts and flows into another area applied with stronger colours. Here and there the pigment clashes and forces adjacent patches of paint to move, causing ragged marks. Thicker, more opaque paint splashes have not mixed into the underlying wash, causing more defined circles of pigment. These untidy, varied combinations of interest remind me of the light and shade of forest.

Right: Back runs and blotting.

Irregular markings are formed within variegated washes by adding new diluted pigment or water as the initial colours begin to dry. Similar blotchy effects, like those seen in areas of foliage, foreground or tree trunk patterns, can be made by blotting damp areas of wash.

Dribbles

I do love to dribble! There is something very satisfying about allowing paint and water to find its own way around a surface. It can be a completely random ramble, or you can use a modicum of control by creating pools of liquid colour, then tilting the board and letting gravity do the work in different directions. If you are using a flexible surface like paper, you can bend or curl it to encourage the movement and flow in a way that suits your composition. It is a perfect technique for conjuring branches and tree trunks in a natural way. Dribbles can be made on a plain, dry white surface for crisp marks, or on a damp background for more diffuse linear impressions. Alternatively, a coloured background could be painted first, with the dribbled effect added on top in a separate layer.

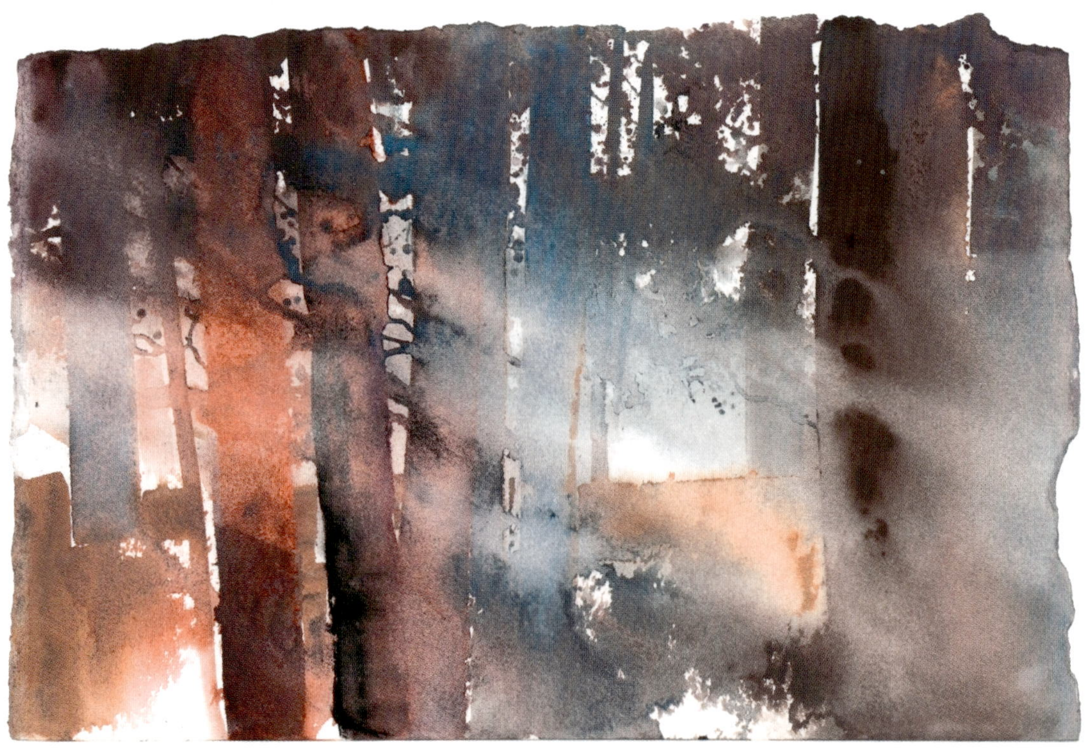

Above: Woodland Sunbeams

I painted a pattern of tree trunk columns using a big flat brush then drifted clean water over it, from the left-hand edge, in a diagonal direction that washed out soft stripes of pigment into a misty kaleidoscope of light.

It is exciting to dribble paint and inks but water itself can also be employed
for a different look. Try dripping water down the surface then drop colour into
these wet streaks. It is thrilling to see the pigment shoot along the transparent
fluid. Water can also be used to flow through drying washes, disturbing and
shifting them into atmospheric light patterns. Judging the wetness of the paint
is critical to the result. If the background is still too wet, you can end up with
a very soggy woodland. If left too long, the dry paint will stay in place. If the
latter happens you could gently blot or lift off colour with your brush – but
that would not count as a dribble!

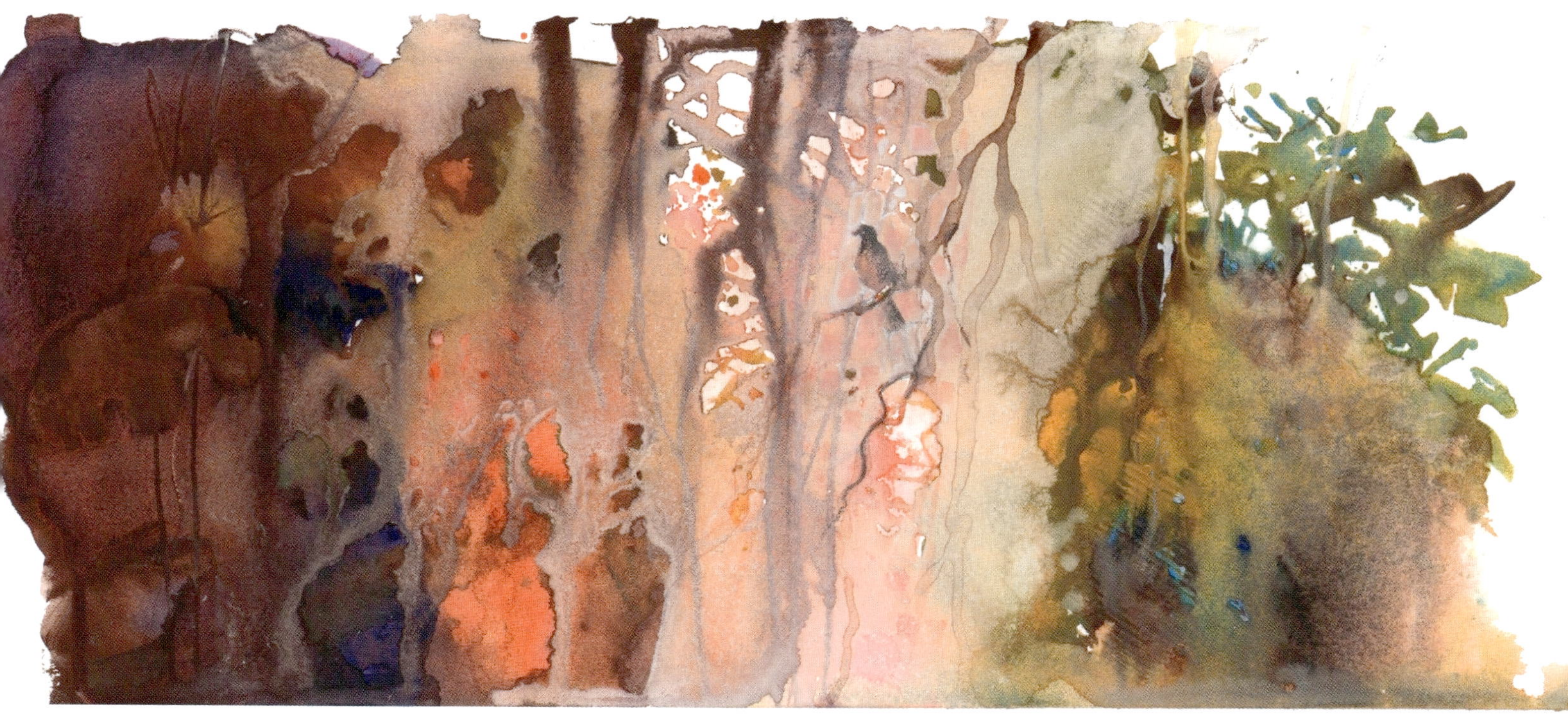

Above: A Bird in the Coppice

*Variegated washes of colour were applied including a few marks to suggest
leaves. I then dribbled opaque liquid gouache over the first layer, which smudged
and shifted the underlying wash in unexpected but satisfyingly drizzly ways.
I added a bird later to create context.*

Getting into the flow

As artists I believe we often focus too much on the end result. I think we can learn a lot and stimulate our creativity by just playing and painting for the hell of it. If we paint a series of similar pictures with no aim other than to 'go with the flow', it can be surprising what emerges. Fear and expectation are probably the two worst killers of creativity. Painting, almost as a meditation, is a great way to resist negative thoughts. It also helps us to be free and loosen up. When you paint a series of exercises you can work your way through initial, perhaps obvious pre-conceived thoughts, and move more deeply into other variations. When you work with a view to creating a series, the individual pieces do not each become so precious, and you are free to learn from your mistakes and achievements in a more relaxed way.

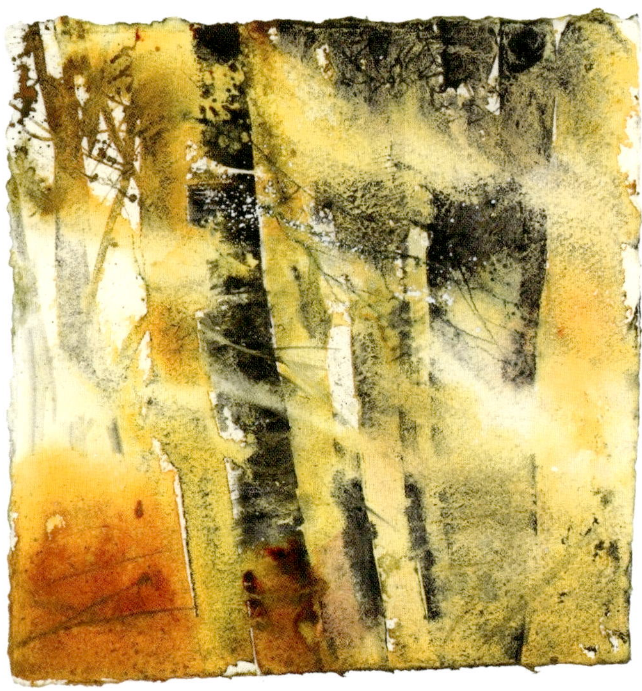 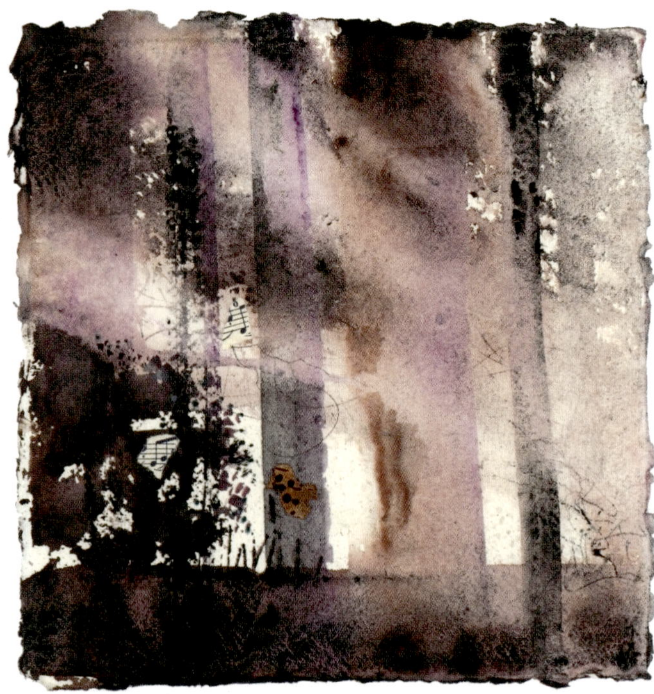

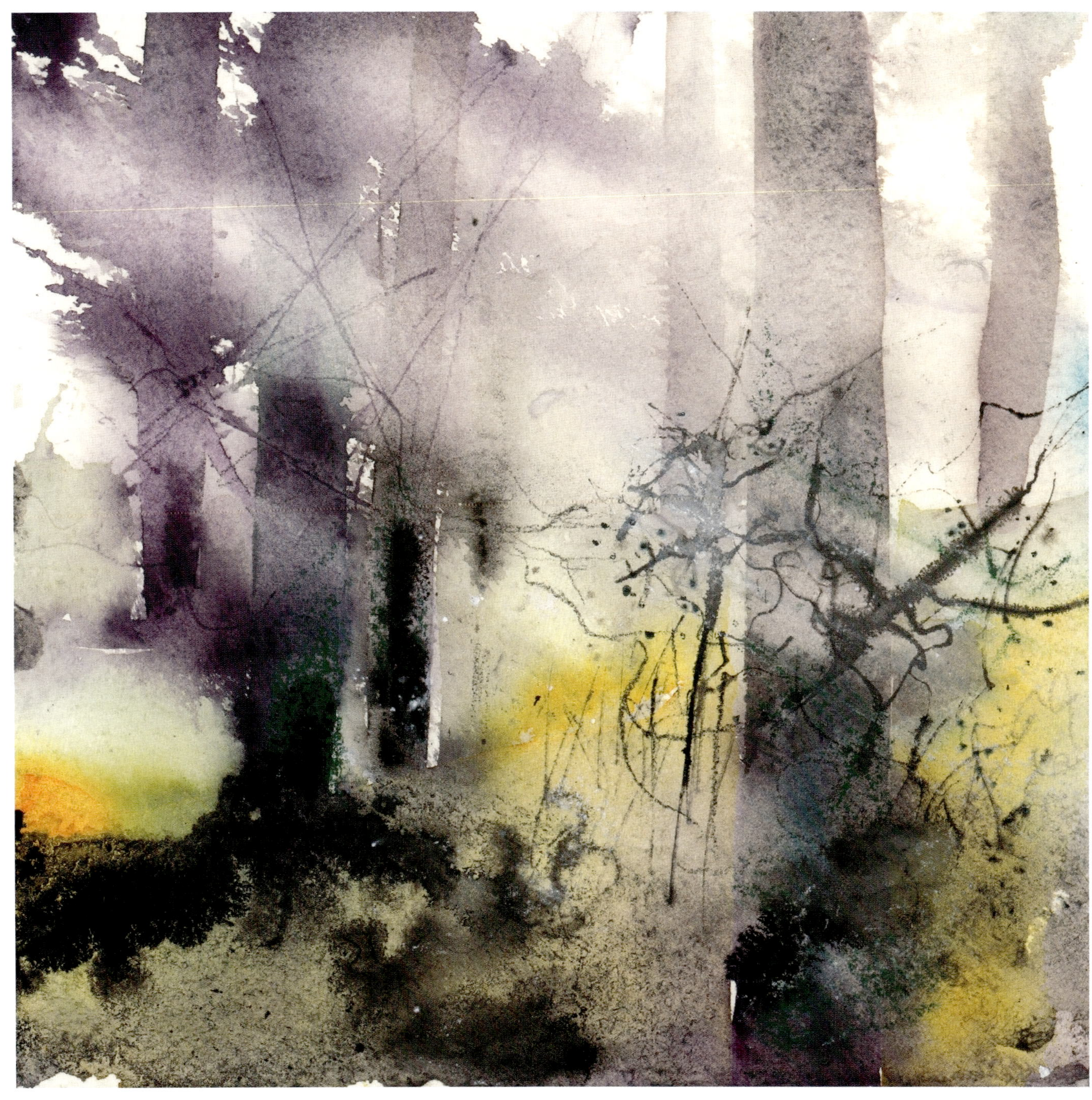

In this series of mini watercolours painted on Khadi paper I began with the vague idea of painting the light shafts filtering through the trees. As I progressed, my imagination took over, and I became increasingly engrossed in the act of making marks for their own sake.

Water spray

Try spraying surfaces with water then drop colour into it. This creates a wonderfully mottled texture that is perfect for recreating the look and feel of a woodland canopy with light shimmering through. It is best to do this with as little brush intervention as possible as brushwork tends to flatten the texture. I recycle spray bottles from the cleaning cupboard but make sure to wash them thoroughly first. In my example, I have also allowed the wet ink to dribble around the page over dry areas to form meandering, branch-like shapes.

Left: Waterspray effects

The joy of this technique is that each time is different. It is good to experiment with the amount of spray. A little often works better than more, as too much water can simply make the colour flood together into a more conventional wash.

You can gently encourage the pools of colour to travel using a tool, such as the end of your brush, or even use found material like a twig. You can try this with any wet medium, such as watercolour, gouache, acrylic or ink. Alternatively, you might try combining different mediums and watch how they react together. I have used a single monochrome ink in my examples, but you can be as creative as you wish with your colours.

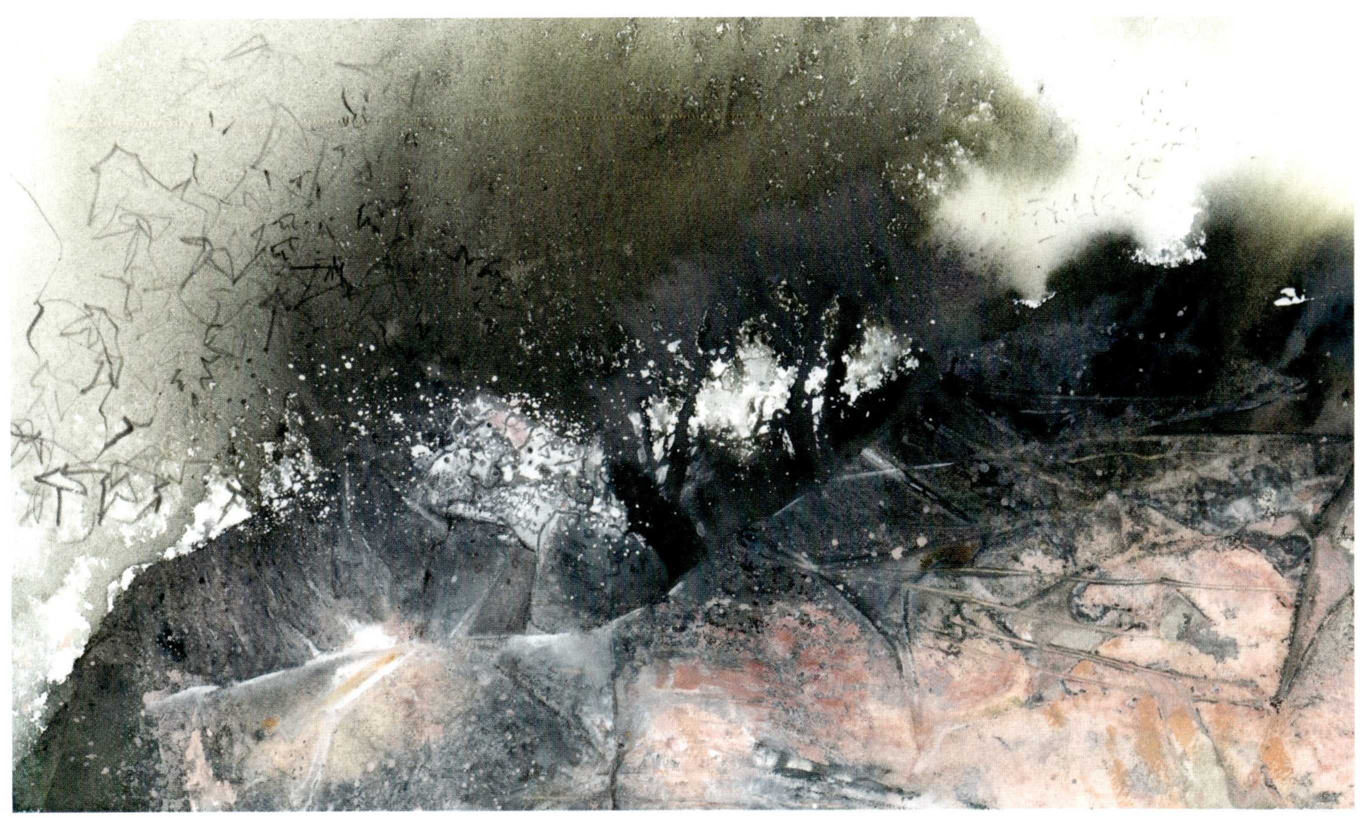

Above: Mountain Thicket *(detail)*

I poured ink onto the upper half of some sprayed paper speckled with water globules. It spread into a soft, mottled effect, like foliage blending into sky. Pigment was painted onto the dry lower area and craft tissue paper laid on to create rocky cracks and crevices. This was removed before it dried to prevent sticking. To create some movement, I pencil-scribbled into the inky section, which was now dry.

Salt

Many of you will have used salt before in your watercolours. It creates a tactile but rather recognizable effect that can dominate a painting. Salt is sprinkled into a watercolour wash at the point where it is still damp but not too wet. Let's see how we can use these ideas in ways that are not so obvious, as they can facilitate very appropriate textures for woodland subjects. Washes can be transformed into atmospheric representations of leaf, foliage, lichen and, depending on the colours used, certain tree trunks or foregrounds. You can use different-sized salt crystals, including table, rock or sea salt. I personally prefer to use salt sparingly. However, if you do use a lot, it can push wet washes into back runs, which is sometimes useful to create the idea of distant groups of leafy summer treetops.

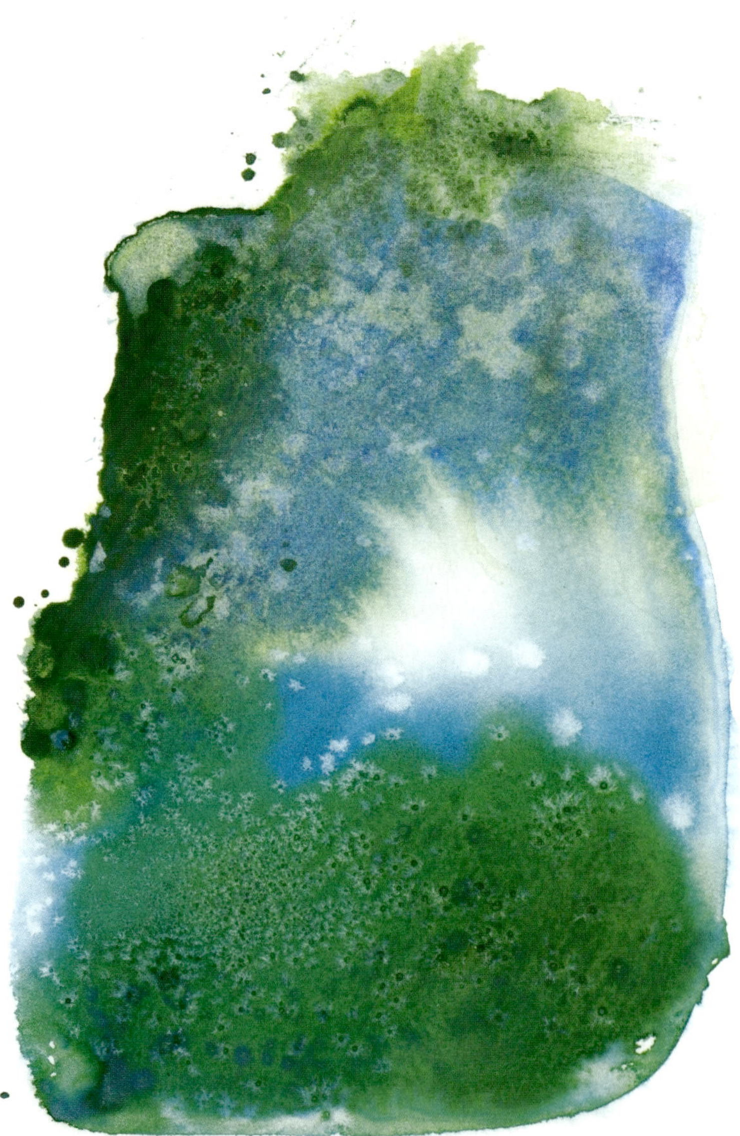

Right: Salt texture 1

This demonstrates salt added in the usual way to develop tiny, pale freckles. However, I used different-sized crystals to vary the texture and dabbed some of the salt away as it dried, which made softer shapes towards the top. The crisp 'sparkles' come forward and the blotted marks recede like the greenery of trees.

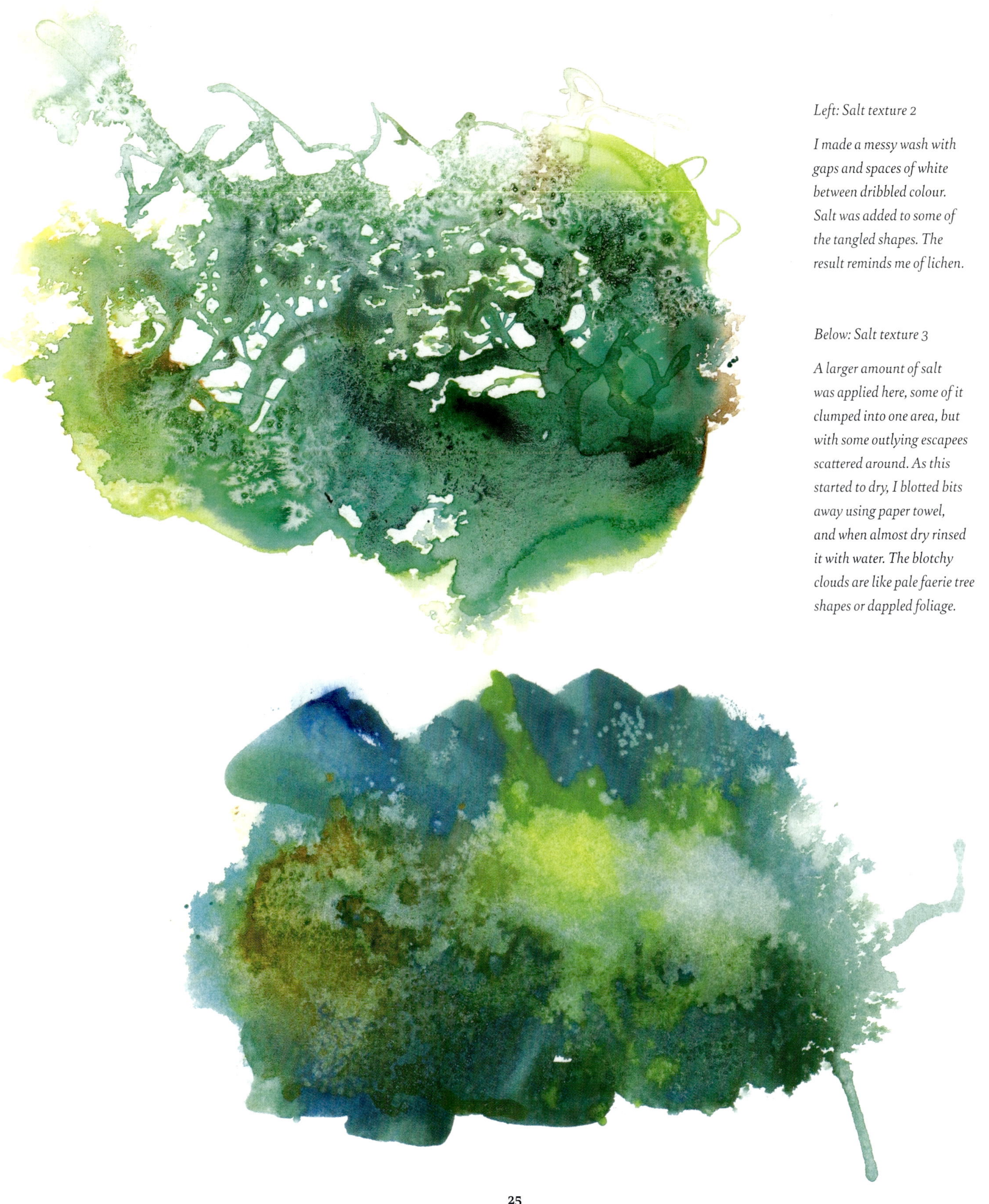

Left: Salt texture 2

I made a messy wash with gaps and spaces of white between dribbled colour. Salt was added to some of the tangled shapes. The result reminds me of lichen.

Below: Salt texture 3

A larger amount of salt was applied here, some of it clumped into one area, but with some outlying escapees scattered around. As this started to dry, I blotted bits away using paper towel, and when almost dry rinsed it with water. The blotchy clouds are like pale faerie tree shapes or dappled foliage.

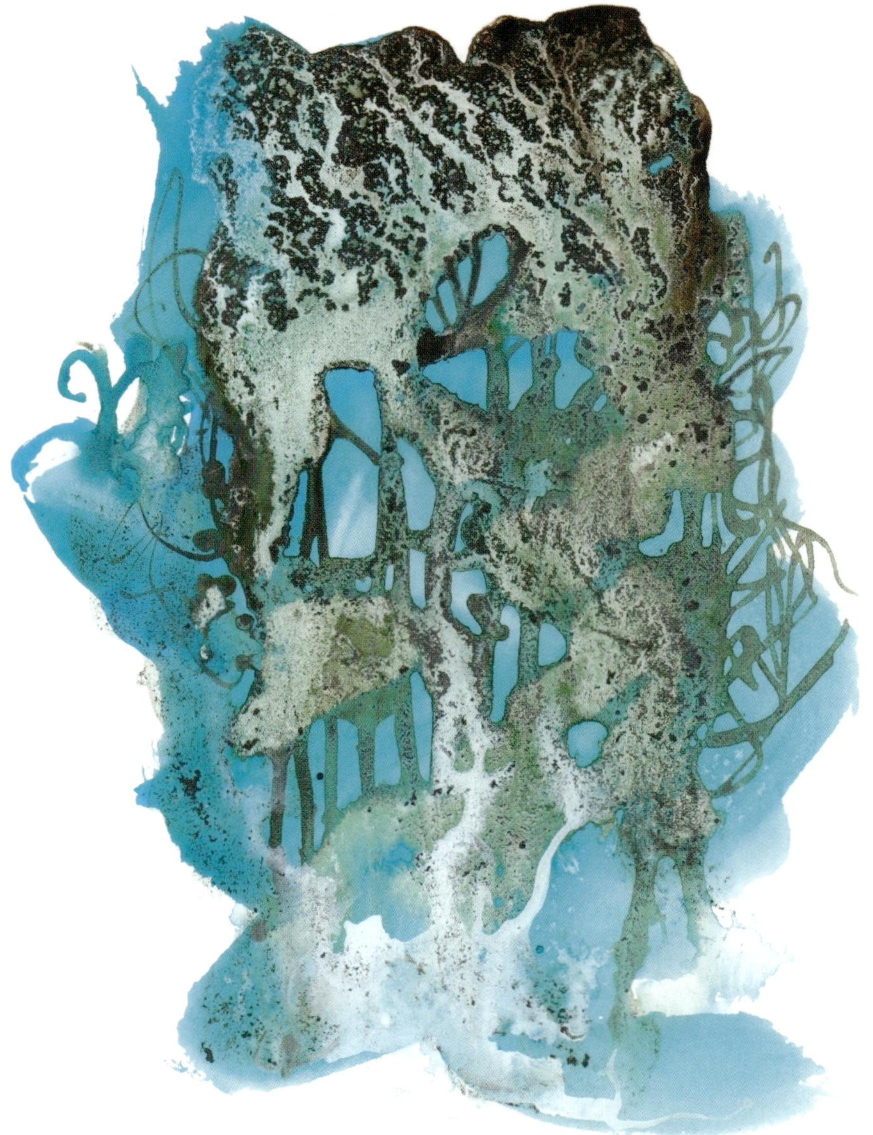

Granulation

Some paints granulate naturally. I am more interested here in making granular
marks using Winsor and Newton's granulation medium combined with
certain inks. Fairly opaque inks seem to work best as they have more sediment
in them to separate and flocculate (form small clumps). I paint a watercolour
wash first, drop ink into this while still wet and add the medium immediately
afterwards. Move the paper about to help the granulation flow through the
ink and paint, trickling in tributaries or rivulets to make root-like tendrils and
boughs. The textures can also be highly reminiscent of those in the bark of
tree trunks and the earthy leaf mould of the woodland floor.

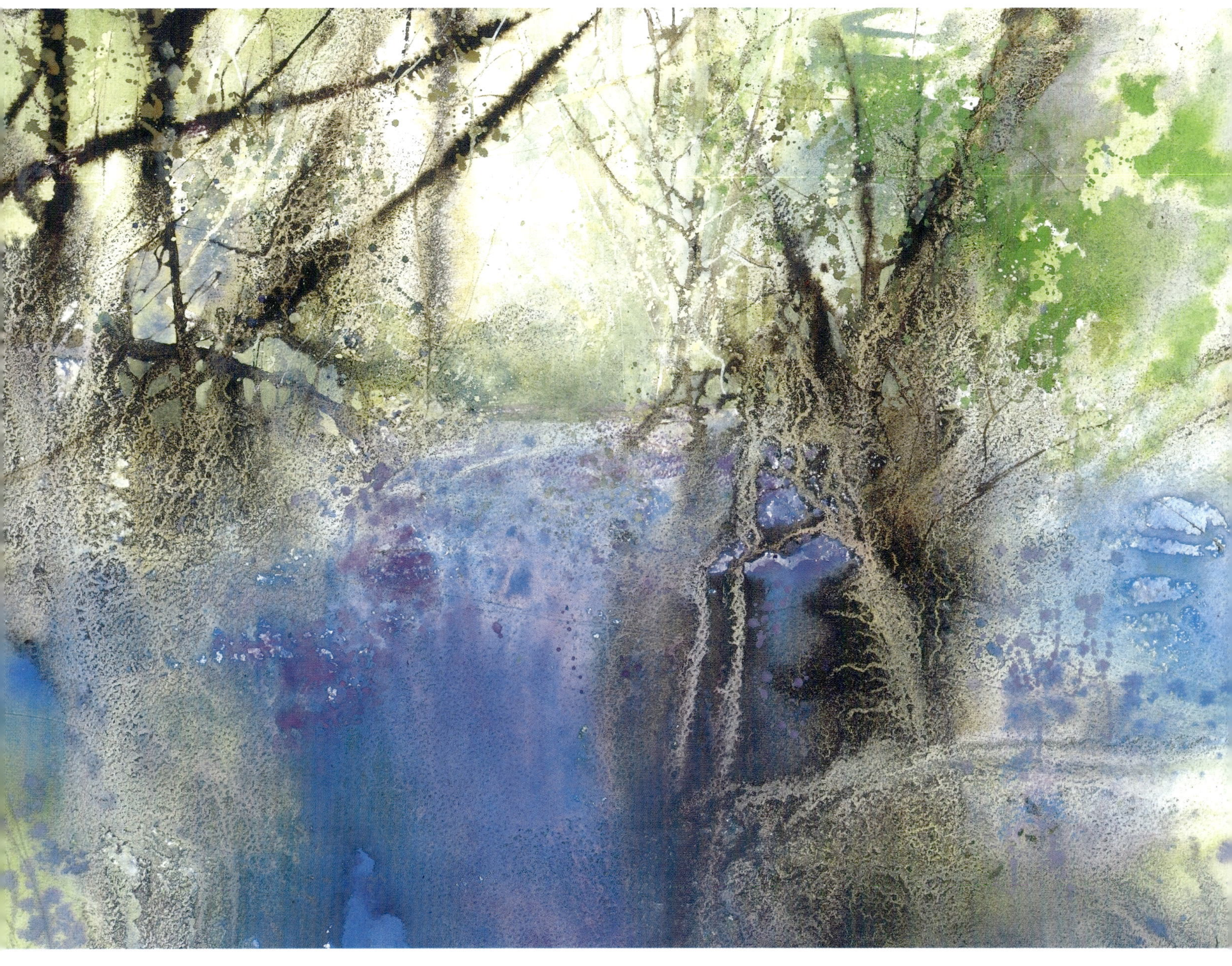

Above: Bluebell Wood Haze

*I added sepia acrylic ink to a wet watercolour wash, drawing it into tree
trunk and falling branches. I immediately dripped granulation medium
into the inky areas, moving and tilting the surface to help the mixtures
shift organically and flow in an appropriate direction. Always be
prepared for the unexpected with this method and go with the flow.*

Spatter and scrape

Here are a couple more fun methods that are great for hinting at all kinds of woody, tree-like parts. Spatter can be used to represent the shimmer and dance of foliage or the spangles of blossom. It can also add movement and an air of lively activity. Perhaps it might simply suggest the humming of bees or the urgency of fleeing birds. A basic form of spattering is to shake a loaded brush over your surface. This tends to create larger marks or blots. Smaller, more delicate specks can be made by loading the tip of a palette knife and gently flicking it or scraping through a paint-laden toothbrush to cast showers of paint dots. The medium needs to be thin enough to leave the preferred tool but concentrated enough if you want to make a strong statement. Any undesirable castaway spots can be quickly blotted or toned down while still wet.

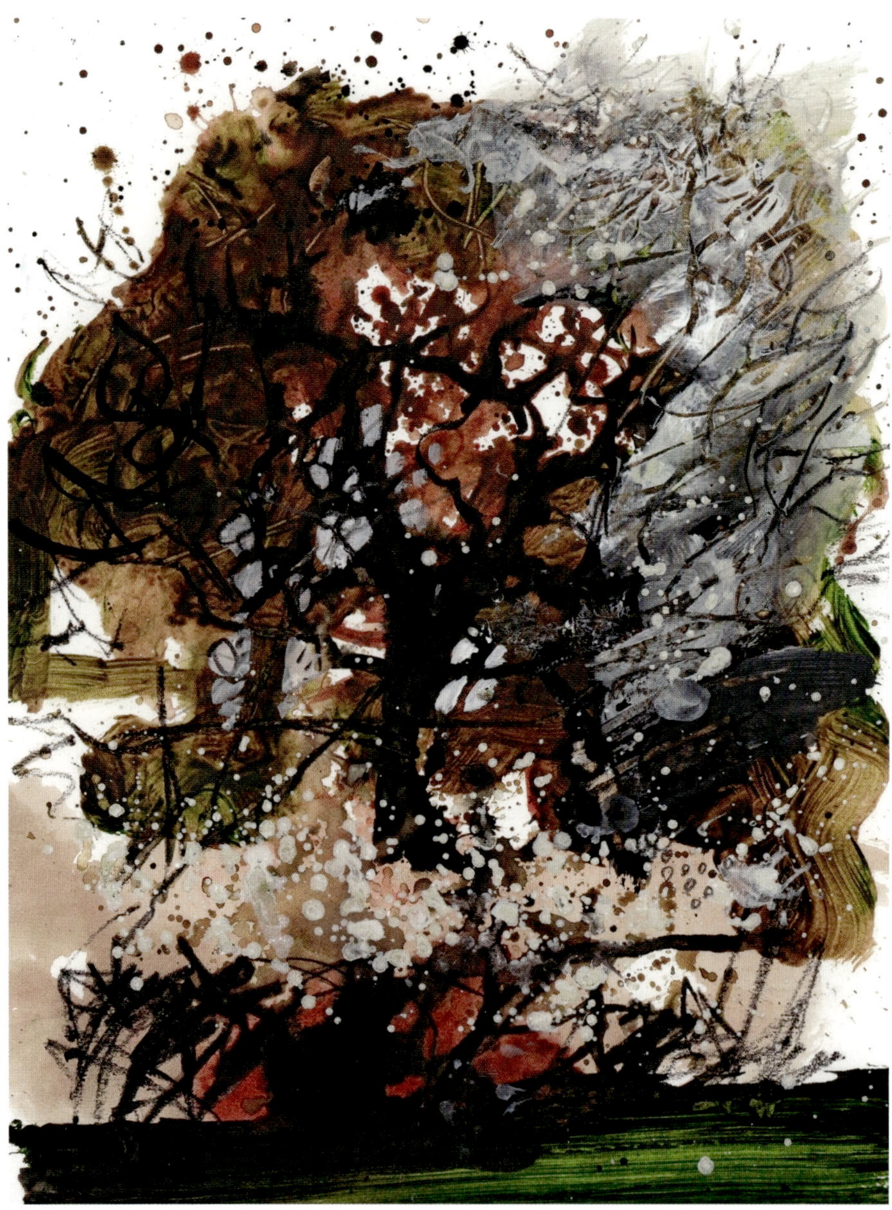

Right: A Sprinkle of Blackthorn Blossom

I made paint sketches outside in March, working quickly because it was cold. I hastily scrubbed paint onto paper using found materials as tools and spattered layers of opaque white gouache on the lower area to indicate the froth of blackthorn blossom. Darker spatters were added on the treetop behind to give a sense of urgency and movement.

Scraped marks can be used to indicate pale twigs, stems and branches. They are usually made through thicker, damp layers of paint with enough body that you do not simply dig into the surface below. I use the edge of a palette knife or scalpel but avoid using the sharp tip. If the paint is too wet, it will flood back into itself, so timing is important. You can keep testing bits in different places to see when it has reached the optimum moment. If you have used thick paint but it is already too dry, you can dampen it with a spray and try again. Remember though that this only works with mediums like watercolour or gouache that are not waterproof.

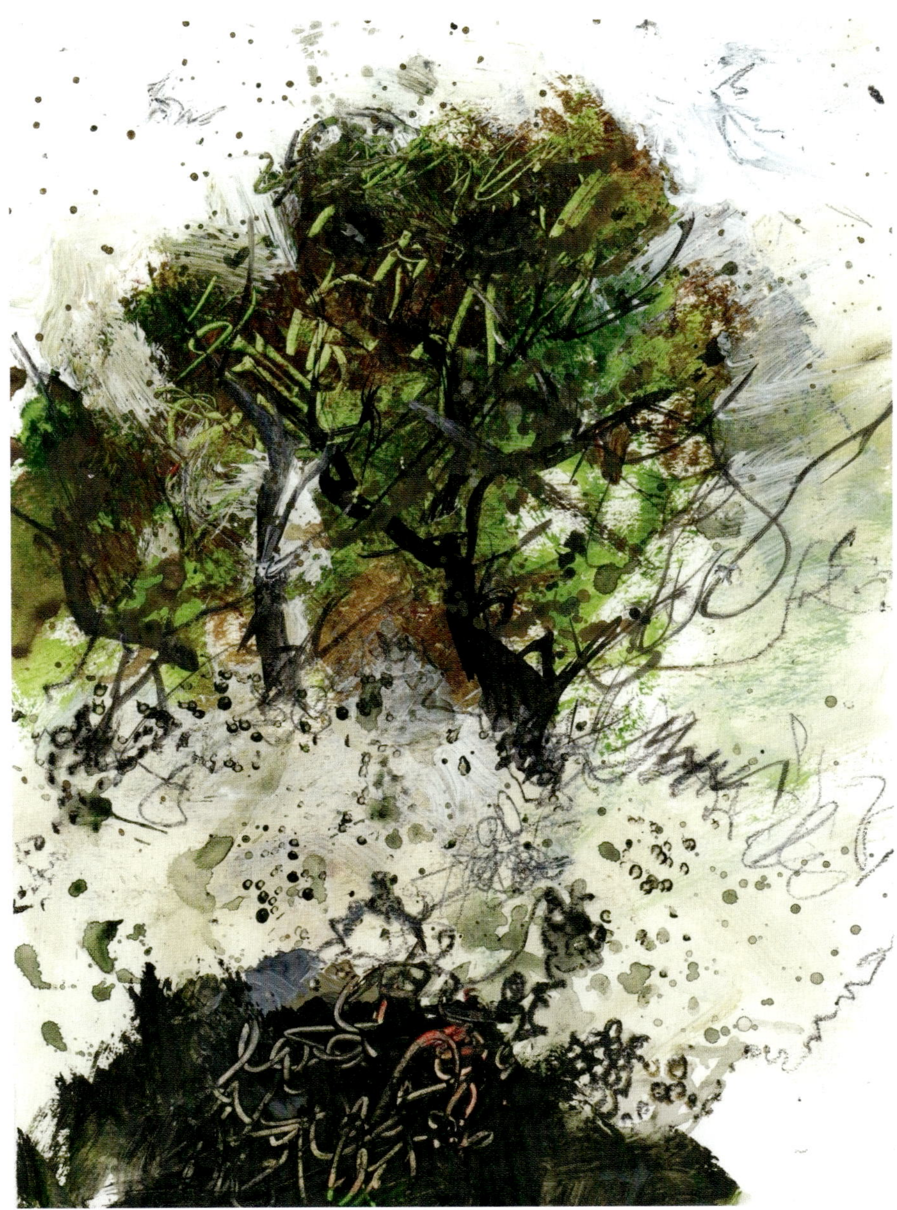

Left: Blackthorn Winter

These sketches may be scruffy but do capture something of the moment. The thick paint dried quickly in the March wind, and I was able to scrape through it almost immediately using almost calligraphic short, straight strokes or scribbles as a nod to the branch and stem shapes.

Choosing colour

Colour completely alters the atmosphere and character of a painting and choosing your palette is a critical part of planning. When water-based colours mix themselves together on the page they often create gorgeous combinations of their own, but I usually have a basic plan before I begin. As artists we can interpret a scene using poetic licence. If we want trees to be red or purple that is our creative prerogative. Your chosen palette can be based on reality or imagined versions of the subject or a combination of the two. Ideas for supplementary hues might be based on flashes of something seen near the scene, even on a previous occasion. You could, for example, add smudges of purple to over-verdant greens because you once saw orchids growing there. In woodland scenes you sometimes need to be inventive to create interesting interpretations. Although autumn woodlands can be very colourful, it is easy to fall into the trap of thinking woods are only green and brown.

I always think that by summer the trees have grown lazy, only dressing in the same old swathes of boring emerald. In certain light or in varying weather conditions, at twilight or dawn, in golden sunshine or morning mist, tedious greens magically change to many hues. It is important to remember or make note of this when the light has dulled the woods to a stagnant green torpor. In your poetic interpretations, using a variety of pigments helps to create a livelier statement. Blend blues and yellows with hints of black or reds for plenty of diversity. Make cool greens that veer towards blue and warm versions with golds and yellows. Below is a list of watercolour shades that I frequently use to mix greens. Experiment and make a note of which combinations work for you.

Right: So Doth the Woodbine Gently Entwist

This was made using several methods shown in this chapter. I began by spraying the background to create shimmering greens. These were mixed from combinations of cool blues such as Phthalo with warm Indian Yellow or Quinacridone Gold to spice up a scene that was really all one shade. The gold of the honeysuckle suggested the addition of further warm yellows within the background. This was offset by the granulated Indian ink tree trunk.

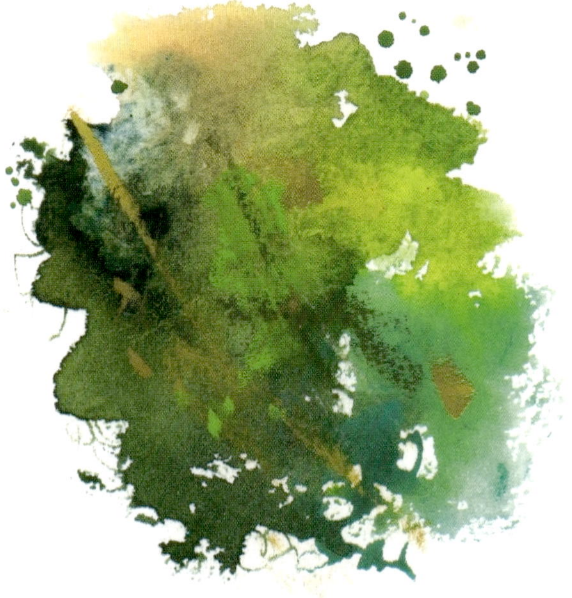

Right: Cerulean Blue, Cobalt Blue, French Ultramarine, Phthalo Blue, Indigo, Turquoise, Quinacridone Gold, Indian Yellow, any cool translucent yellow, Burnt Sienna, Brown Madder and Sepia. I do not use ready -made greens often but I like Perylene Green and Winsor and Newton's Green Gold.

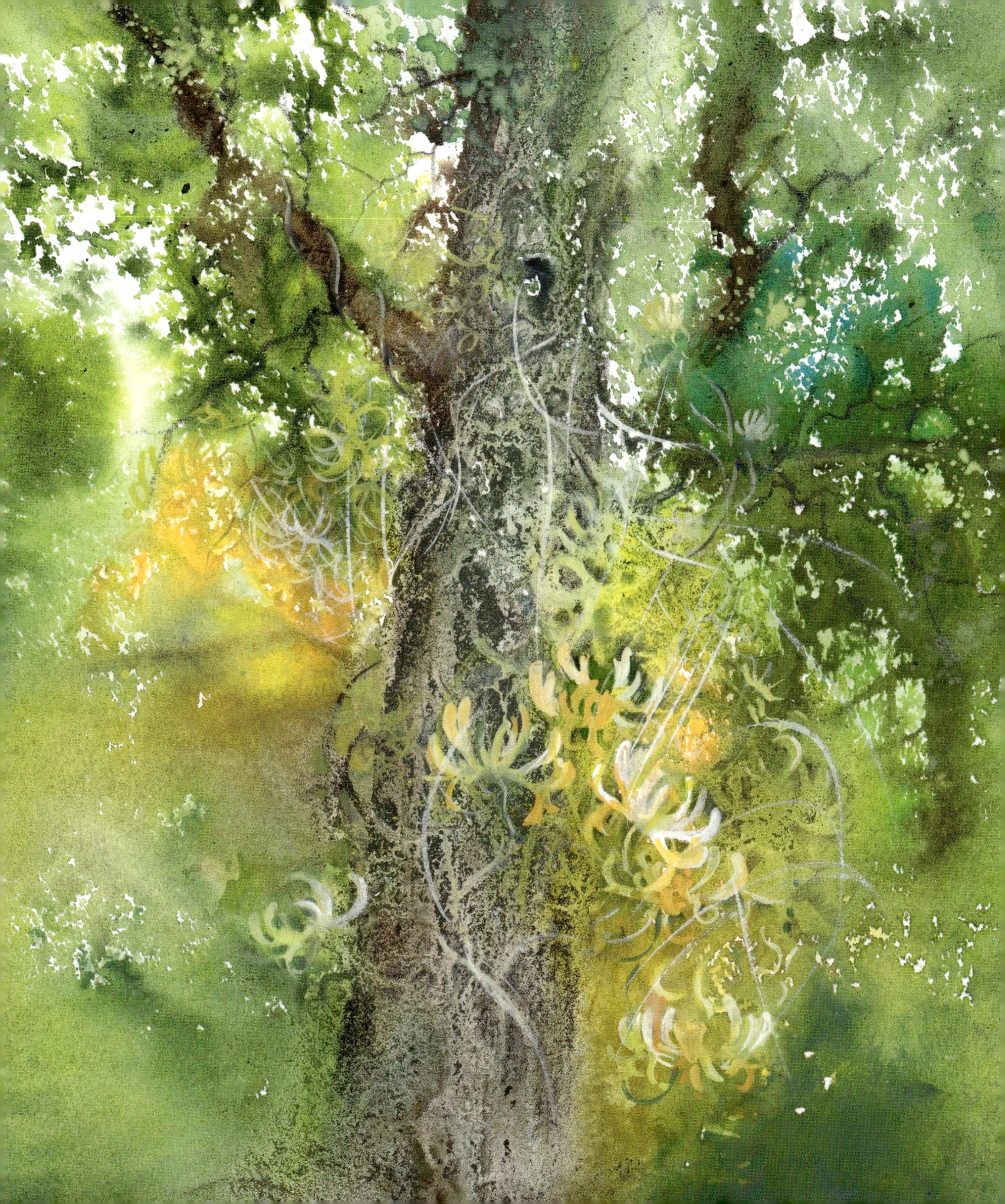

White gesso

Most manufactured gesso is acrylic-based and I only use it with discretion when it has a particular use. A big advantage is that you can paint it over all or part of 'failed' work, which avoids waste and relieves pressure to perform. The gesso layer can be scraped or drawn through while wet to reveal lines or patches of the original colour underneath. You can also try applying gesso thickly then press thin scrap paper on top. Peel this back immediately to pull the wet gesso into raised feathery effects that can be painted over when dry.

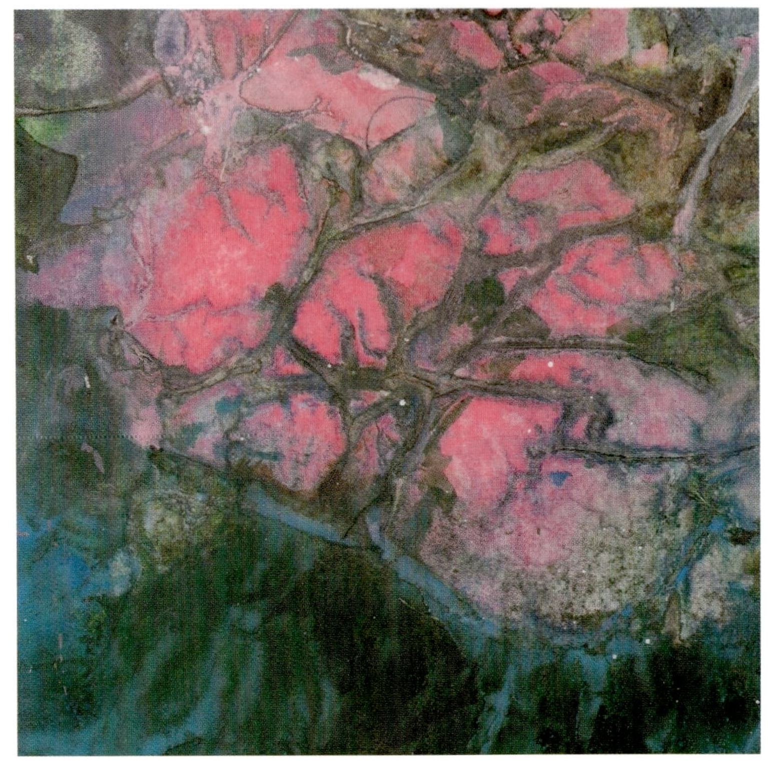

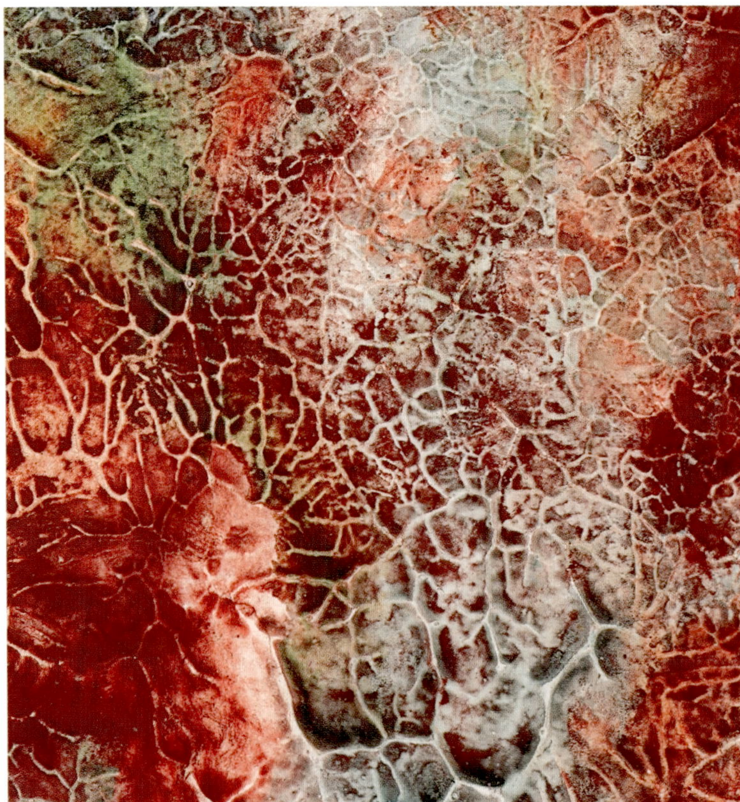

Above right: Tissue paper (and gesso) branches

Paint applied over dry gesso gathers along the raised crumpled folds of tissue paper embedded in it to describe delicate filigree branches.

Right: Textured gesso

Raised fractals created with thin printing paper and gesso can be used to represent bracken or mossy forest floor.

Flat or small natural finds can be sandwiched between layers of gesso, ensuring they are fully encompassed. Manmade materials can be included in a similar way to create unique surfaces. Crumpled thin paper like craft tissue can be thoroughly 'glued' down with gesso. The folds of each crinkle are useful for imitating the linear patterns of branches and undergrowth. When any of these initial layers are dry you can paint on top – I find that thicker paint consistencies work better on top of gesso than a thin wash. You can experiment on top of dry gesso with any of the techniques discussed in this chapter. See how the reactions change on the altered surface.

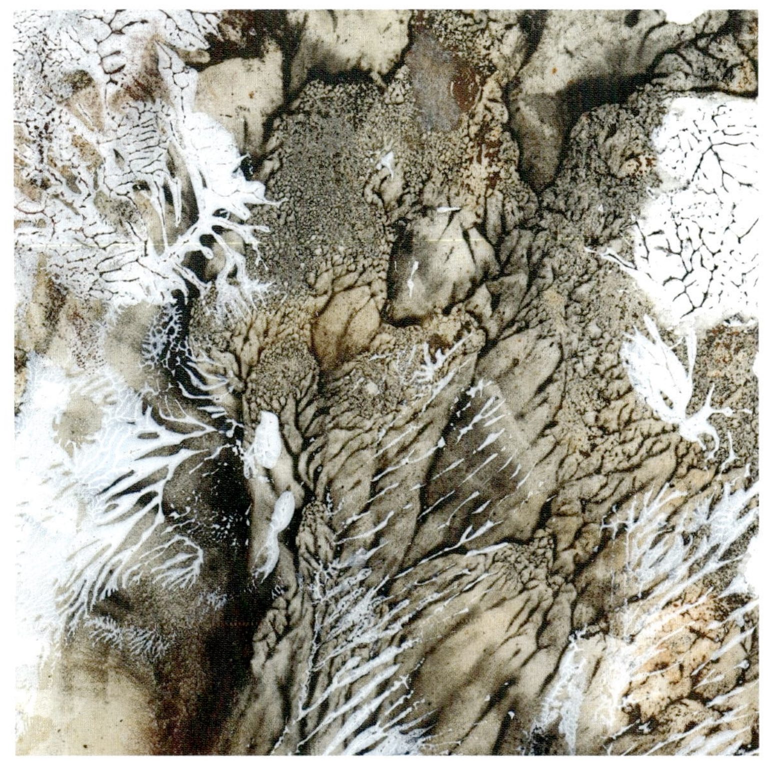

Above left: Bark texture

When creating feathery gesso marks as described above, the thin paper, used initially as a tool, acquires its own gesso markings. If pressed down while still wet onto another painted surface, it transfers the gesso patterns. It reminds me of tree bark and lichen.

Left: Lacy blossom

Lace featuring blossom and leaves was encased within gesso then painted over when dry. Crayon was dragged over the textured surface to abstract the pattern.

Foliage ideas

In the context of this book where botanical accuracy and detail play a lesser role, let's look for ways to describe the clusters and masses of leaves that you find in deciduous broadleaf woods. The idea is to discover shorthand transcripts of reality. The method might depend on many different factors: the general size, scale and shapes of the leaves or setting that you are hinting at. Also, the density and colour of the foliage groups might be different through the seasons. The style of artwork will also dictate your choice of methods. An abstracted interpretation may offer more quirky solutions or opportunities than a traditional style.

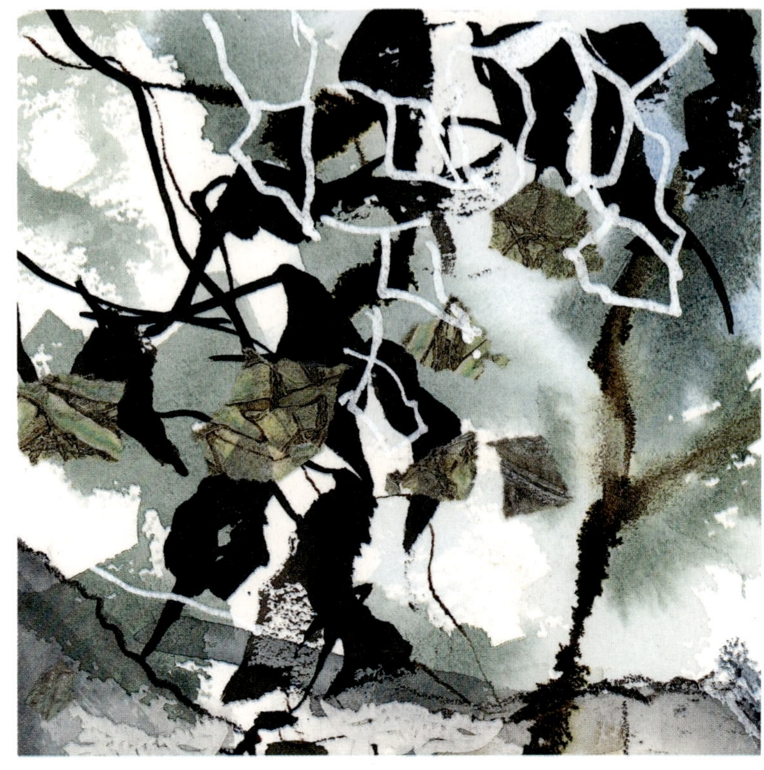

Above right: Combining layers

This sketch detail of dangling leafy branches began with a loose wash. Dark shapes were added when dry. Next, I tore up pieces of coloured tissue paper into foliage shapes and stuck them on. Finally, I used an opaque white felt tip called a Posca pen to draw further linear leaves.

Right: Crumpled tissue paper

I rarely use clingfilm as I avoid using plastic if possible. I used to crumple it over wet paint, disturbing it into geometric shapes reminiscent of foliage and foregrounds. A similar look can be made using craft tissue paper. Unlike clingfilm, the tissue must come off when it is still damp to avoid it sticking. I have used this technique here and then painted into the resulting pattern to enhance the leaf design.

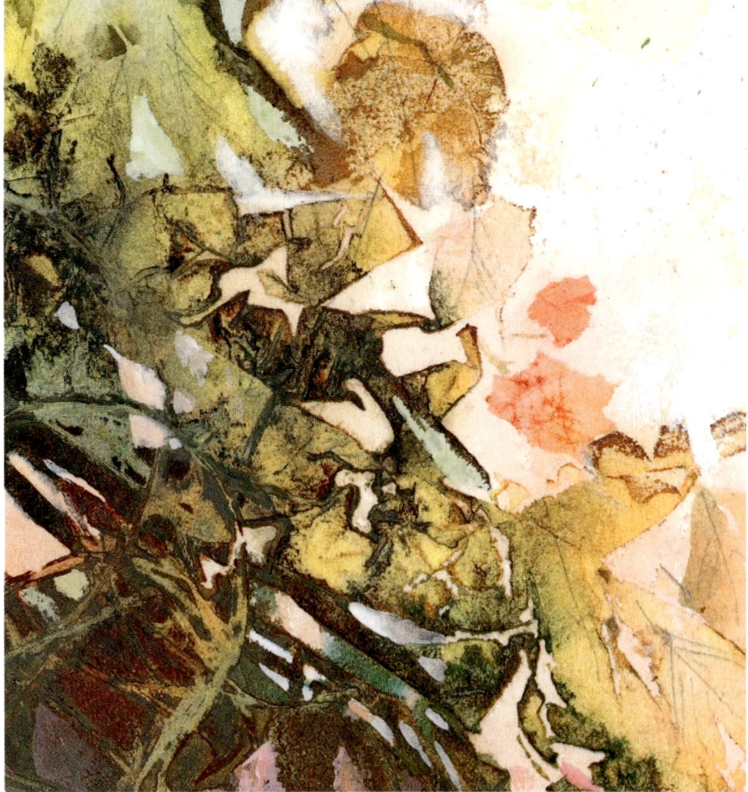

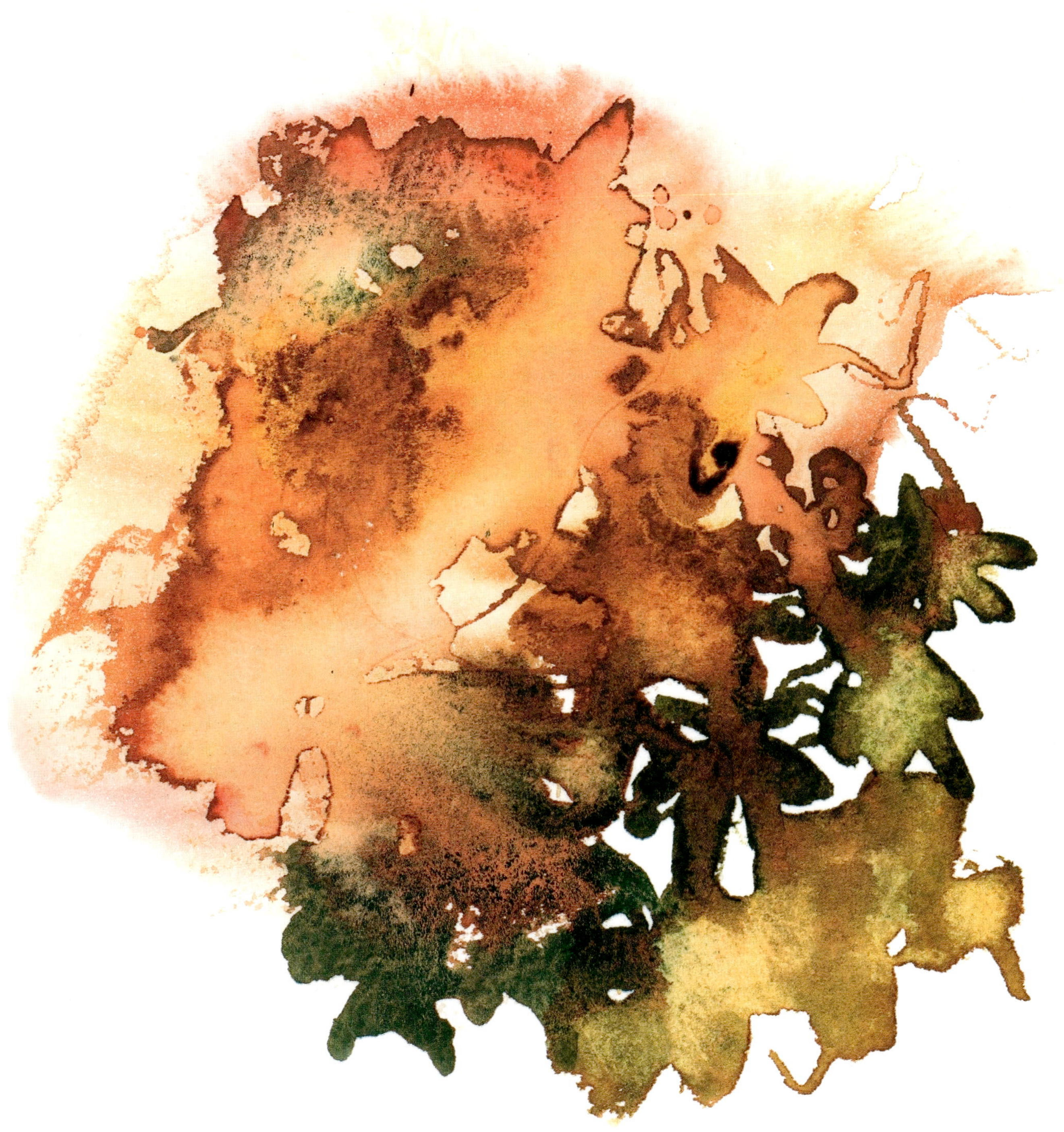

Above: Washing out

The washing out technique creates a fusion of soft and hard shapes. Here, I painted a watercolour wash mixed to a creamy consistency, into the jigsaw shapes of autumn hawthorn. I poured water over this before it dried, to wash away the central, damper part of each area, leaving dark, crisp colour around the drier edges with pale smudges within.

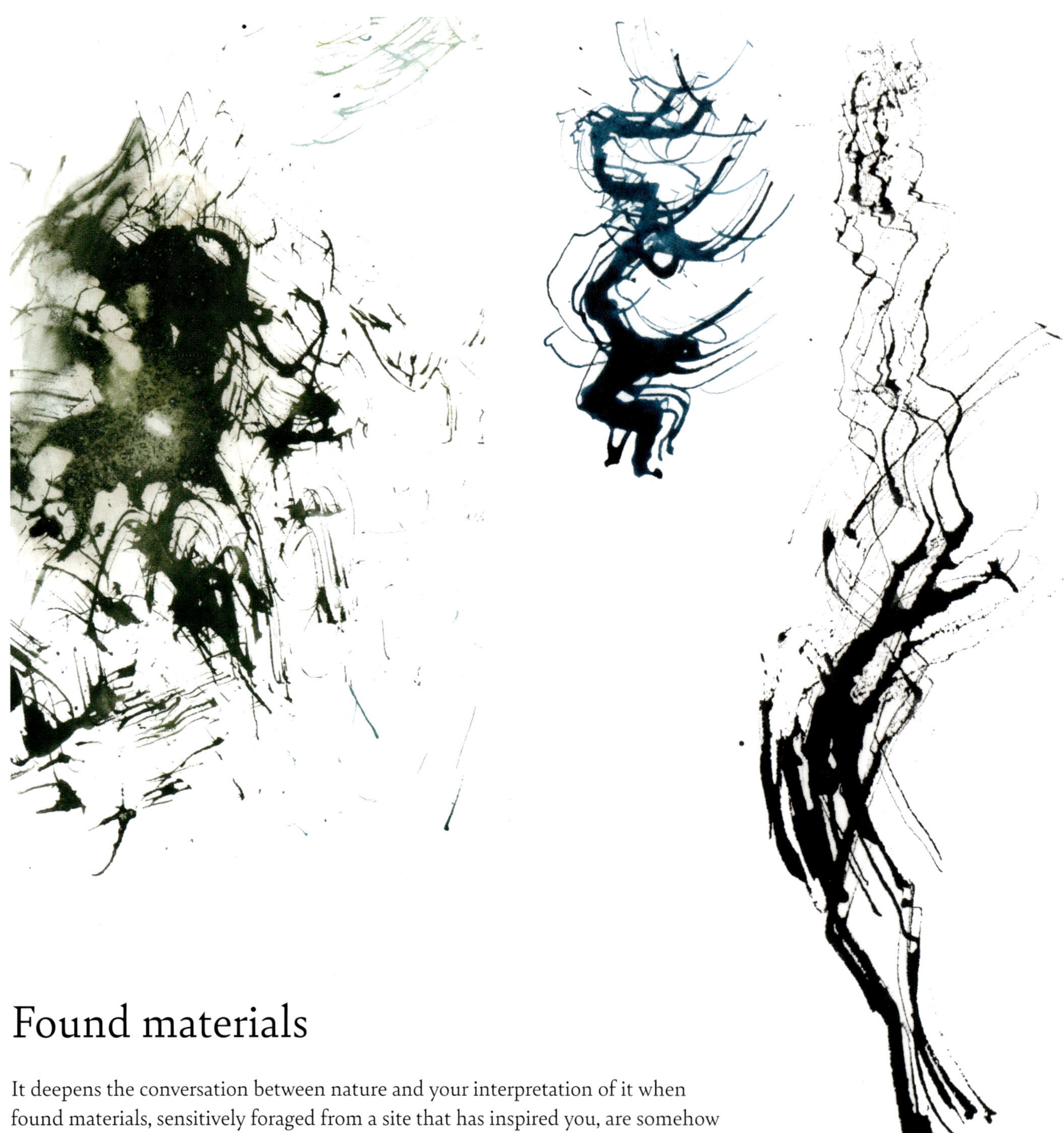

Found materials

It deepens the conversation between nature and your interpretation of it when found materials, sensitively foraged from a site that has inspired you, are somehow used or incorporated in ensuing images of it, either made *en plein air* or taken back to the studio. You can use forest materials as tools, such as feathers, bunches of pine needles or gorse, to drag paint or draw with. Experiment with single gnarled sticks, or tie together a few slender twigs like birch, for more broken, scratchy effects. The paint marks will echo the very material used as a tool.

Above and left: Marks made with fallen sprigs of gorse, conifer and Scots-pine needle.

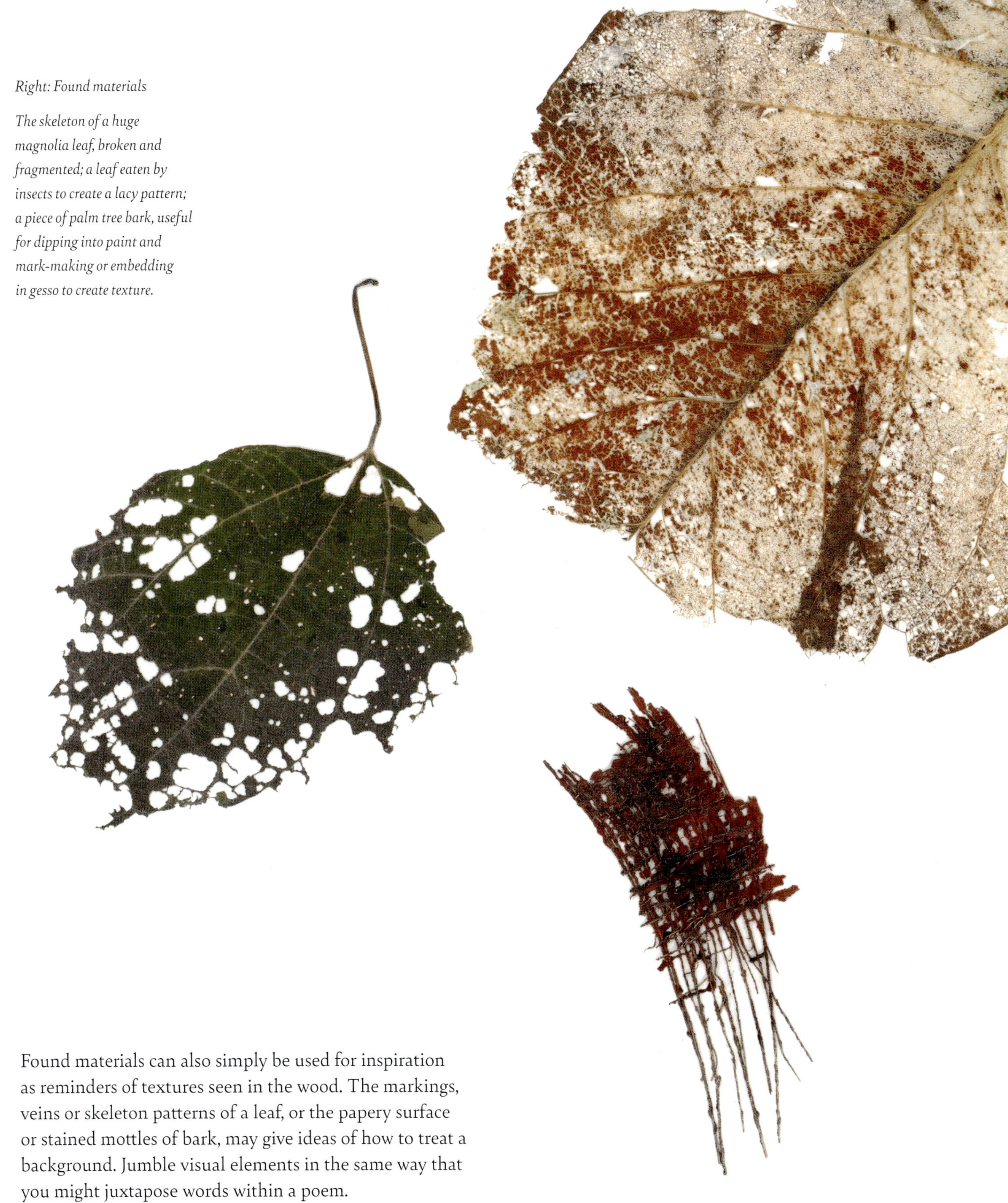

Found materials can also simply be used for inspiration
as reminders of textures seen in the wood. The markings,
veins or skeleton patterns of a leaf, or the papery surface
or stained mottles of bark, may give ideas of how to treat a
background. Jumble visual elements in the same way that
you might juxtapose words within a poem.

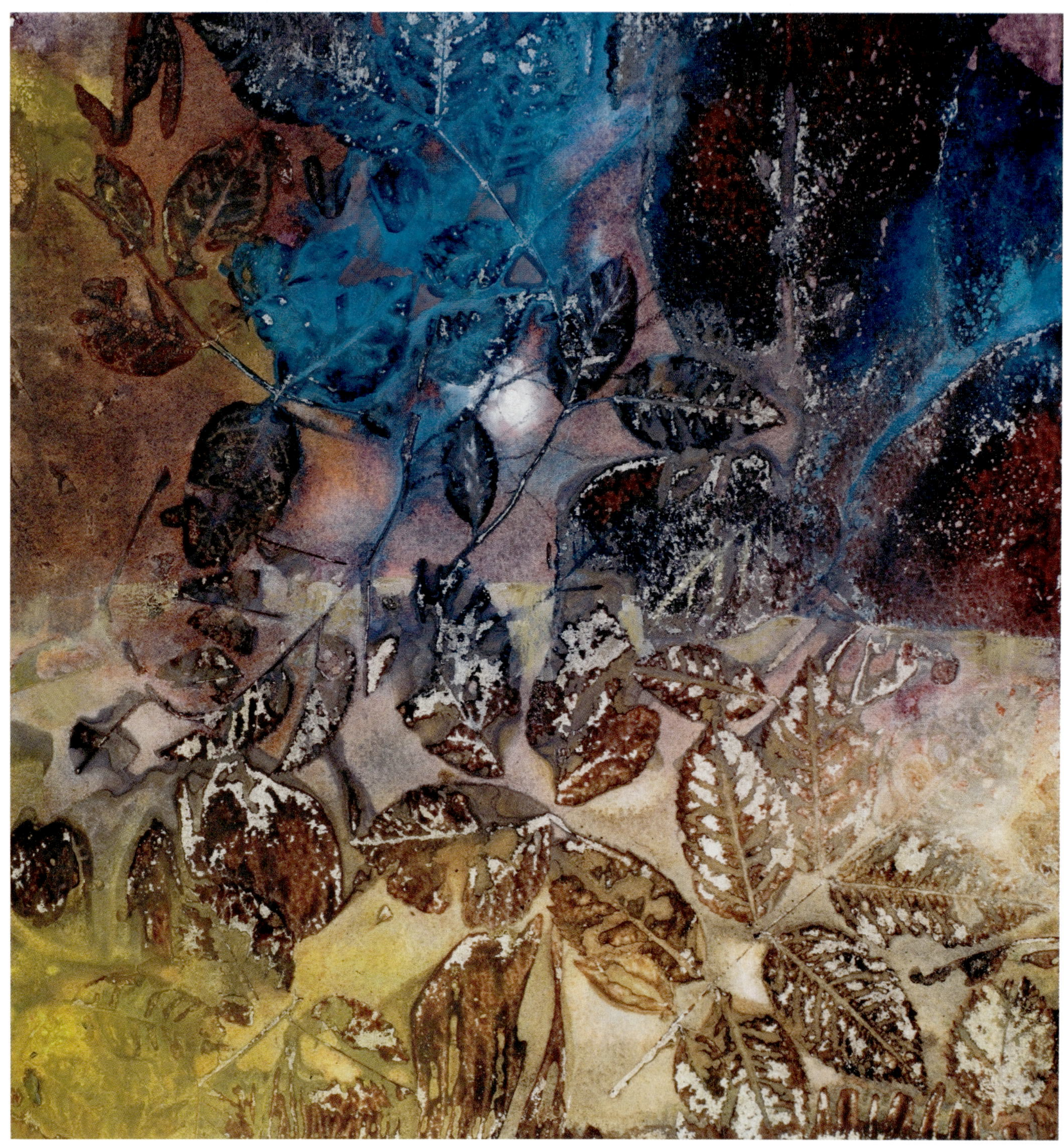

Above: Moonlit Leaves

Wild rose leaves were used to make this watercolour print. The moonlit effect was a lovely, serendipitous 'accident'. I worked into this to create a more defined moon and a landscape horizon.

Nature printing

Continuing the theme of connecting artwork with place, try printing directly from natural, flat materials, judiciously gathered from the landscape. In the woods there are many subjects suitable for such experiments. I have tried leaves, simple flowers like snowdrops or primroses, and flat evergreens such as conifers and sprinklings of pine needles. Be careful to gather only a limited quantity of material, even when it appears to be abundant.

Make prints by generously painting your surface with ink, watercolour or both. Smooth paper works well or even a board covered with flat gesso. A very rough texture can hinder you making a sharp impression. Randomly place materials onto the wet paint, or more carefully if you have a composition in mind. Be prepared to be flexible though as the printing is often wayward in its results. Cover it while still wet, in craft tissue paper or recycled plastic. You can introduce more colour, or spray water under the edges or through torn holes in the coverings, if you need more liquid or pigment. Press flat under a heavy board, leave it until almost dry and then peel away the materials to see what you have. The result can be developed into a picture or the best sections added to your collage collection.

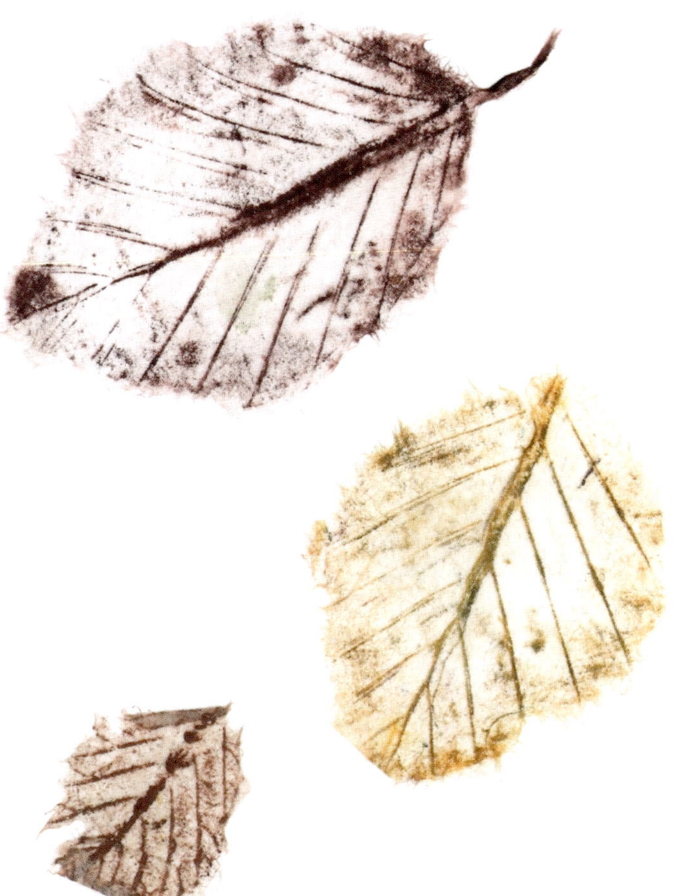

Above and below: Lay flat woodland goodies (above) on a board with thin paper on top and rub the side of a crayon over them to pick up any raised marks and edges. These were made on translucent paper scraps, which if used as collage will seamlessly blend into the background. The impression below was made by brushing mud (you could use thick paint!) onto a leaf and firmly printing it onto paper.

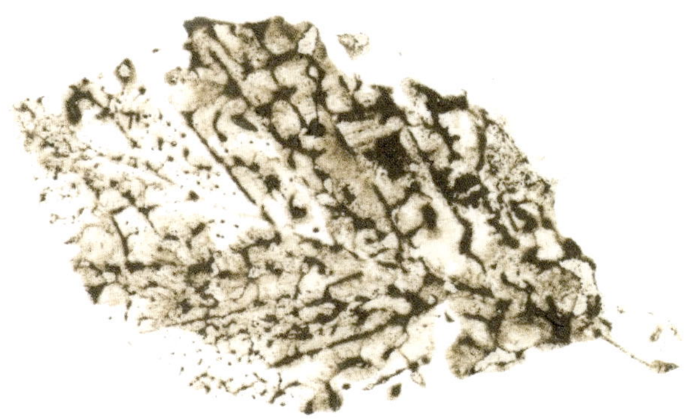

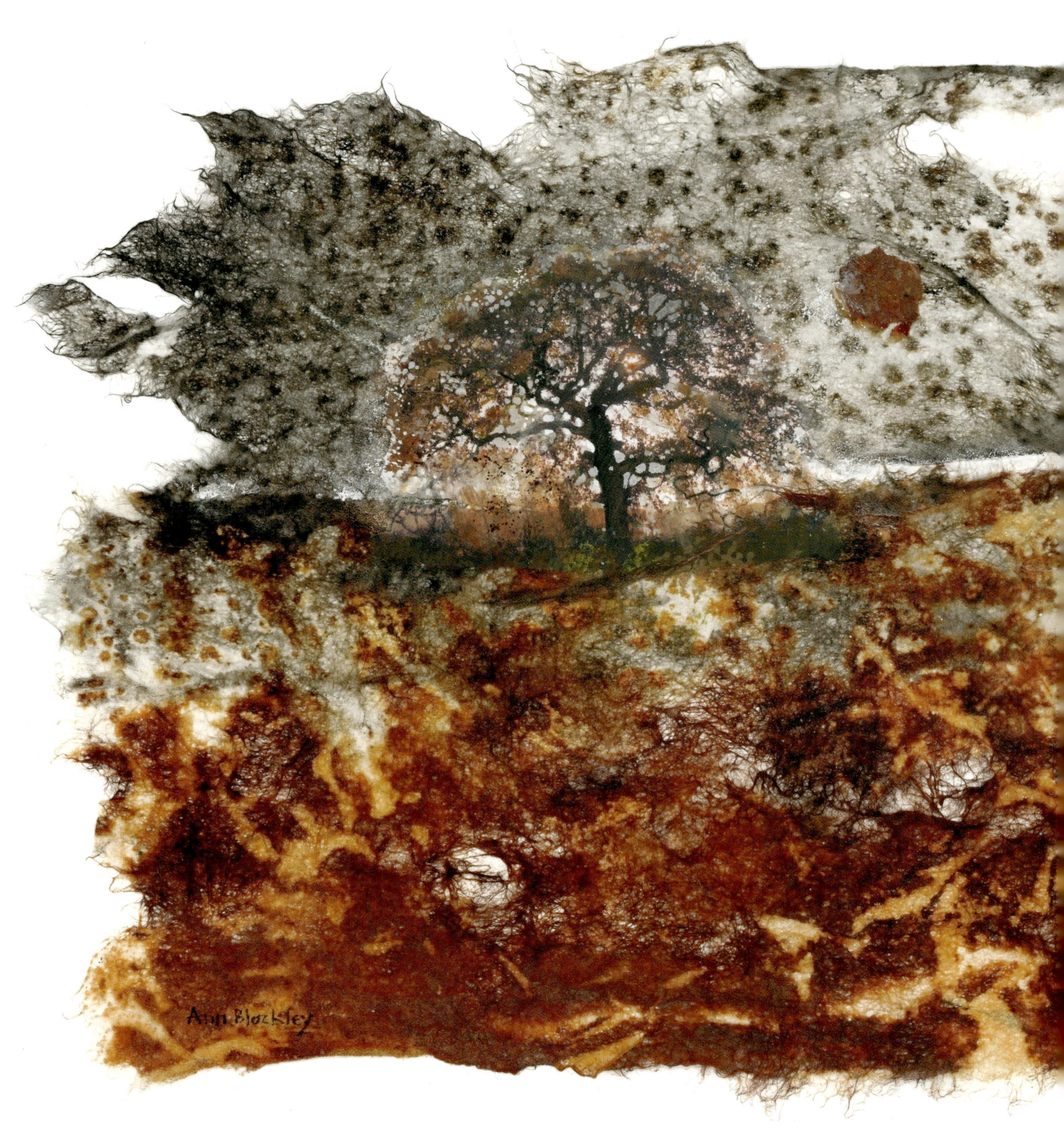
Ann Blockley

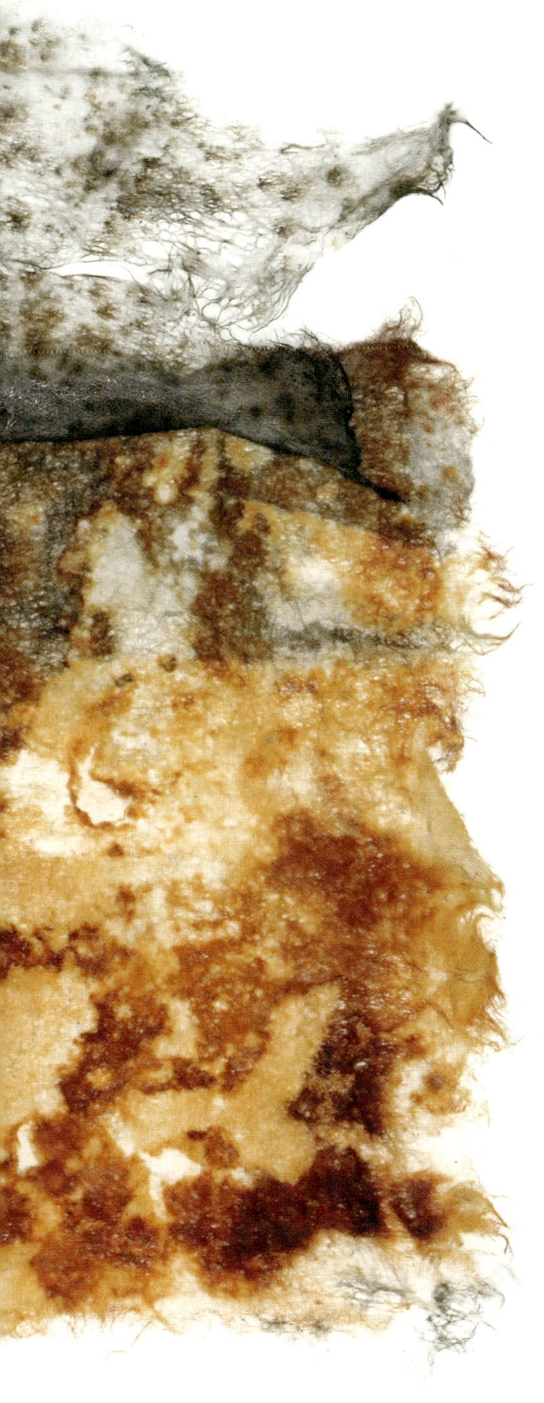

Collage

Collages are like visual poetry made using image fragments. Piecing these together can help us to be more inventive and open to the unique or unusual. Some poets stimulate creative ideas for their writing by making a habit of collecting words everywhere they go. This medley is then placed or jumbled to create poetic relationships that might not normally have been conceived. In a similar way, you need to collect a range of potential visual material before you begin to collage them together. You will find some already in the studio, but look also in the bin, kitchen cupboard, garden shed, sewing box or bookcase. You can look in charity shops, craft fairs or on the forest floor too. In particular, collect papers of different weights and textures and think twice before discarding any paintings.

Remember: any art, bark, bracken, collagraph, doily, doodle, dried leaf, envelope, fabric, feather, frottage, gift-wrap, hair, label, lace, litter, magazine, map, music, newspaper, packaging, poem, print, recipe, remnant, seed-packet, sun-print, sketch, thread, watercolour, X-ray or zodiac – might turn out to have a collage purpose! It is helpful to collate these materials into categories to make it easier and quicker to find suitable combinations for inclusion in a particular piece. You might file according to colour, texture, surface, subject, season or mood.

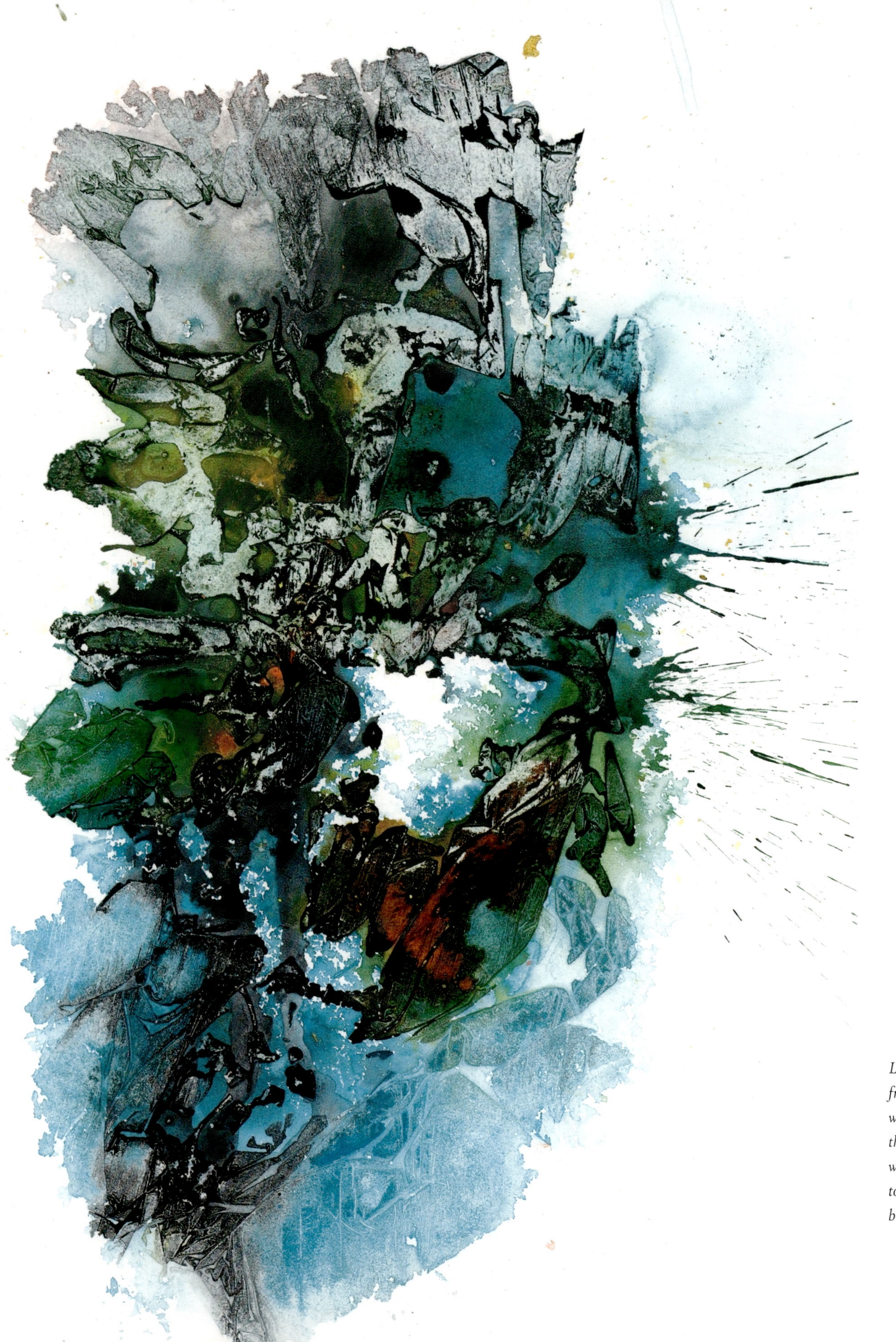

Left: A piece rescued from the bin. Sometimes we can be too hasty in throwing artwork away without allowing time to consider how it may be re-used.

Accidental mark-making

Pieces of 'accidental mark-making' can be added to your collage materials library. By accidental I do not mean the unintentional but gorgeous happenings that sometimes occur in a painting. These should often take precedence over the original plan and are moments to be relished. However, in the context of collage, I mean the overlooked and incidental auxiliary pieces made as part of other processes. These are the leftovers that you might discard unless you look at them with refreshed *wabi-sabi* eyes. It may be humble ephemera, but there is beauty in the textures and patina that might otherwise be seen as stained rubbish. They were probably not intended to be 'artwork', but viewed afresh for their imperfect but tactile qualities, colour and marks, some of these make valuable contributions to a collage. It is a truly rewarding, ecologically sound and efficient use of wastepaper, which I think our trees would approve of!

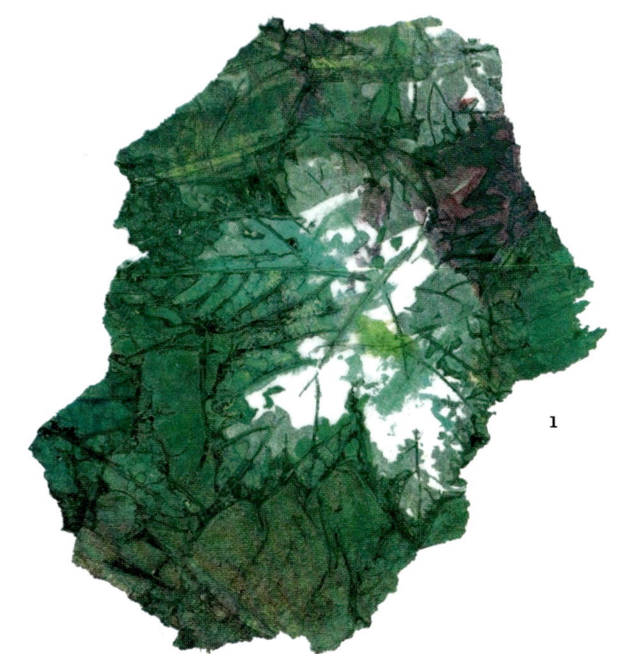

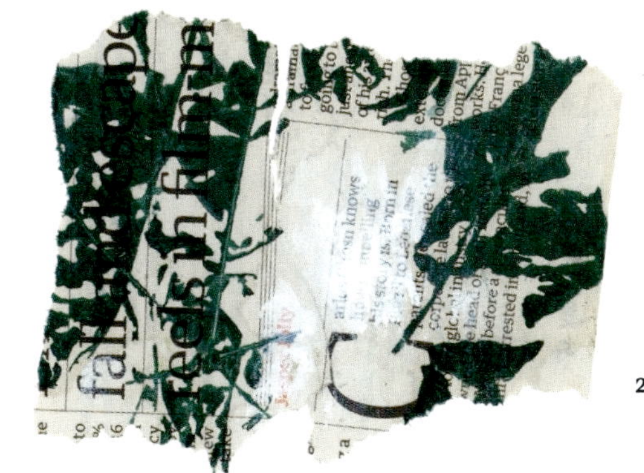

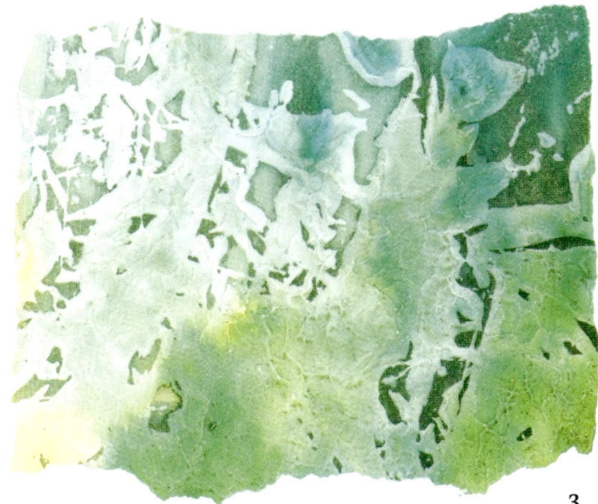

Right:

1. *Tissue paper, in the process of printing leaves, has itself absorbed traces of the print.*

2. *Newsprint used to protect the table has acquired quirky paint marks. The text beneath the paint adds a further dimension but can be partly obscured if needed.*

3. *Paper used to lift gesso into textures (see page 32) has gained interesting marks of its own, which I have emphasized with paint.*

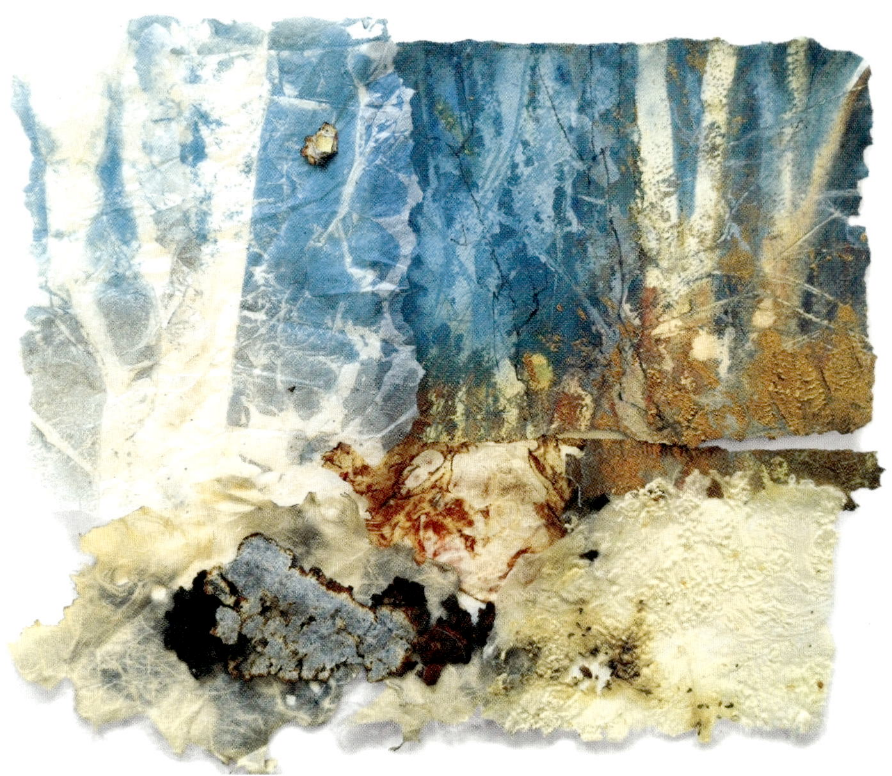

Poetic collage

In the making of *Rusty Moon* I had amassed an array of material that shared organic, textural qualities that mirrored and reverberated with each other. The sum of the parts lent an air of pale fragility, complemented and warmed by golds and soft teal hues. Frail, handmade washi paper was made less translucent by adding diluted washes of sepia. A piece of torn tissue paper left over from a printing session contained the unintentional, white, negative shapes of a ghostly tree. These and further scraps of handmade paper sat comfortably beside an old paint experiment in which tree trunks had been scraped out of turquoise watercolour and old bronze paint used up, before it dried out. I pasted the varied collection onto heavy watercolour paper.

When this was dry, I realized that although there was a twilight woodland theme, there was no strong focal point. That evening, I wandered into our wooded garden where the moon began to peer between the trees. I looked at the moonlit ground and saw a small piece of eroded metal. Its rusty powdered surface reminded me of the unfinished collage. I broke off a circular fragment and used it to play the part of moon in my collage tale.

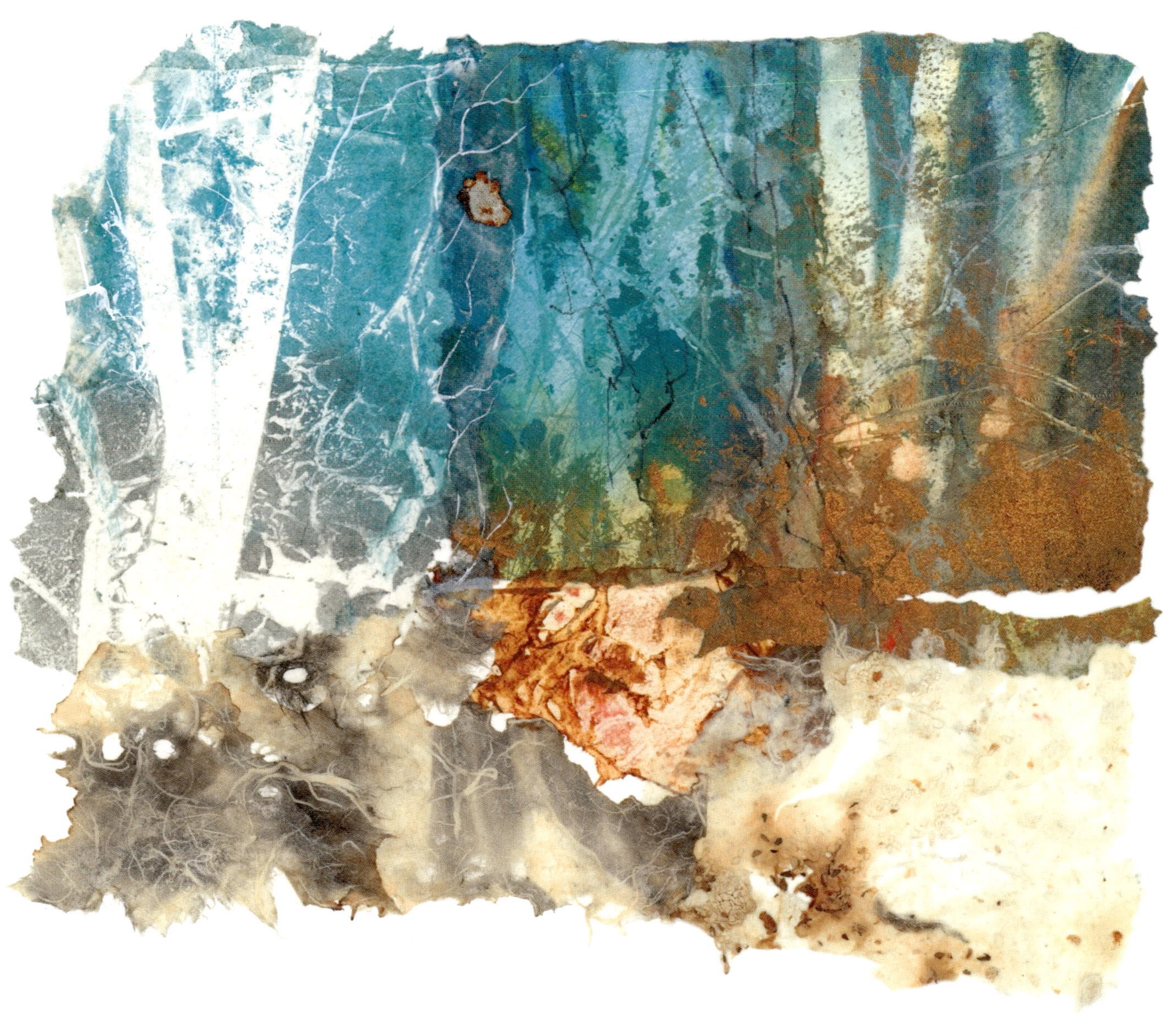

Above: Rusty Moon

I always stick pieces onto a sturdy surface like this, or mount board which will stay flat. PVA is good for gluing heavy material, but wallpaper paste is an option for fragile ephemera. Layers can be covered and weighted down to avoid cockling, and to ensure they adhere properly, but do ensure there is no excess glue along edges.

Storytelling

The layering and connections of separate pieces of visual material make it possible to tell poetic stories through collage that have seams of meaning not so easily communicated through a straight painting of a single scene. It is like the difference between poetry and prose. A poem might incorporate hidden messages and allusions that are not immediately obvious to decipher. The collage shown here, called *Money Doesn't Grow on Trees*, is an example of a how a series of thoughts, ideas and beginnings have been assembled in this way.

I had made watercolour prints using ferns, primroses and beech leaves throughout the year. I later tore them up to retain the most interesting sections, collaging them back together on a board. I noticed in my collection of potential collage material that a damaged, unusable bank note shared similar colours to the pinkish brown area of the image. It seemed appropriate that the English naturalist, Charles Darwin, was featured on this banknote. I was careful to retain a glimpse of his name and dates at the eroded edge of the composition. We have evolved into a species dominated by money, in a world where profit is more important than rainforest and tree. The addition of recycled material reflects the urgent need for us to reduce what we use. I also used the note because its disintegrating edges remind me of shredded, decomposing winter leaves. The assemblage is a comment about the cycle of the seasons and its colours reflect the changes in the turning of the year.

As summer turned to autumn
My mother sang to me:
'You need to know that money
Does not grow upon a tree.'

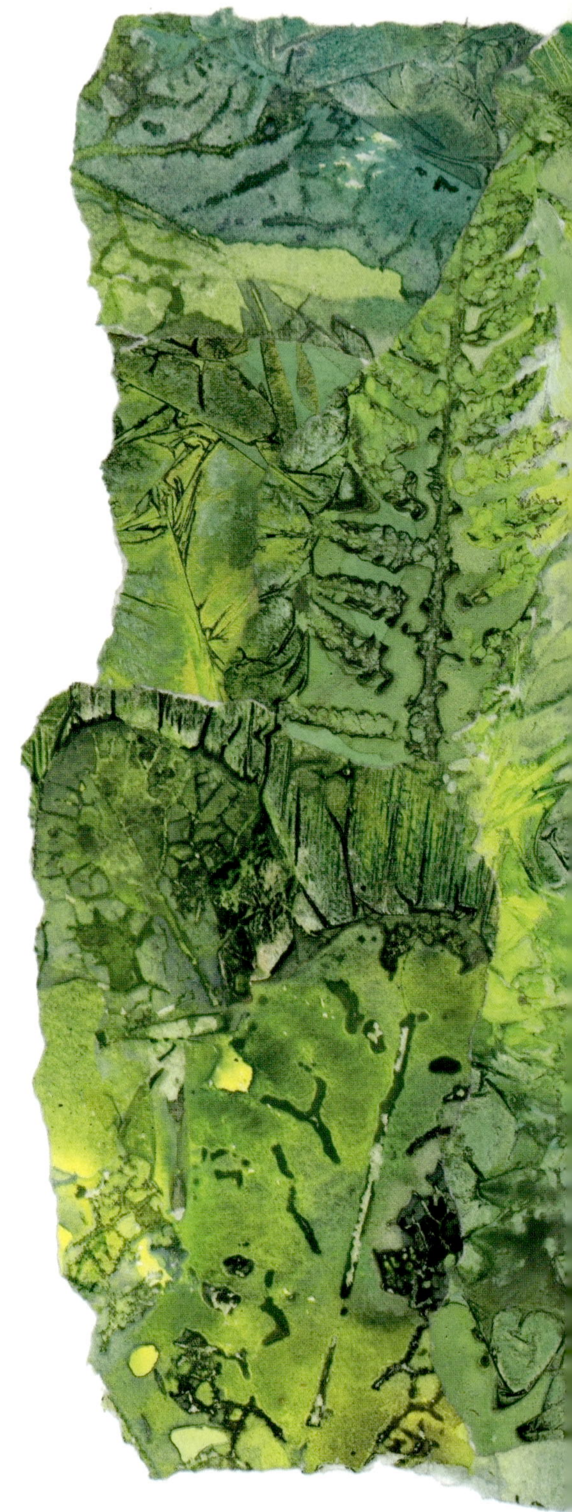

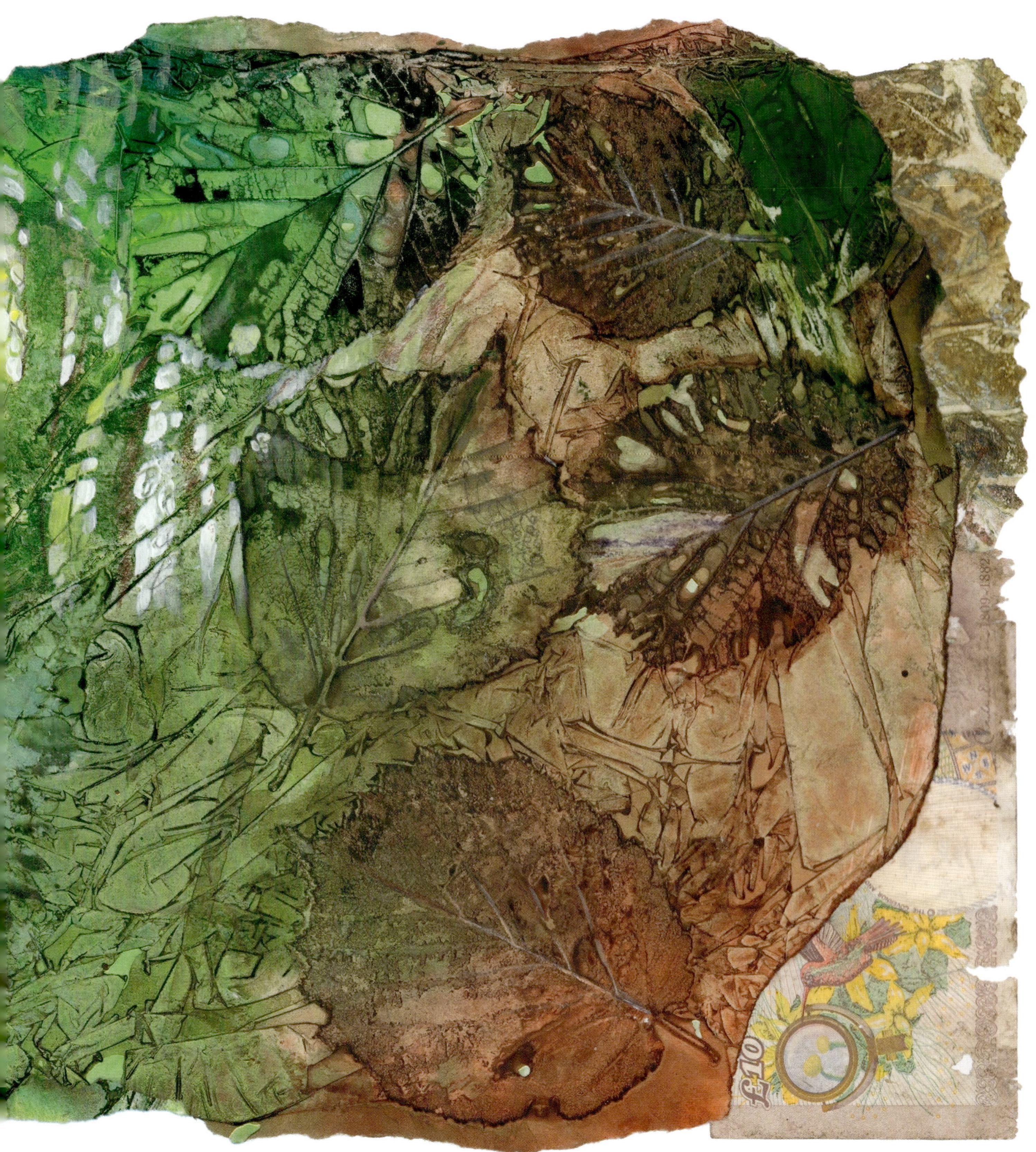

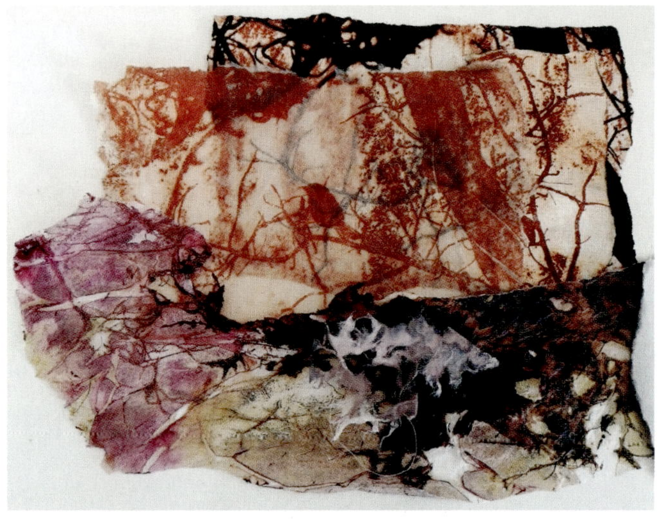

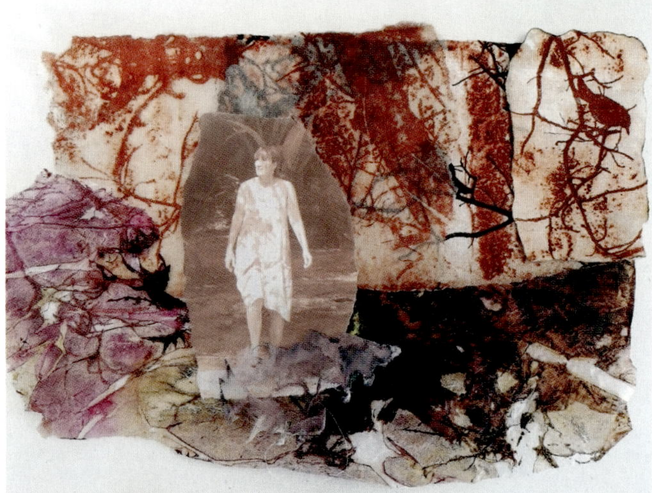

Collage layers

On a November ramble, a long time ago, as I wove a path through a tangled covert of neglected undergrowth, I looked up and glimpsed a deer, staring at me nervously through the twisting maze. It almost instantly disappeared into the woody labyrinth, but I had just enough time to snap a photograph. Years later, I was searching through my library of collage materials and discovered a selection of mauve and warm brown papers; tissues covered with watercolour, handmade papers with textured ink and print-making samples on a translucent surface like tracing paper, which I had made at an experimental workshop. Layered together, the pieces reminded me of tangled woodland and I remembered the deer I had once fleetingly seen. I tracked down the photograph and played with it on the computer, changing its greens to a sepia tint. This suited the collage palette, but I also liked the way that the sepia tone reminded me of old photographs of someone that is only a distant memory. I used this as reference to paint the animal shape within the collage, using similar colours so that it was almost camouflaged, just as the real deer itself had vanished into its surrounding habitat.

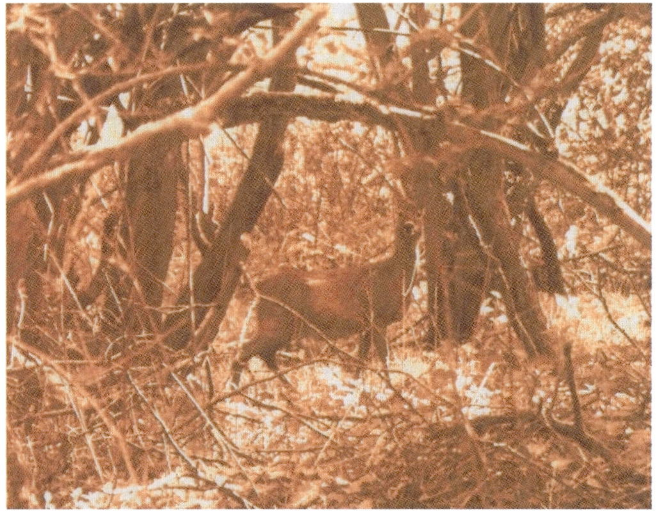

Left: In other auditioned versions I had played with the idea of incorporating a bird or even a self-portrait within this collage before deciding upon the deer. You can see the self-portrait that I eventually created on page 140.

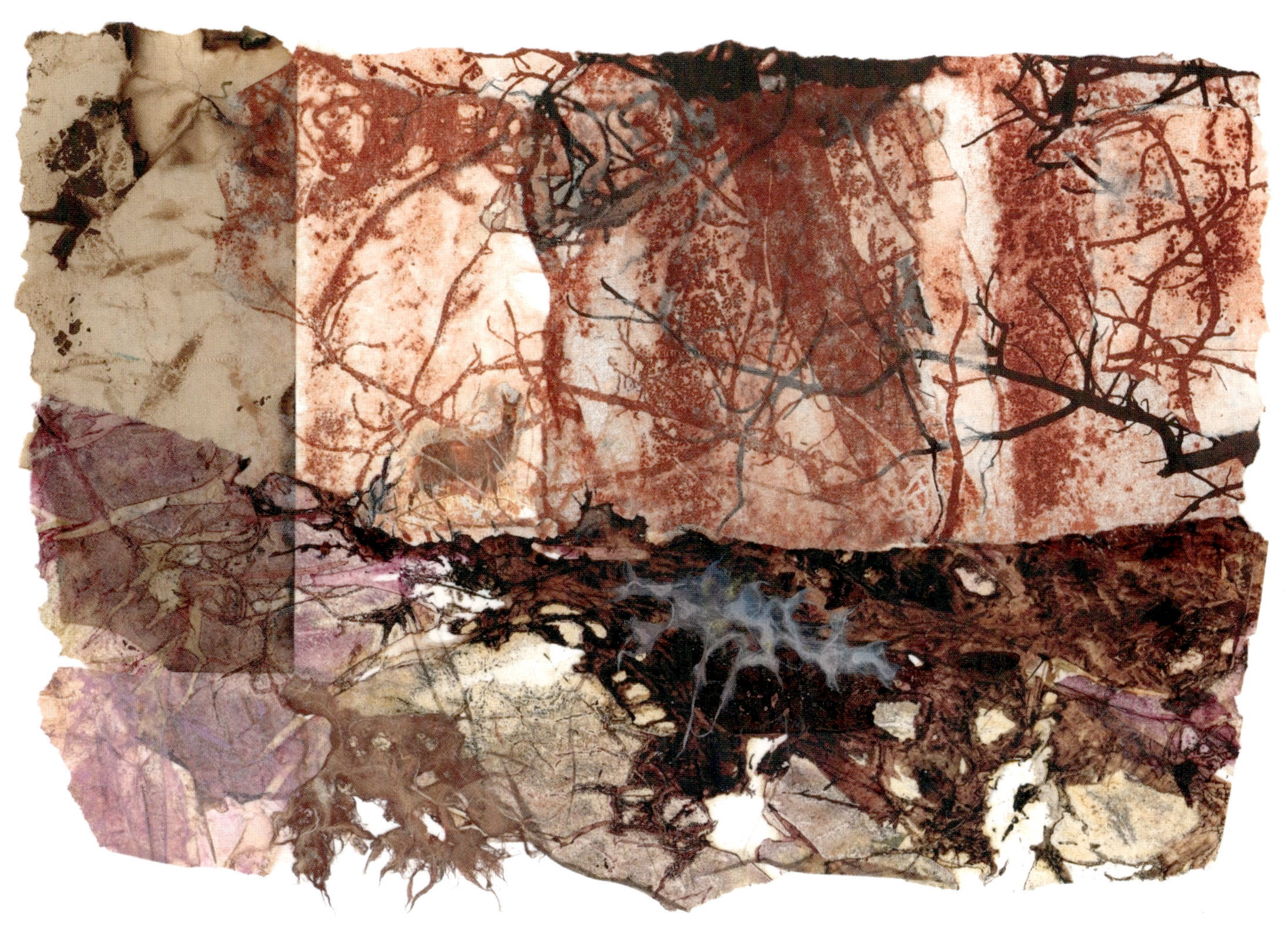

Above: Deer in the Covert

Stitch and fabric in collage

Adding stitch to layers of collage is gratifying in many ways. A practical advantage is that it can supplement or even replace the use of glue to stitch pieces of collage material together like a form of patchwork. This means you can use less glue and it gives you extra confidence that everything is secure. A degree of planning is needed, as you can only stitch thin, flexible layers of material, but these can subsequently be stuck onto a heavier surface if required. Hand stitching, embroidery, machine sewing can all be done on paper. It is a form of drawing but with thread and needle replacing conventional tools. Stitch marks echo those made with pencil, pen and crayon. The mark-making in all these can vary from thick to delicate lines, straight or meandering, defined or fuzzy-edged. Stitch is generally built from shorter, punctuated marks, but I like this quirky alternative in the context of the woodland, where shapes shift, break and embroider themselves into tangles and patterns.

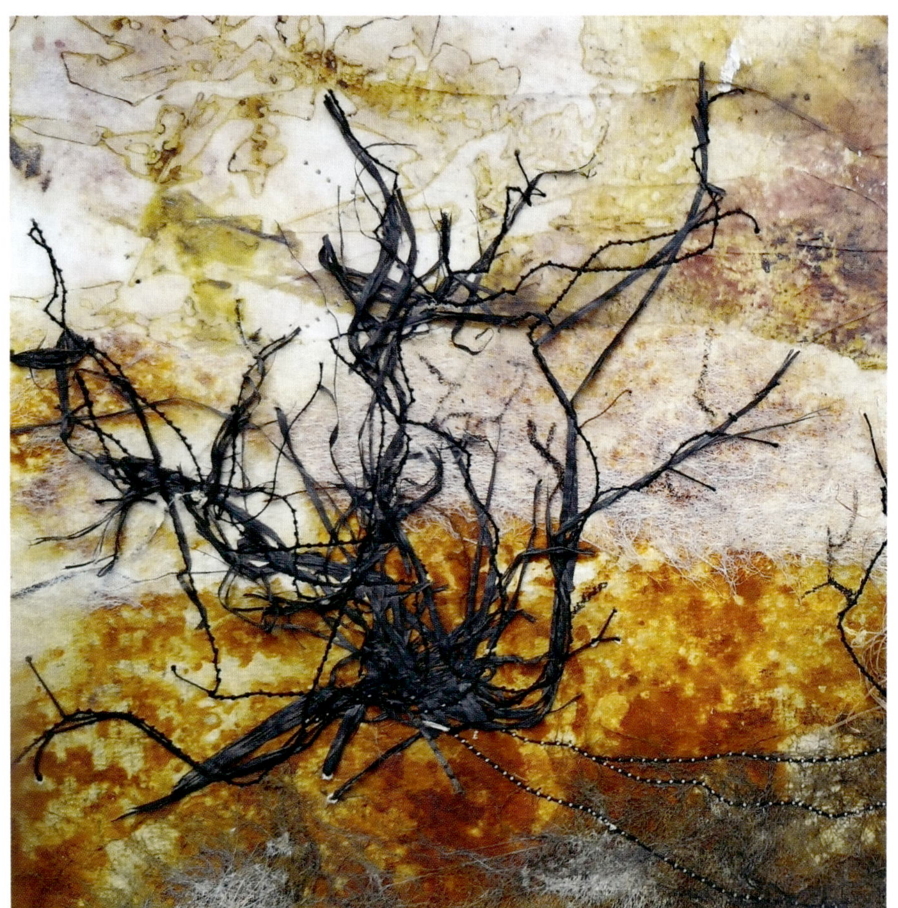

Left: Burnt Gorse *(detail)*

The way threads are made from several twisted strands means they can be split and separated into branching, tree-like patterns. The lacework of frayed black fabric in this detail reminded me of burnt gorse. It was sewn onto a collage background using large stitches to keep it in place.

Right: Turn Over a New Leaf

I machine-stitched organic handmade and painted papers together, attaching a tangled skein of thread remnants on top. Tiny running stitches reminded me of trails left by insects in tree bark. I added a leaf skeleton and a dried maple leaf, as a kind of appliqué, sewing around the edges and along veins. Finally, I embroidered the word 'leaf' by hand, enjoying its rustic 'homemade' quality.

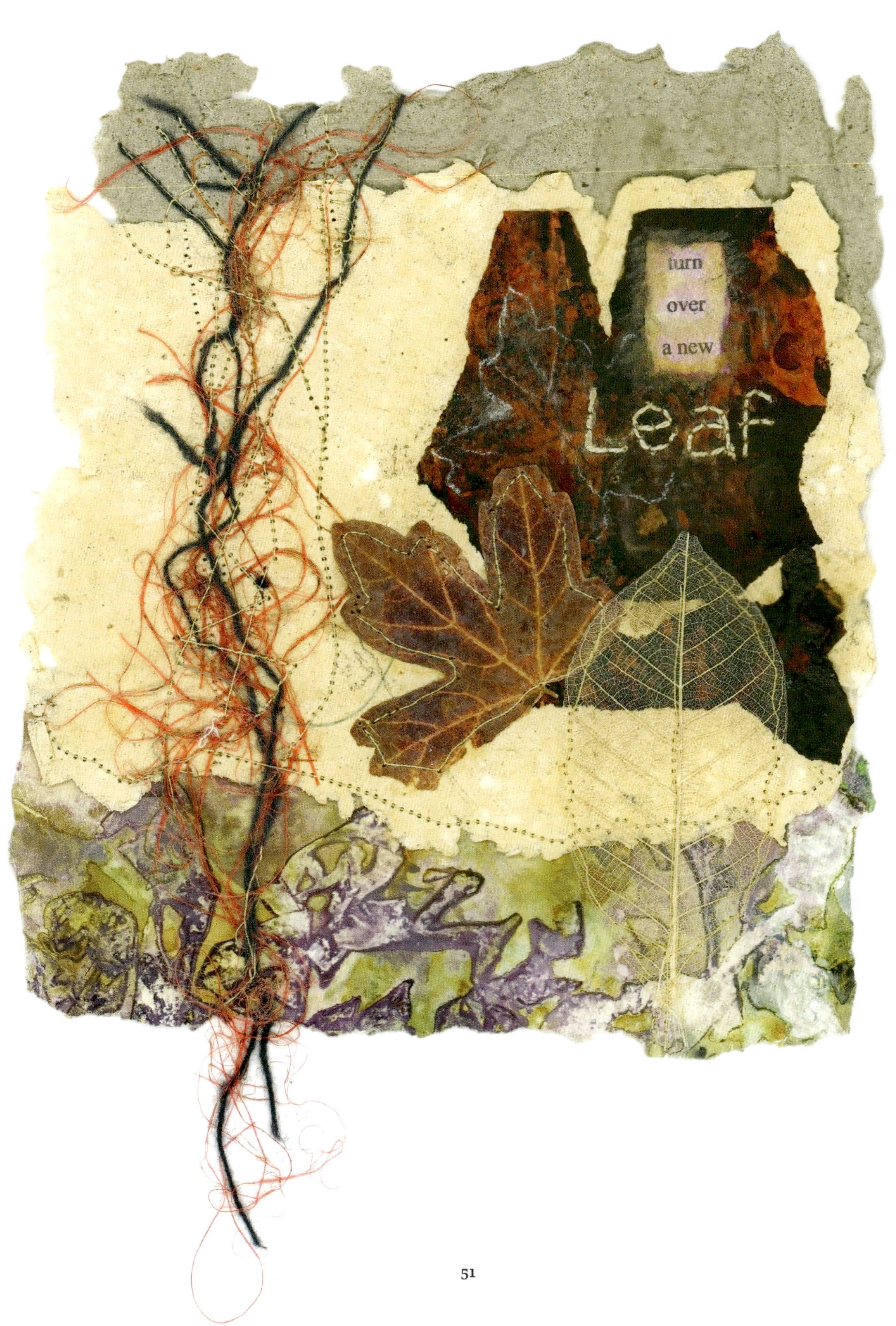

turn
over
a new
Leaf

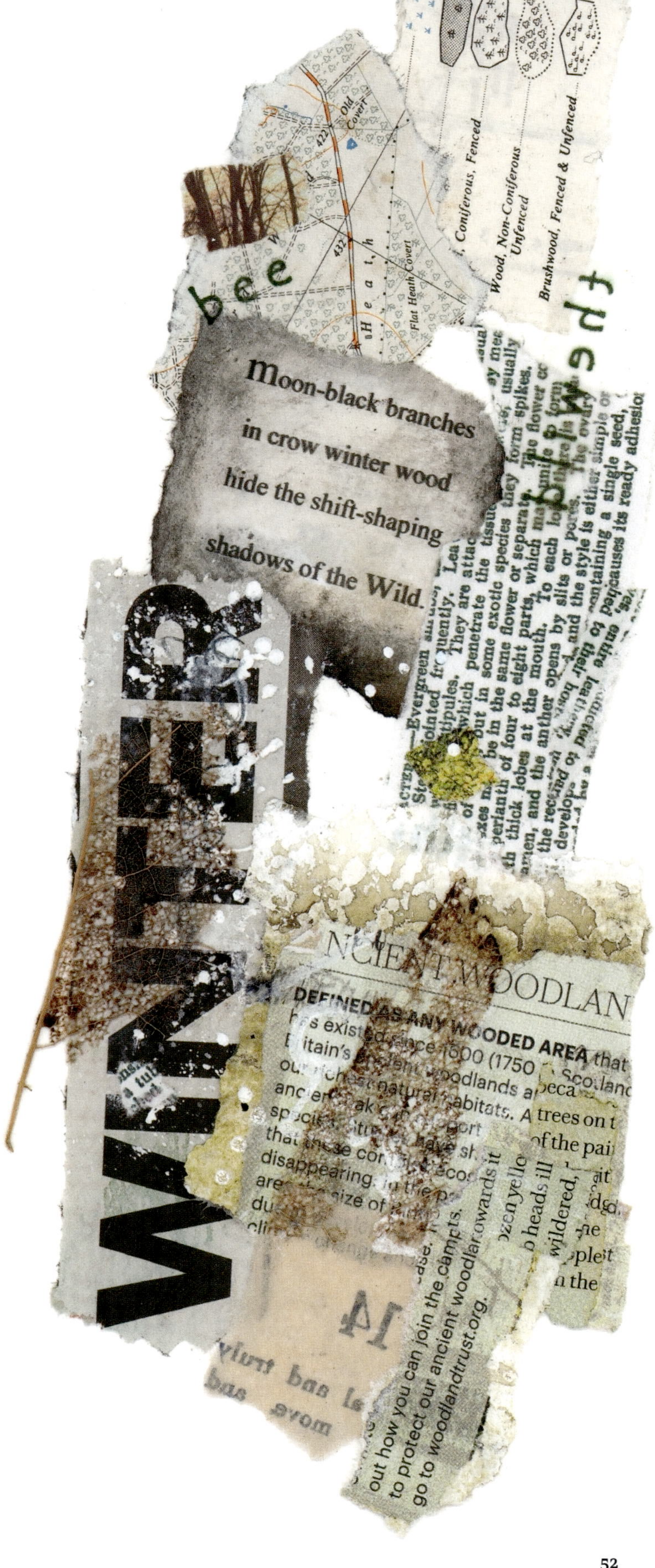

Combining words and image

We have looked at ways to make marks to represent reality in poetic or atmospheric ways. Messages and moods can be highlighted by including words or text. Writing directly into a painting is one way of doing this. You can practise calligraphy, use your own handwriting, employ capital letters to create formality or large letters brushed on like graffiti. Try scribbling into thick paint or use pencil to discreetly write over plain areas, perhaps varying the direction of text to suit the subject. The writing can be done first then painted over, allowing some of it to shine through. The process could also be done in reverse. The order of play and materials used affect the outcome. For example, if you paint on top of words made using water-soluble or waterproof ink, it will either blur or remain crisp.

The printed word is everywhere and can also be included as collage at different stages, either underneath or on top of artwork layers. Alternatively, print your own creative writing in a suitable typeface using a weight and size that suits the image.

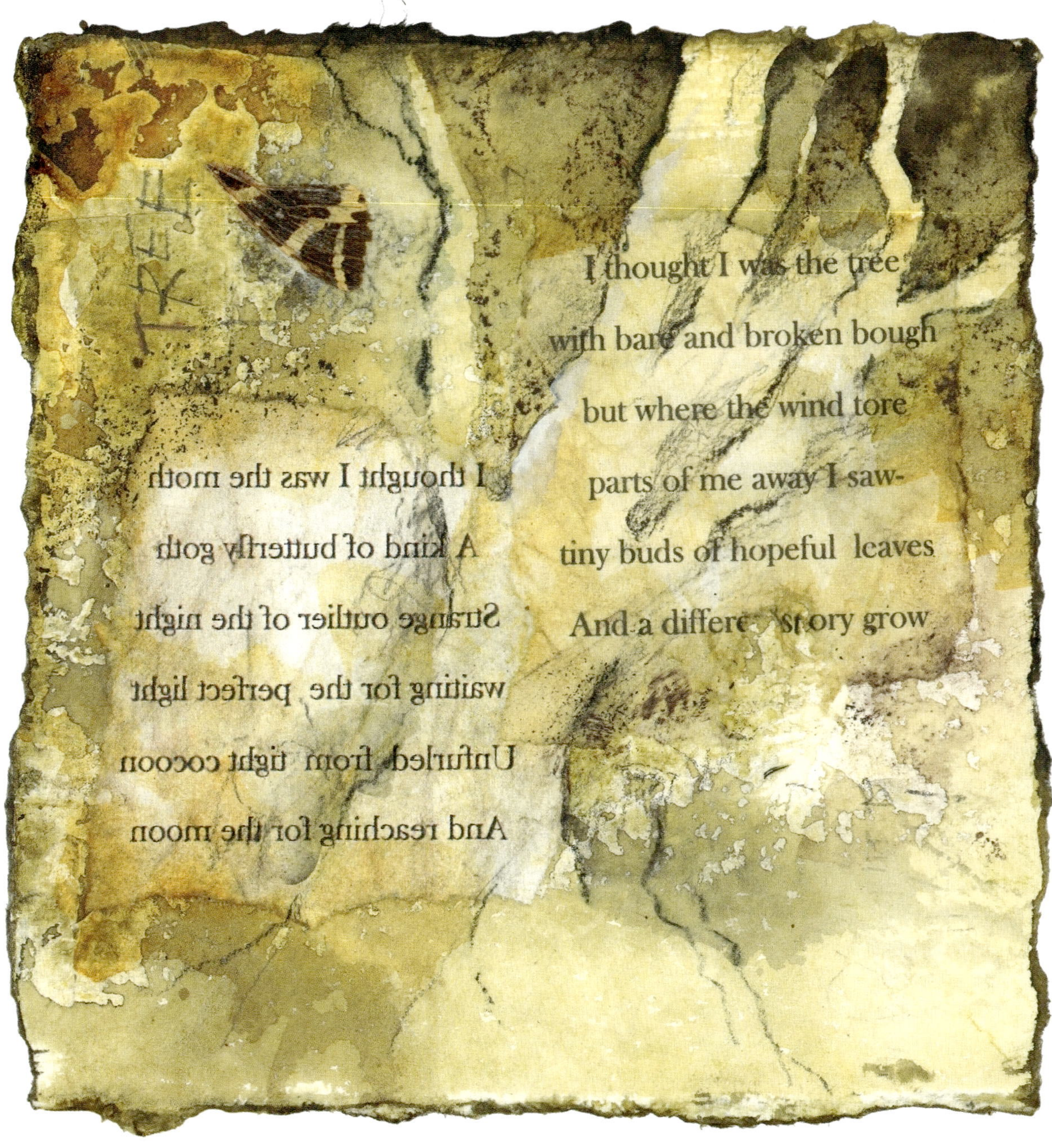

Above: With Bare and Broken Bough

After printing a verse from one of my poems about a tree, I played with ways to blend and fuse it with the image so that it did not dominate the picture. I printed another verse using reverse text as camouflage then tore and stuck the pieces onto rough paper, whose surface had been altered with a smearing of gesso. This was stained with weak ink so that the text could still be read before I drew a tree on top.

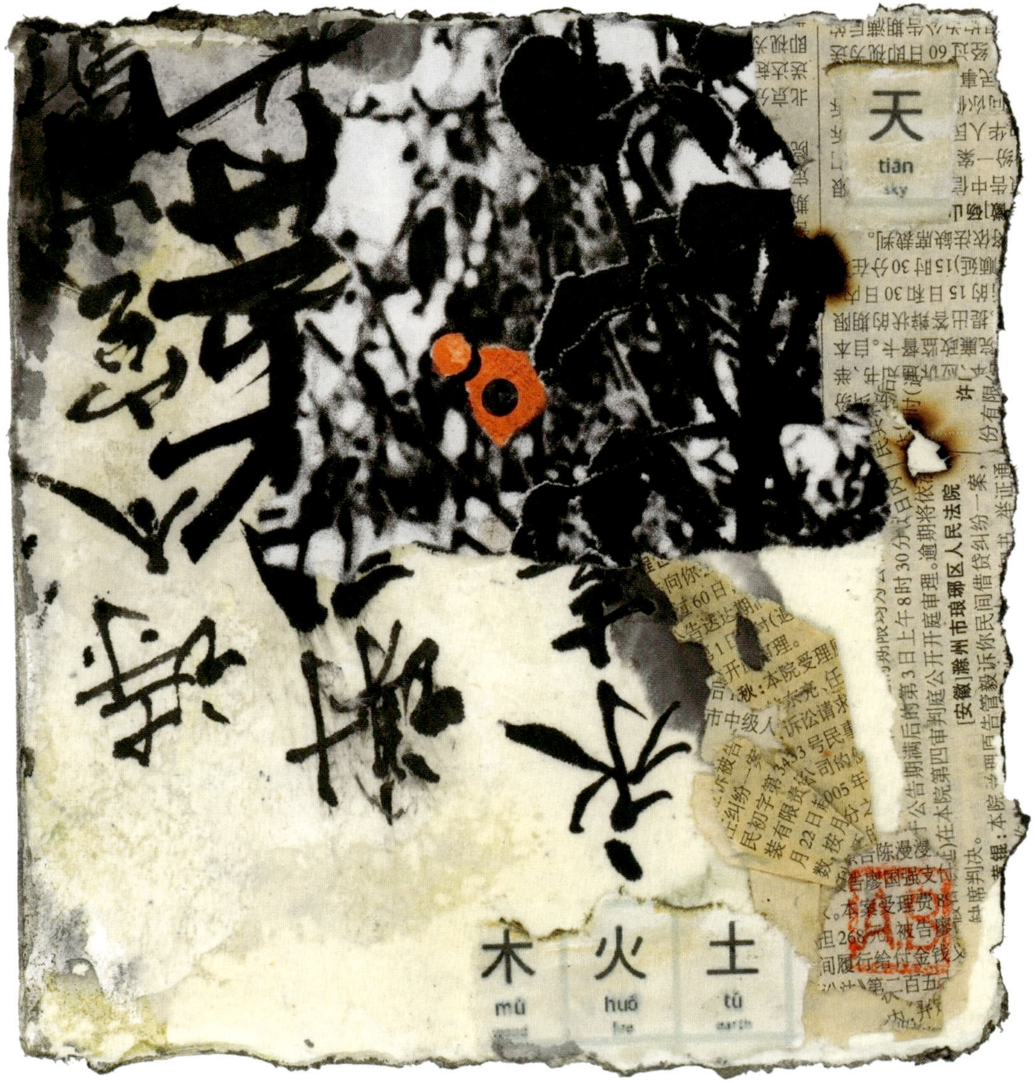

Left: Sky, Wood, Fire, Earth

Using script and characters from other languages is a useful way to add a certain flavour to collage. On a trip to China, I practised some calligraphy on rice paper. The angular shapes and patterns of the marks, although abstracted, reminded me of the silhouettes of winter branches and twigs, and I overlapped and jumbled the two visual ideas in this abstract collage piece. I also burnt holes in some strips of Chinese newspaper to distress them and added a few symbols to echo the other marks.

Disguised or altered words

When I add text or words to an image, I want it to only insinuate and hint in a way that I suppose is in keeping with my painting style. My aim is to create romantic interpretations that I would like to be considered magical and poetic. Therefore, I enjoy the idea that any supplementary words remain slightly hidden and camouflaged. I want to keep an air of mystery in the same way that I might soften any other kind of mark. Words added to images can be blurred. Smudged with gouache or charcoal. Partly obliterated with paint or gesso.

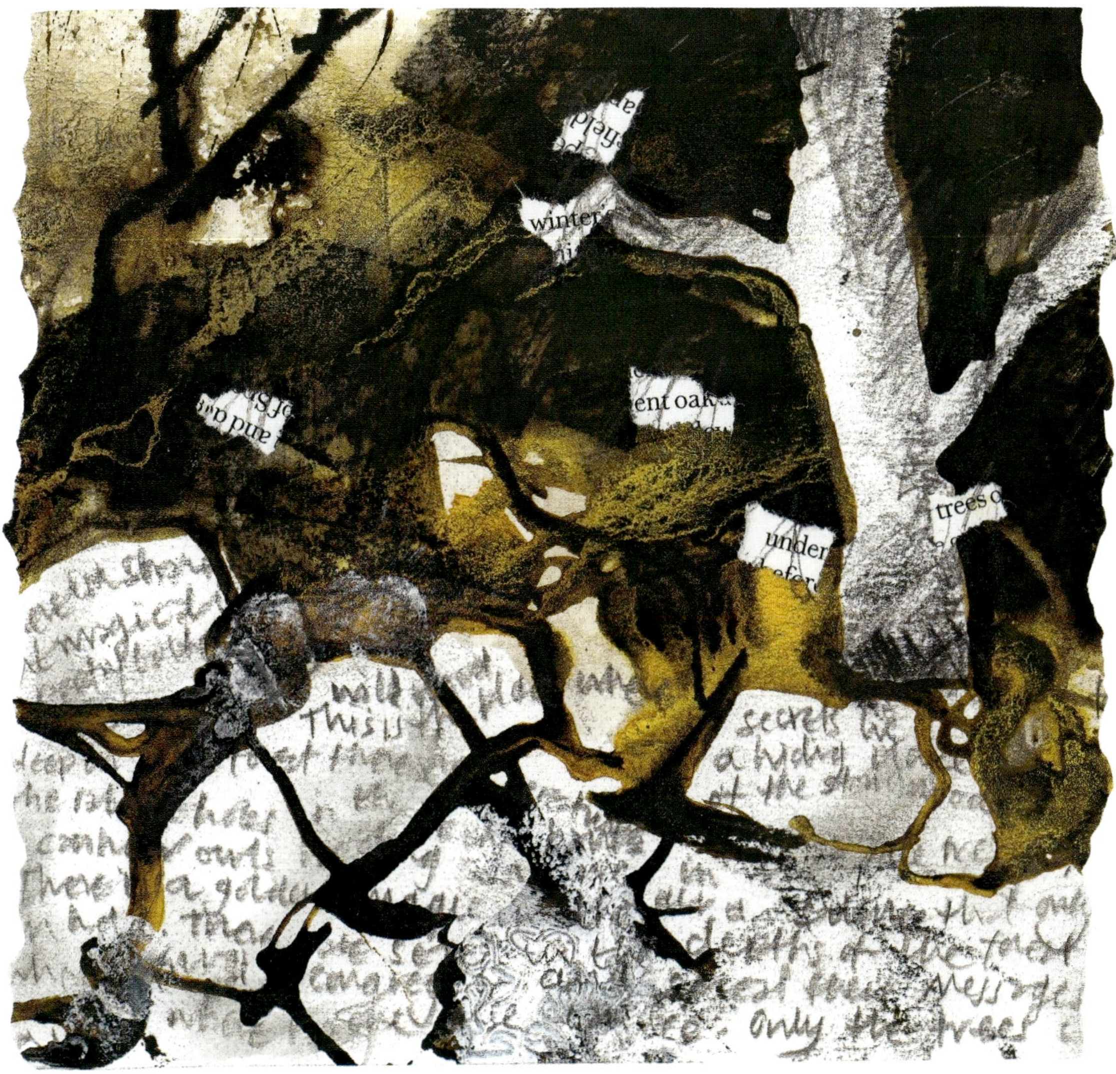

Left: The Forest Edge

I added another dimension to an ink sketch of a wall at the edge of a forest. In my drawing, the stones were simply white shapes and I filled them in with hand- written text describing the scene. I wrote over the whole area with pencil, but the letters were invisible in the lines of ink drawing, only showing up as written texture in the empty spaces. I collaged in a few extra floating words to balance the composition.

Scribbled over. Sanded. Burnt. Solid text can be broken up and altered by covering up or excluding some of the words. Pieces of text can be torn through to make them indecipherable. All these methods dampen the impact of these linguistic forms, but you need to consider whether this suits your own voice. I love to see artists speak loudly using impactful, strong, dark, graphic words. So be brave and make your own wonderful statements in your own voice.

Re-assembling an image

Most artwork usually needs some degree of editing, and this can be done with further layers of paint or collage to adapt and alter the initial image. The aim might be to improve it or emphasize a particular point. Another method is to physically reassemble work into collage by cutting or tearing pieces away, moving sections around and perhaps re-using pieces in more unexpected, poetic ways. It may be as simple as tearing artwork in two and sticking it back together in a different position, for example moving a horizon or forest floor further up or down. There is also the option to completely re-organize various parts of the picture into a more abstract, patchworked design. You may like to reshape a piece, not just by cropping it, but using the discarded sections for collage within the work. These might have been torn into smaller bits as abstract leaf shapes or long strips that mimic logs or tree trunks. They might be re-positioned and stuck down to break up normal straight edges and so create a more randomly shaped piece. It is a great way to keep areas of work that you are happy with and discard or re-purpose the rest. You can use this technique to create quirky interpretations for 'exhibition' work or to clarify or simplify your areas of interest in working sketches.

Left: Reassembled sketch

In this piece I combined sections from two different paint sketches of the same subject. Each contained areas of interest but neither quite summarized my full interest in the scene. Tearing them up, discarding certain areas and sticking them back together was a stimulating and satisfying solution.

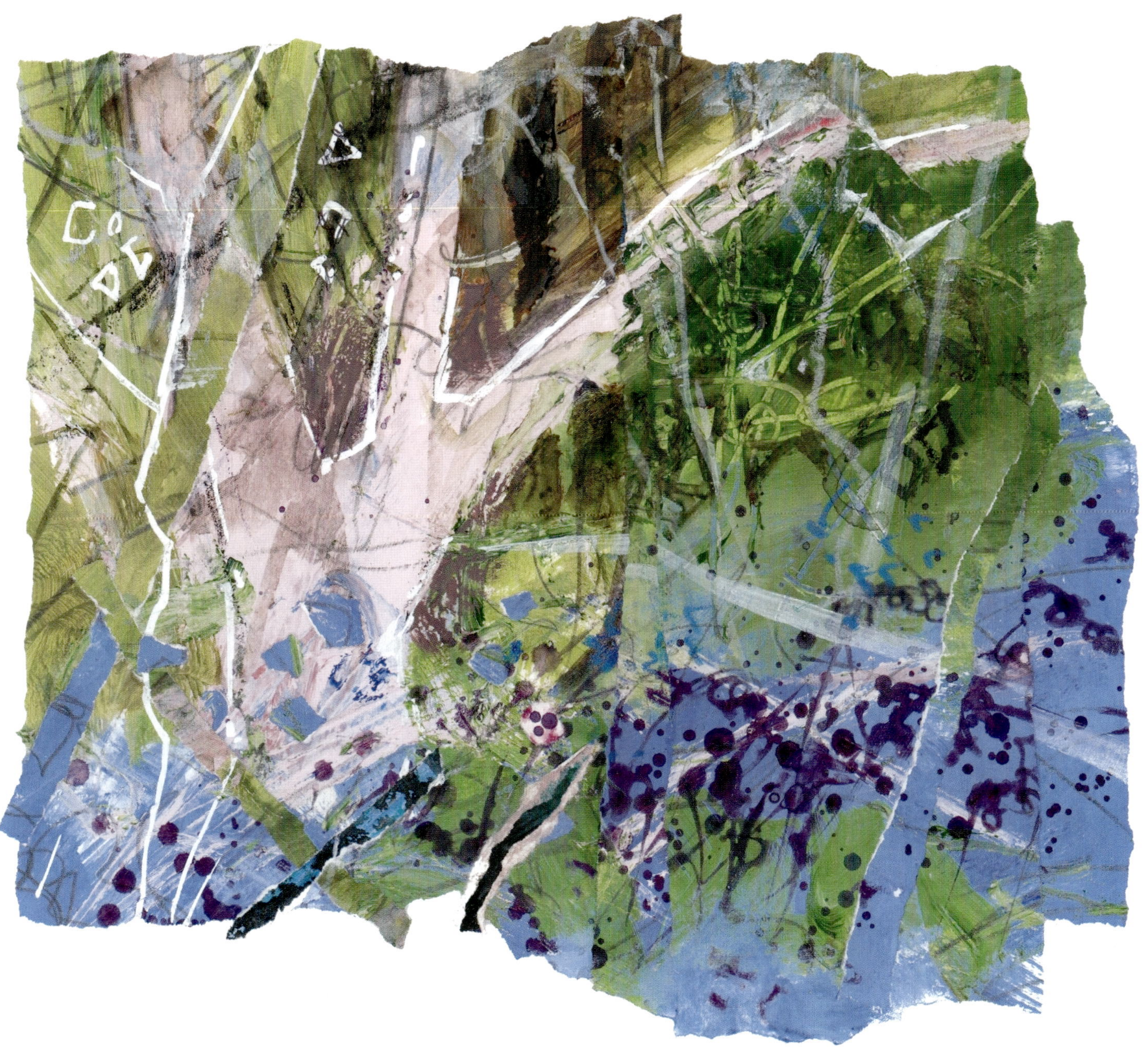

Above: Patchwork sketch

The woodland contains surprising elements of geometric pattern in the shapes of its branches, trunks and gaps in-between. I enjoy the way these random, geometric shapes can be echoed in a re-assembled sketch.

Woodland sketching

When sketching outside it is rewarding to use
materials that have a connection with the subject.
Charcoal, created through a long process of burning
wood, is an appropriate medium with which to sketch
trees. Its soft black is ideal for combining the soft
and hard edges, thick and thin linear patterns of
backwoods and thickets. For a complete immersion
into the forest, you could also use inks made from
materials gathered there, such as fungi, oak gall and
walnut. Sticks, stems and stalks can be dipped into ink
to draw with, while charcoal can be smudged with old
leaves or bracken.

I add colour to black and white sketches if there is a
particular reason to do so. It might act as a reminder
of accents, such as magenta rhododendrons shining
through gloomy dark foliage or clusters of lingering
gold leaves on winter branches. This information
is often secondary; using monochrome makes you
concentrate on the silhouettes and patterns of light
and dark in your subject as well as their structures.
I am interested in slightly abstracted interpretations
where the overall mood is more important than
identifying specific species. However, it is important
to stay in tune with a tree's character. Take note,
for example, if their shapes are light and airy or
densely disguised in ivy clumps. Trees may have
been coppiced and grown back with many stems,
rather than a single trunk.

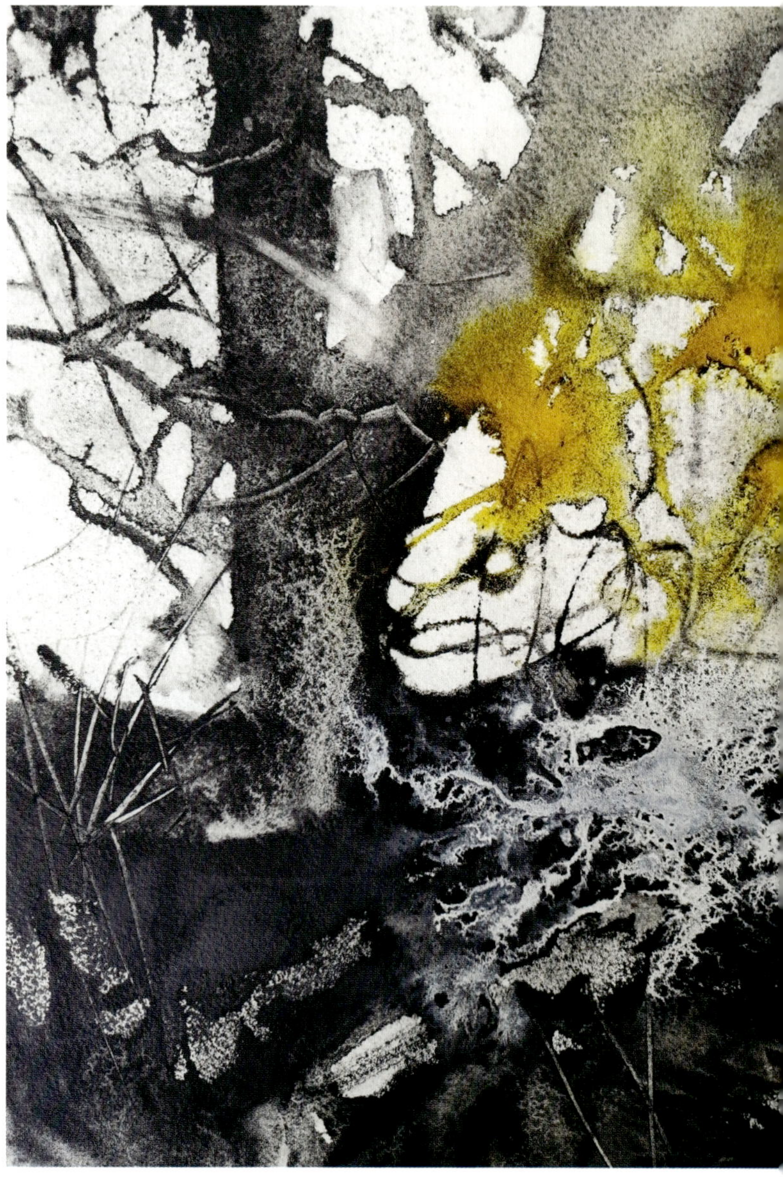

*Above: This 'sketch' was painted using liquid charcoal and graphite powder.
Both mediums granulate with the addition of water and the graphite can be
rubbed out, like pencil, to create pale areas.*

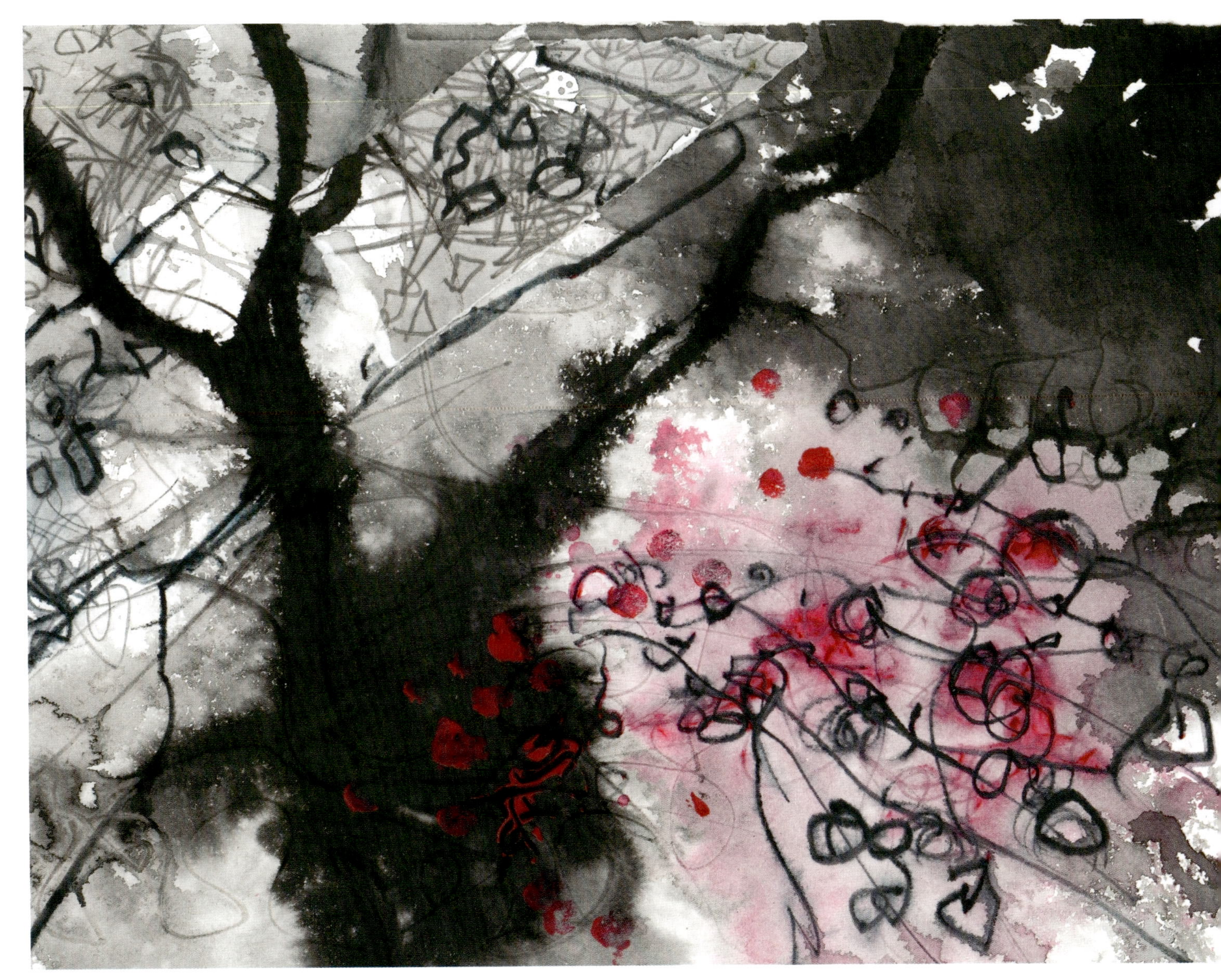

Above: The blurry-edged,
ivy-covered tree trunk was painted
in ink on water-sprayed paper. Angry,
energetic scribbles were drawn with
charcoal and graphite pencils.

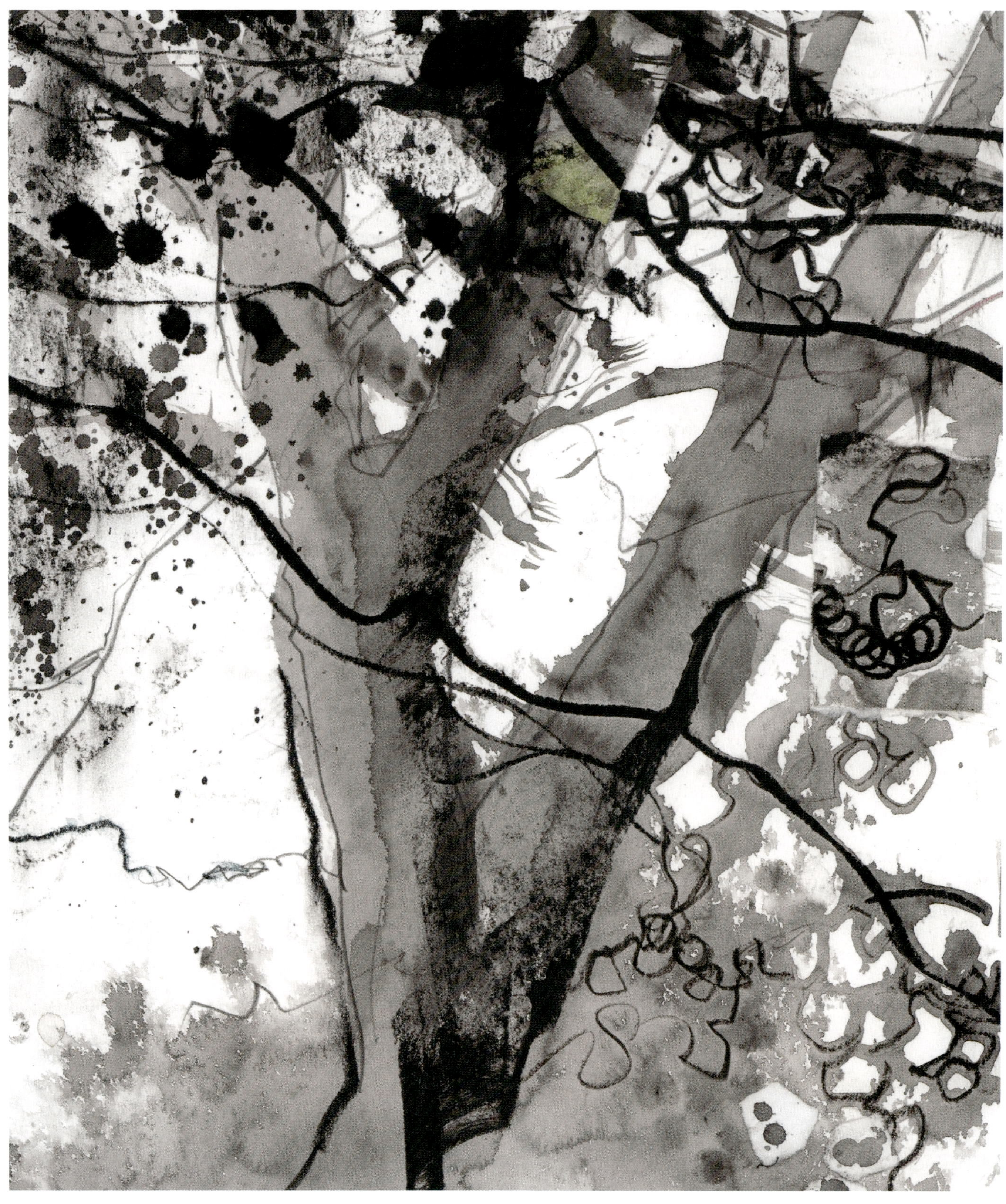

Mindful sketching

Make marks in response to the different sounds of the wood. Your drawings are conversations with everything you hear. Find visual equivalents for the scratchy croak of a rook, the cooing of the pigeons, the rattle of the pheasant, the hum of bees in lime trees, the dripping of rain on the leafy canopy, the rustle of fallen dead leaves, even the jarring noises from outside the wood. Jot down words if they float into your head. You might be feeling calm, sad or angry, and these emotions should melt into your drawing. Make further sketches but this time shift your attention to what you can feel and touch – the softness of the leaf mould on the ground or the sharp prickle of nettles and thorns. Respond again through your materials and marks. Sketching or painting like this, in a mindful way, savouring every aspect of the experience, not only feeds your artist's soul, but the subsequent interpretations made indoors.

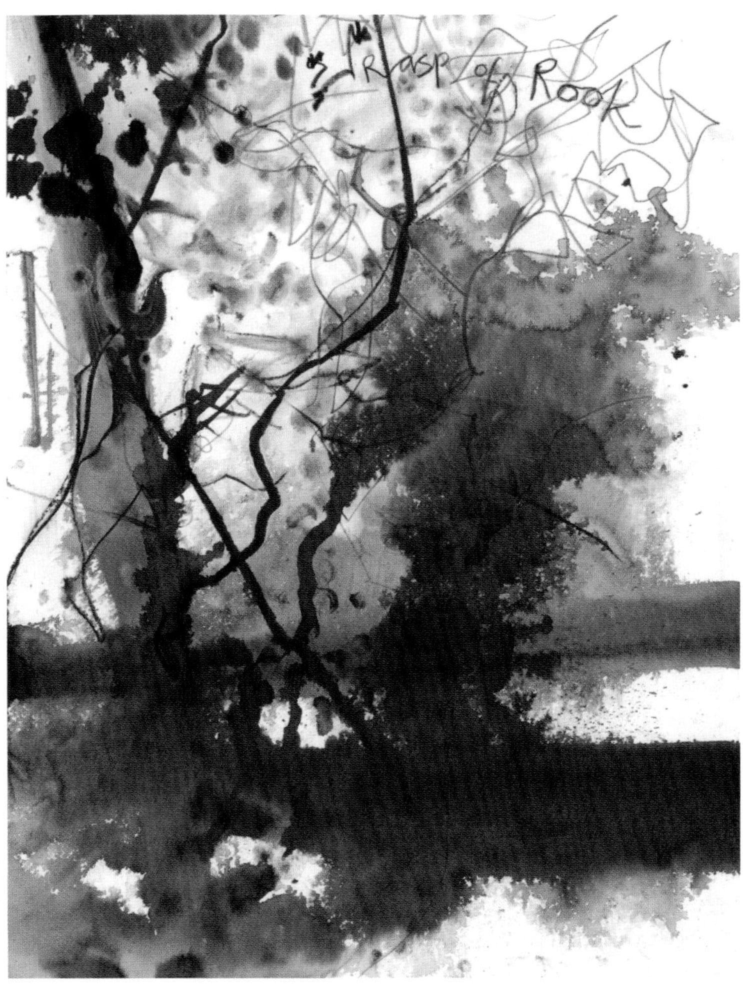

Rooks

Scattered shavings
    of pencil black
  sprinkle
the damp wash of sky
    above the soft-edged cumuli
  of the canopy so high.
These specks and markings
    swirl and fly.

  But unlike dots and dashes
of the drawn,
  this kaleidoscope
    of distant bird-clouds
  shape-shift
as they move and swarm.

Using photographs for reference and collage

Photographs are an invaluable resource for artists that can be used as reference or collage material. However, I think it is important to take your own pictures if you want your ensuing artwork to be intensely personal. If you work using a single snapshot for information, it is more difficult to stay connected with a fuller sense and memory of the scene. For this reason, I often take a series of images to record different facts, perhaps from varied viewpoints and even returning to take similar shots at different times. This makes you less susceptible to being 'trapped' into a finite, rectangular idea. You are not so influenced by any one composition, colour or focal point, leaving you free to make adaptions within your painted interpretations. Photographs are a starting point, just like any other method of recording, but unlike a sketch, which can be selective, the camera documents everything.

As an amateur photographer, most of my selecting and editing is done afterwards. I have looked at ways of doing this digitally and within the painting process. I have been exploring the idea of incorporating elements of the printed photograph itself, as collage, within a painting. I like the idea that an interpretation is a collaboration between actuality and artistry. The photograph can capture a real split-second moment in time, whereas painted elements are based on imagination and experience. It is interesting and fun to play with the juxtaposition of these and tease the eye. The result has a slightly unsettling tension about it – a dreamlike quality where the factual fades into the fictional, in a kind of poetic prose.

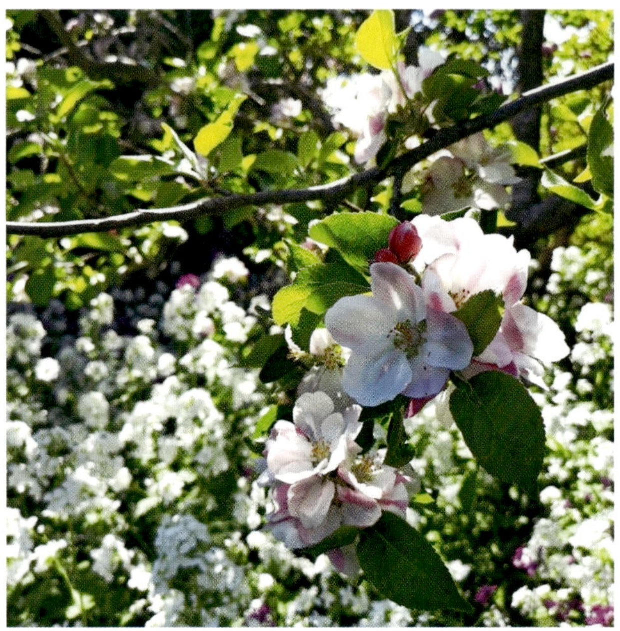

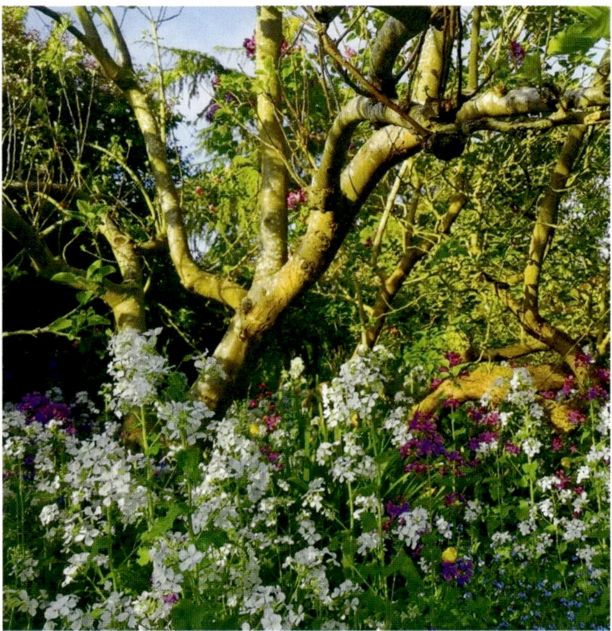

Top: I referred to this and other close-up photographs of blossom when painting the apple tree. I like the way the larger shapes create depth, but I reversed the focus in the painted version so that the blossom became less detailed than the background tree.

Bottom: I printed this snapshot and tore out the section containing the trunk and spreading branches. I collaged this piece onto a watercolour background. Finally, I painted in gouache over and around the collage so that it – almost – blended in.

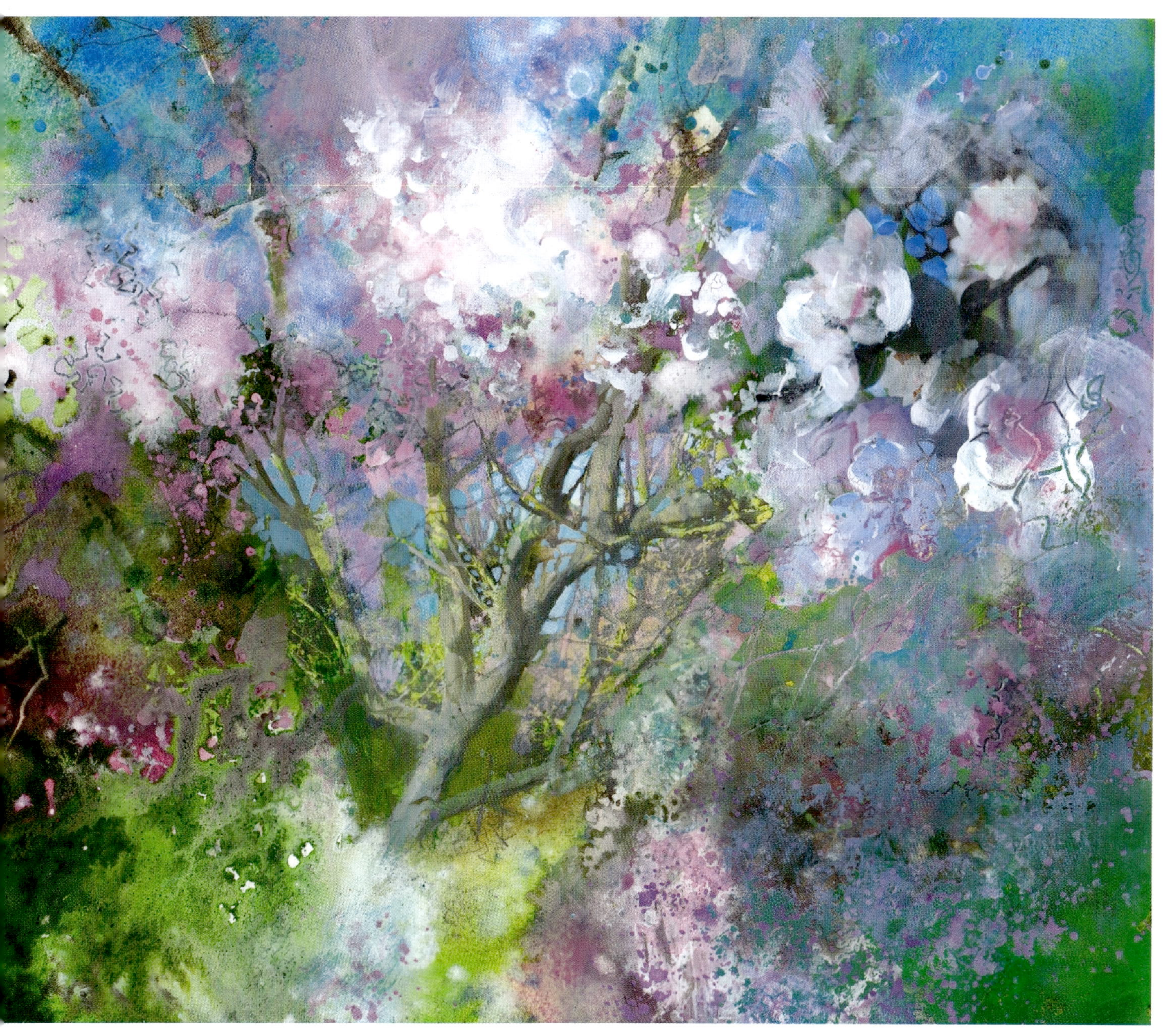

Above: The Old Apple Tree

Manipulating photographs

I am not someone that feels at home in front of a computer and would far rather be outside playing in the woods! However, on the inevitable English indoor days, I find it stimulating to browse through my personal library of digital images for ideas. Although my technology skills are appalling, even I discovered that I could be inventive with some of the editing tools available on my computer. Cropping, changing colour and tonal balance, blurring edges and reversing are all things that can be done in the painting process, but sometimes we need a helping hand to boost our creativity – and I say 'anything goes'. All it took was the simple press of a magic button to discover the transformative power of being 'negative'. In other words, changing the darks to light and vice versa. Where colours are involved in this process, the most extraordinary, fantastical and unexpected combinations appear. White moons are eclipsed. Bluebells mutate to emerald green and grass metamorphoses into shades of blue. Skies turn black and foregrounds are edged in violet. The woodland floor is washed in turquoise. It is the stuff of dreams and poetry.

Try cropping details out of a whole image and enlarge them. Change colours; reverse, fade or enhance the contrast; turn it into a negative or convert the shape to a thin vertical. Make photo transfers out of images. Alternatively, print onto textured papers using archival ink and leave them as they are, or experiment with drawing or painting on top. Stick experiments into sketchbooks of explorations. See how these manipulated photographic images influence subsequent paintings or collages.

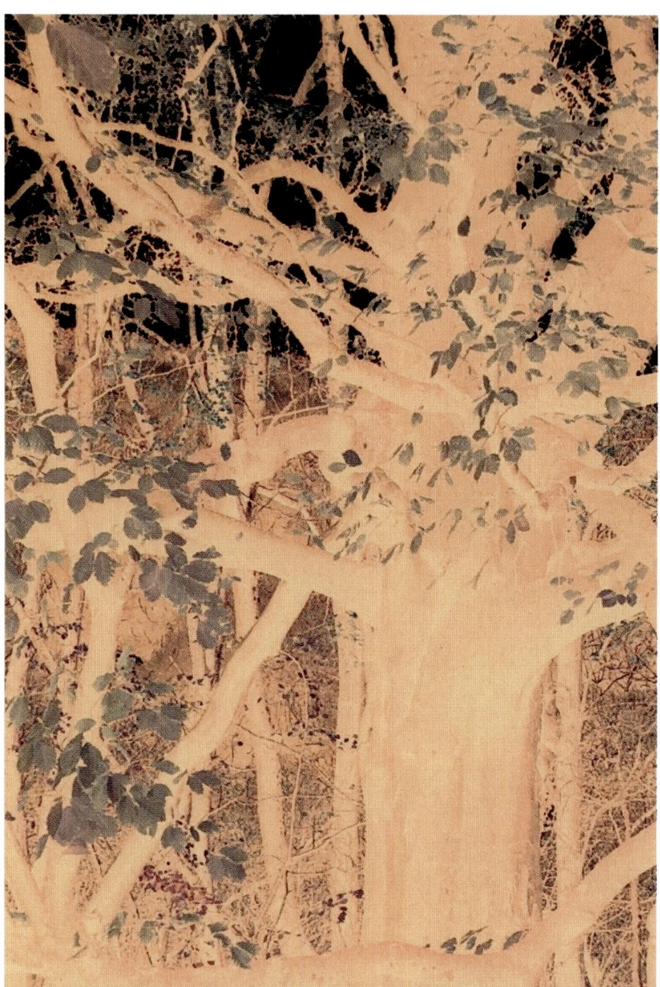

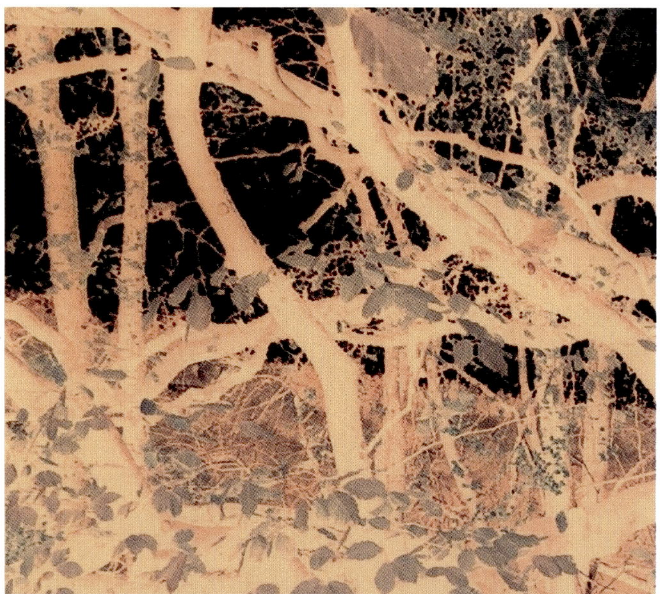

Right: I cropped a section from a pleasant but rather dull photograph of an autumn beech tree to give less recognizable, more abstract patterns. These were turned into a negative in which the colours mysteriously transformed to fairy-tale hues.

Right: Crow Black Moon

Negative printed on handmade paper with lace inclusions embedded.

Below: Photo transfer

*Printed images can be transferred onto another surface that has been
coated in white gesso, acrylic paint or special transfer medium. Place the
image to face the wet layer and leave to dry. Re-wet and gently rub the back
paper away to reveal the slightly distressed image on the new surface.*

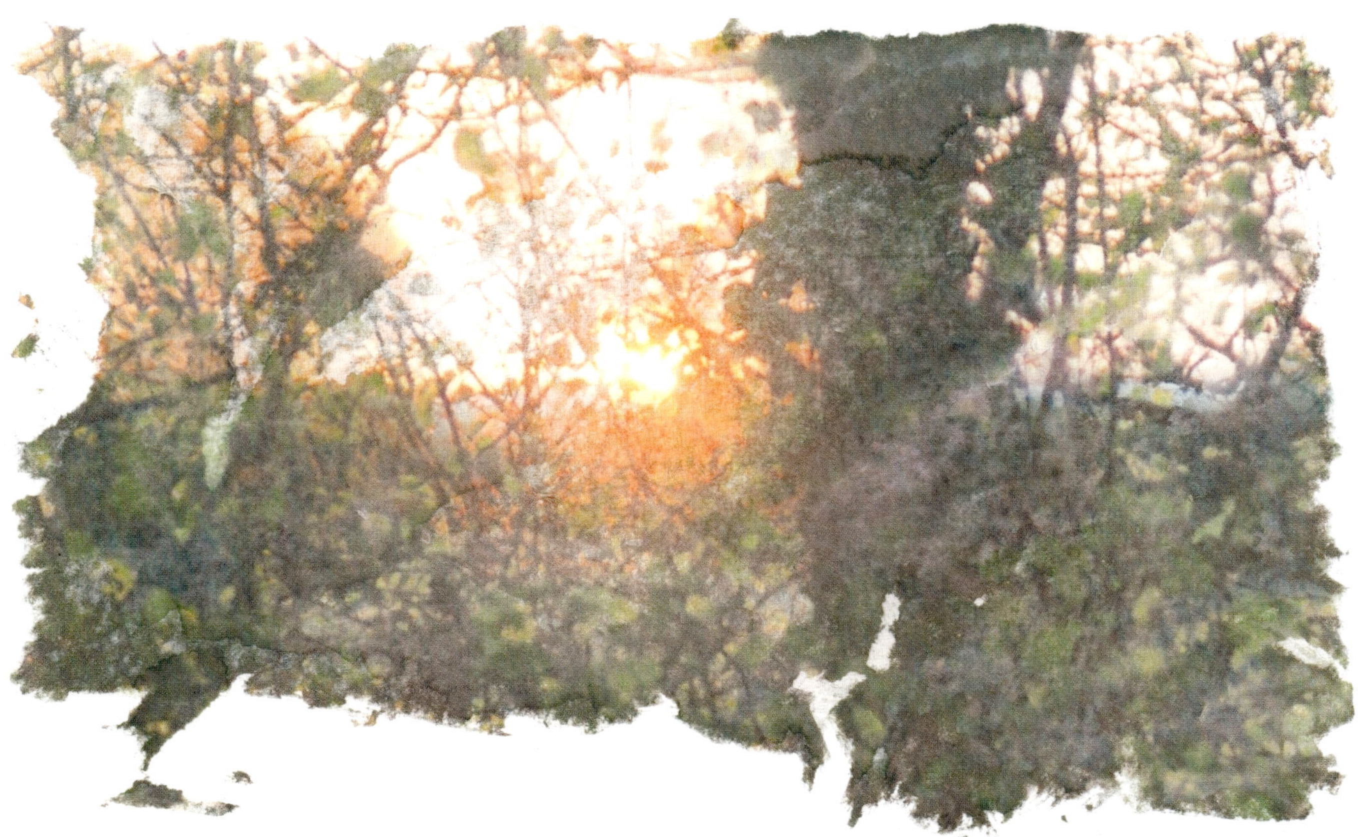

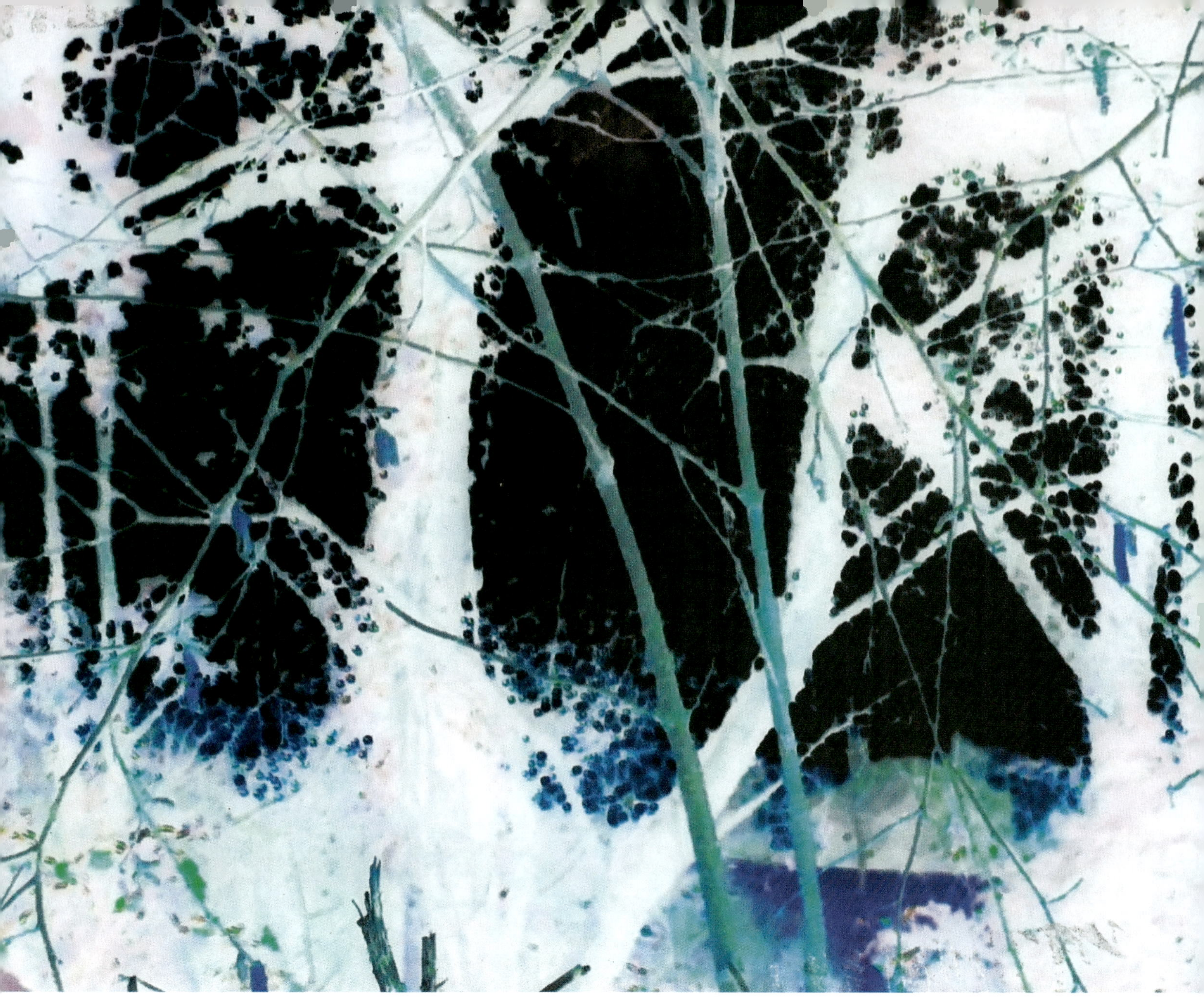

Above: The Entangled Hedge

Manipulated photograph.

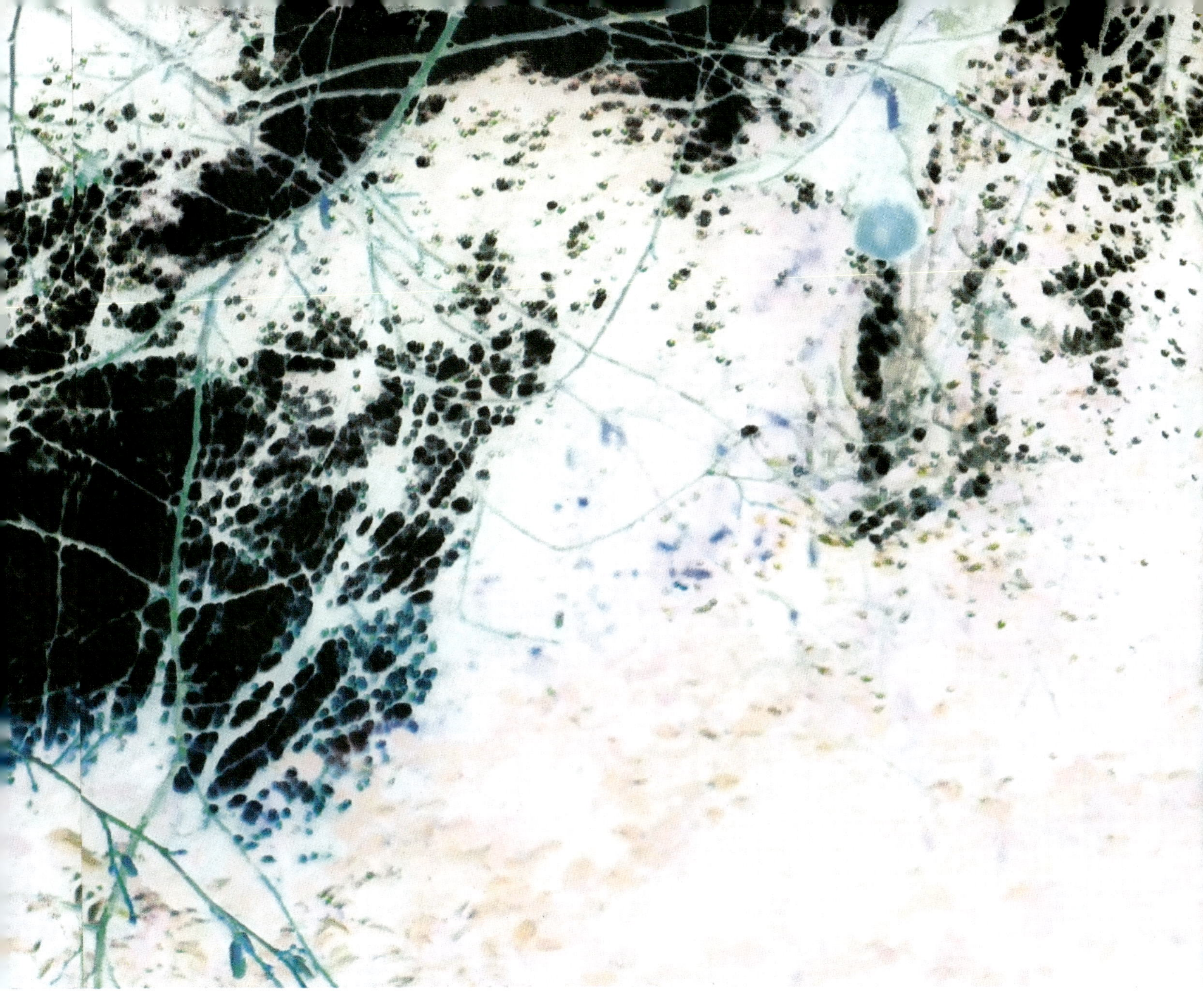

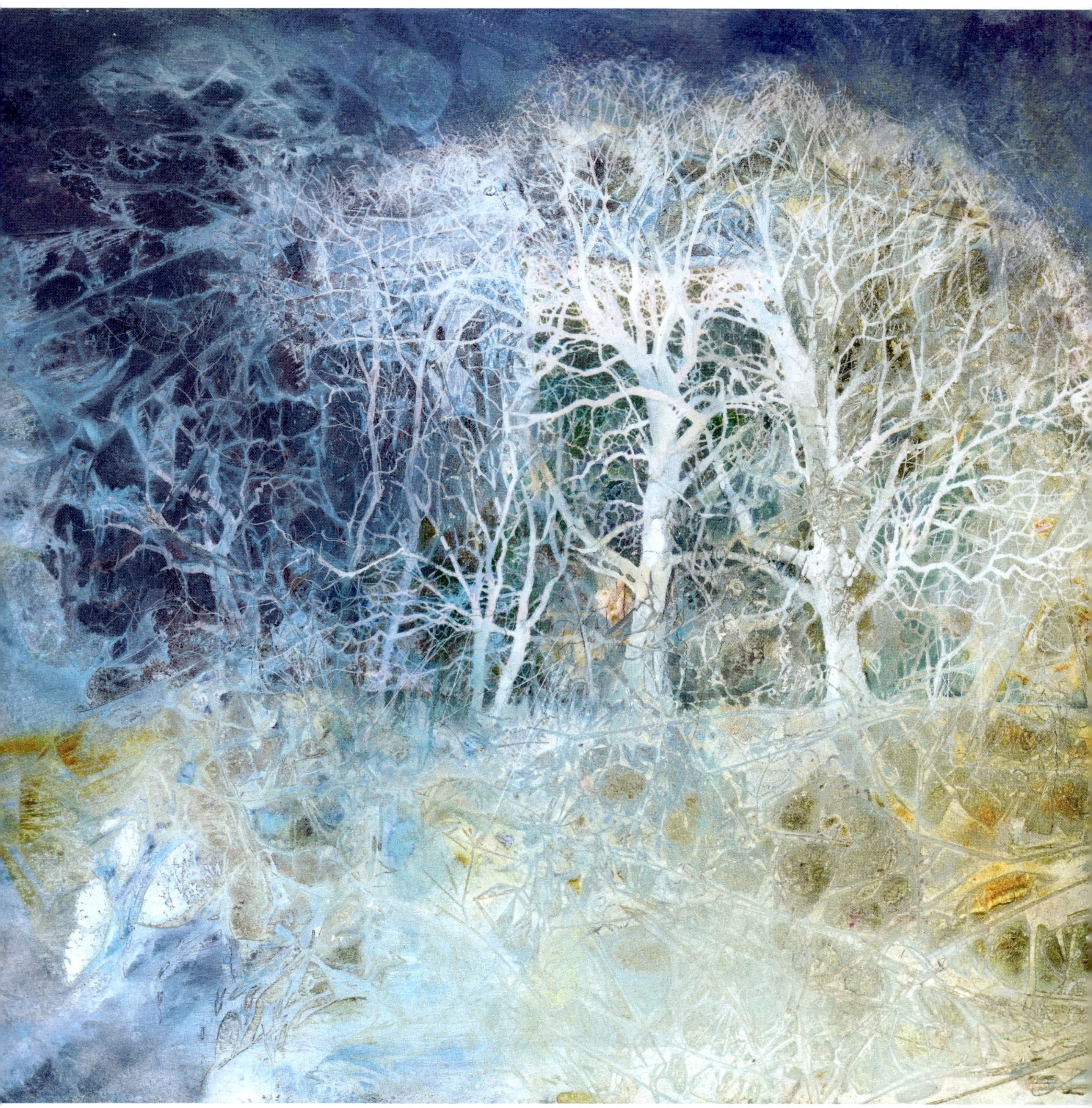

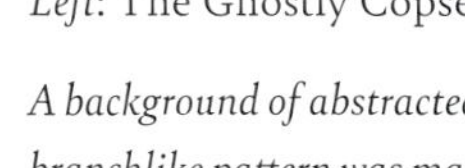

Left: The Ghostly Copse

A background of abstracted, branchlike pattern was made using forest materials and tissue paper to leave imprints in watercolour and gouache. Photographic imagery was used as reference to paint over the marks, but also included as collage.

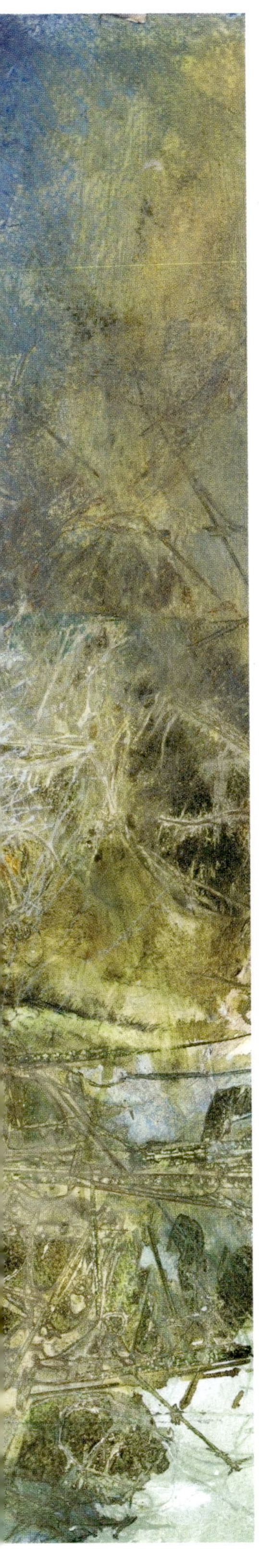

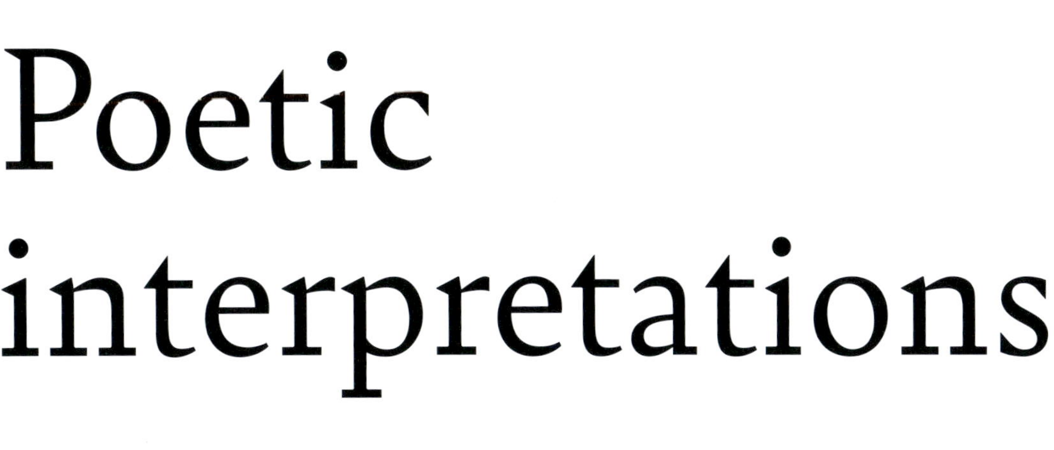

Poetic interpretations

In the previous chapter we experimented with aspects of making and using marks and materials in ways to create visual metaphors for assorted arboreal subjects and woodland experiences, using all our senses. Now let's look at how we might employ these in more 'finished' interpretations. Our starting point is an observation of nature to provide facts. Then we can use appropriate mark-making to translate these as we wish. For example, the quality of light and the grouping or structure of deciduous or evergreen trees are some of the prosaic qualities that we might first notice, but this chapter, while recognizing these scientific actualities, looks at transforming this information into imaginative, pictorial poems. The following pages demonstrate some of my own musings, memories, allegories and celebrations. I have scattered the acorns of ideas that will hopefully inspire you to consider how you can creatively interpret trees with atmosphere and empathy. My passion is the English woodland, copse and covert, greenwood and wooded garden. Yours might be the park, rainforest, jungle or even your back garden. In fact, let's use the word 'woods' loosely – creative thoughts can simply spring from the fertile forests of imagination!

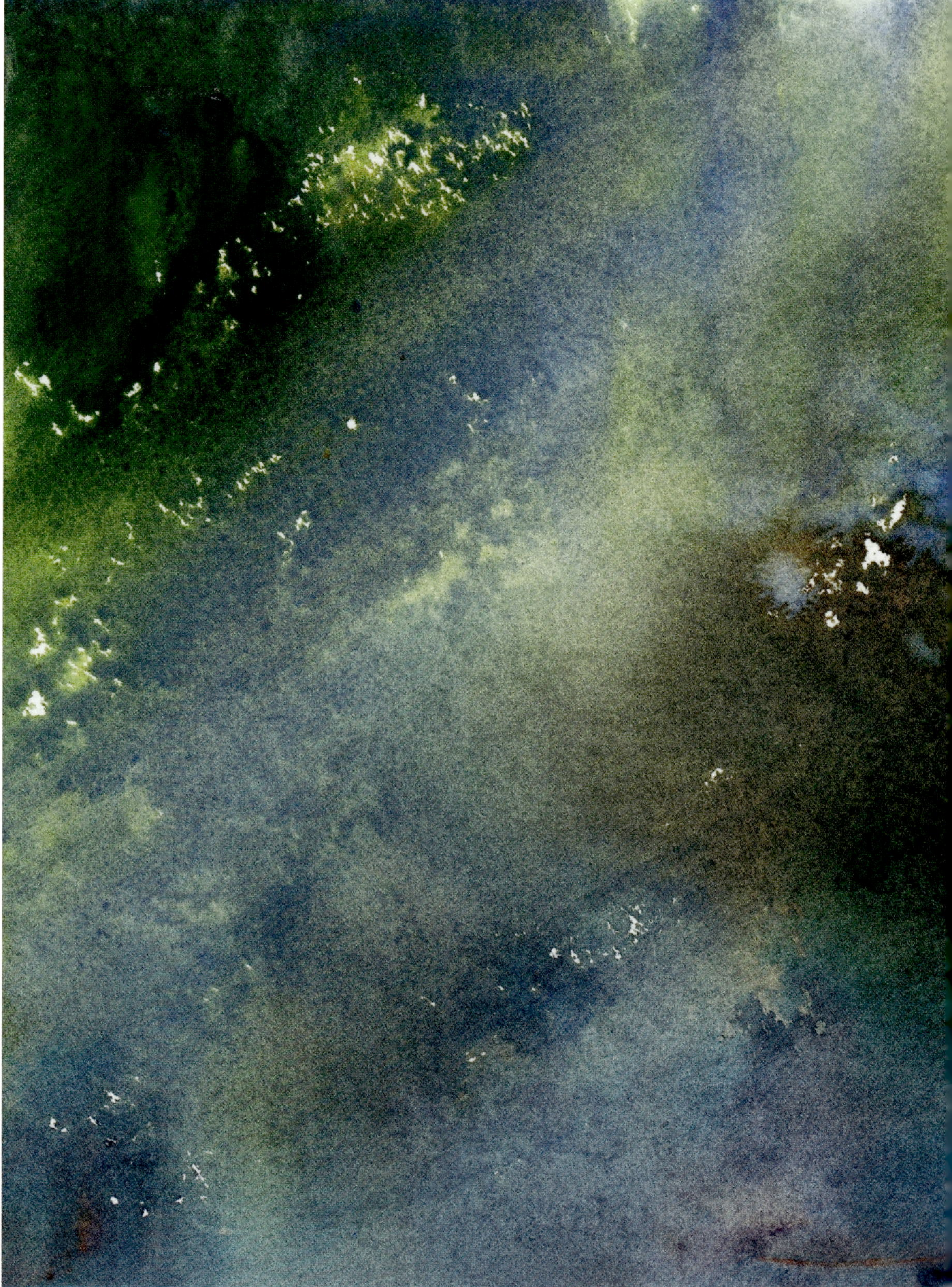

Silent Pond

A dreamy early morning light drifts sideways through broadleaf trees at the pond edge. Water melts almost seamlessly into an earthy bank with only glints of light to help define it. Sprayed paper in the upper section helps watercolour washes gather in ragged, nubby textures that suggest clumps of leaves on slender trunks. Cool lemon yellows and crisp-edged light patterns emphasize this dribbled focal point. Elsewhere, I used a flat brush to spread and lift colour into faded wispy streaks of sunbeam. Large areas with little detail bestow an air of silence and peace, which is further accentuated by the wide, landscape format.

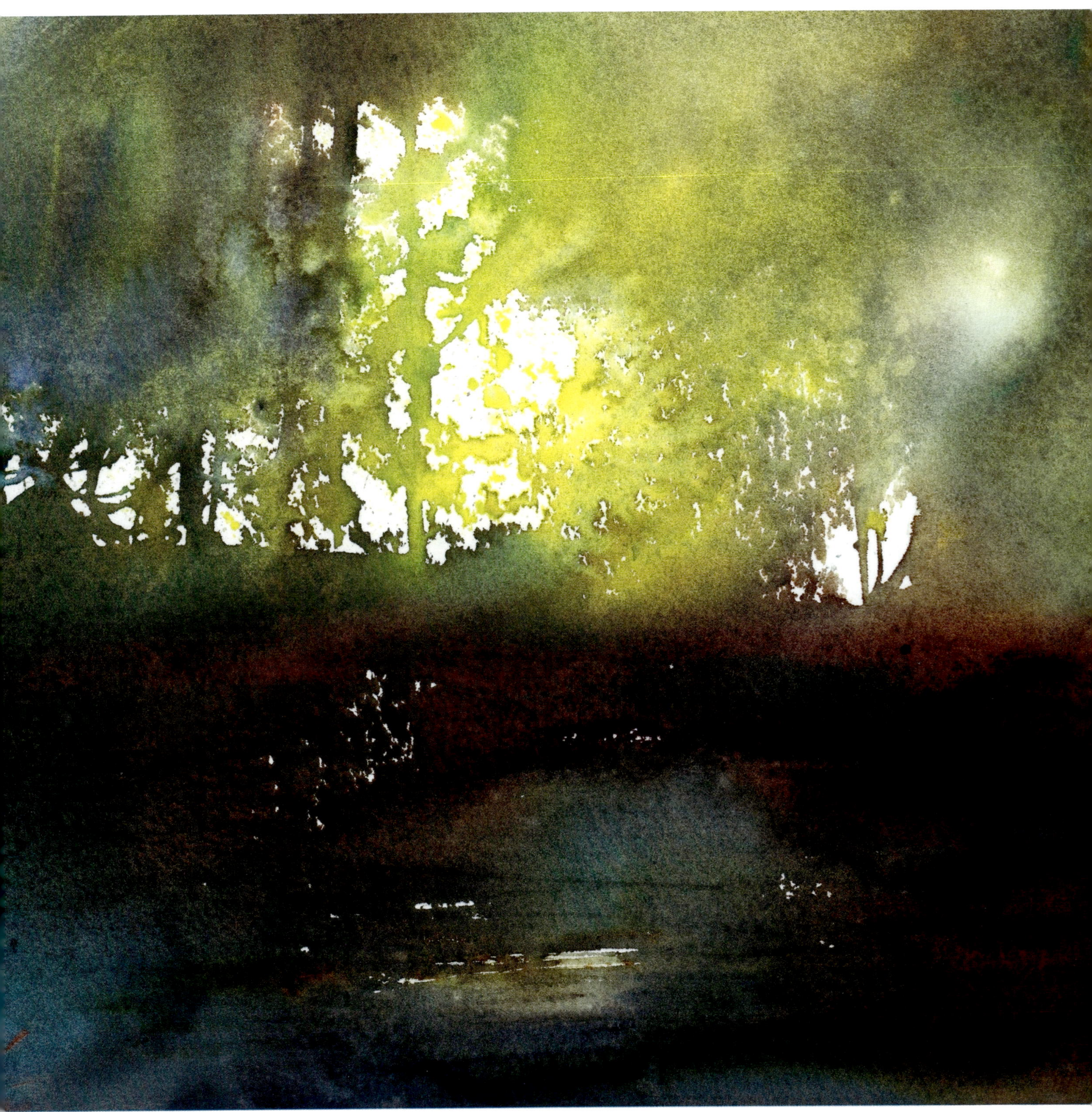

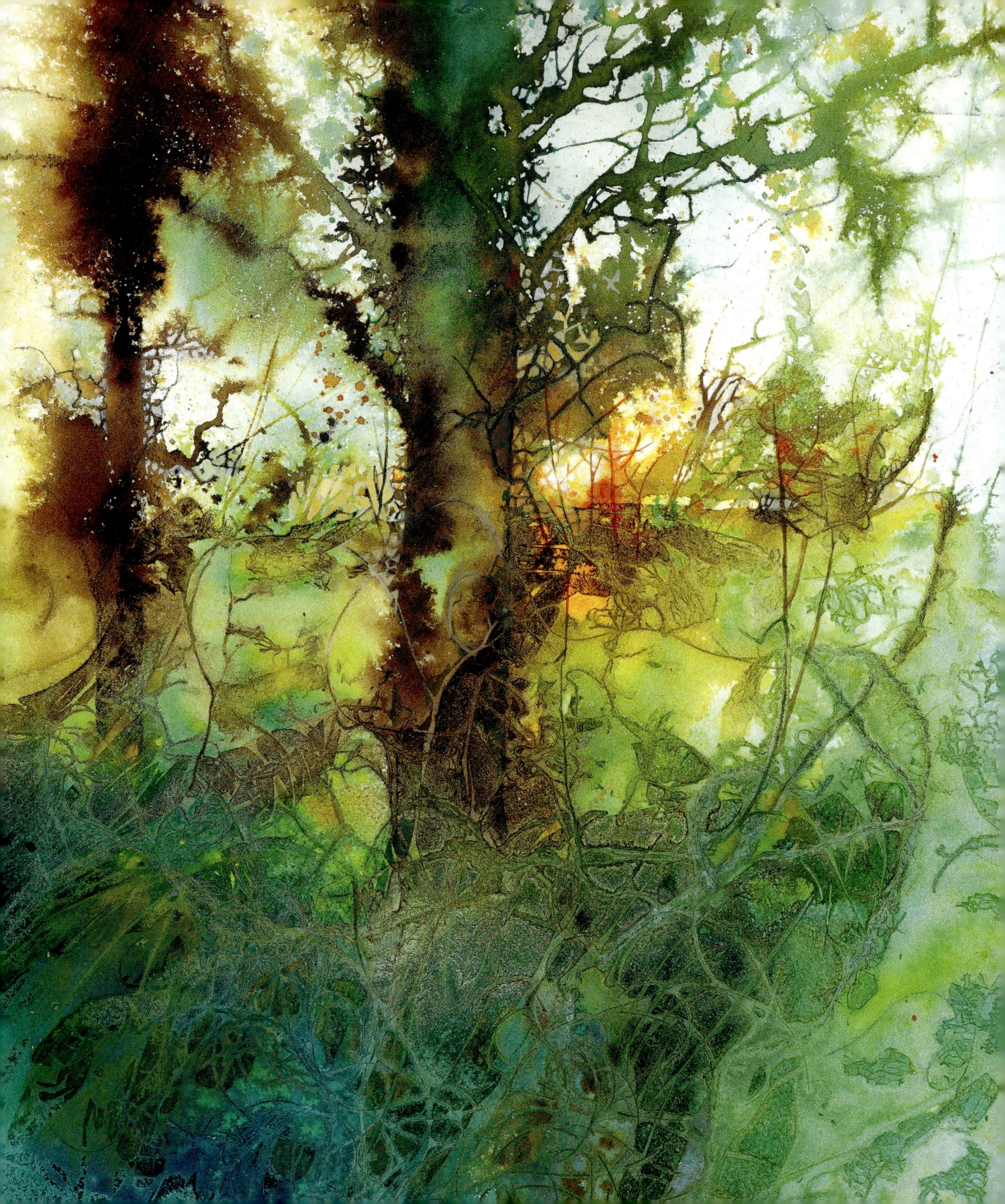

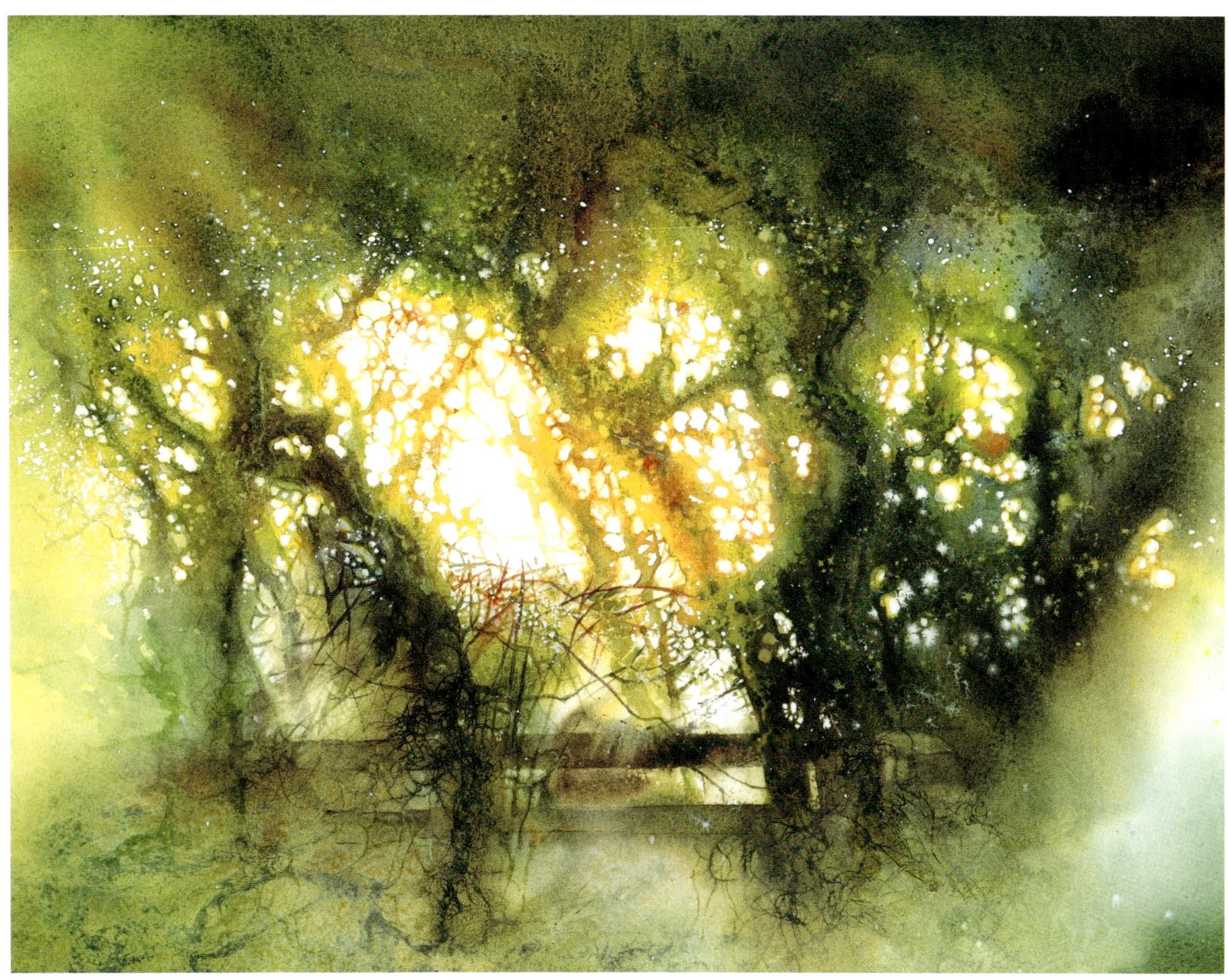

Left: Sunglow in the Greenwood Tree

The setting sun that peeps through a tracery of twigs was the focal point in this painting and as such I needed to carefully consider how to proceed. I could have simply left a small white space and painted around it, even blending the colours to a soft edge. Any trespassing paint flooding into the wrong place could be painted out later using opaque white gouache. However, I chose to use masking fluid on this tiny area as it was essential that it remained crisp and sharp.

Above: Hedgerow Shimmer

There are perforations, holes and spaces between the lattice-work mesh that makes up the framework of a hedge. Light pierces through these gaps to dazzle and glitter. It blinds and distorts perception of the actual shapes it punctures – fading and blurring edges, bleaching and colouring dark stems to shades of orange. In this image the canopy of hedge-growth and the ground below is painted in washes of green. The light shapes and holes were protected with masking fluid to enable the flow of loose colour washes over the whole area. The mask was removed later to leave white paper shining through.

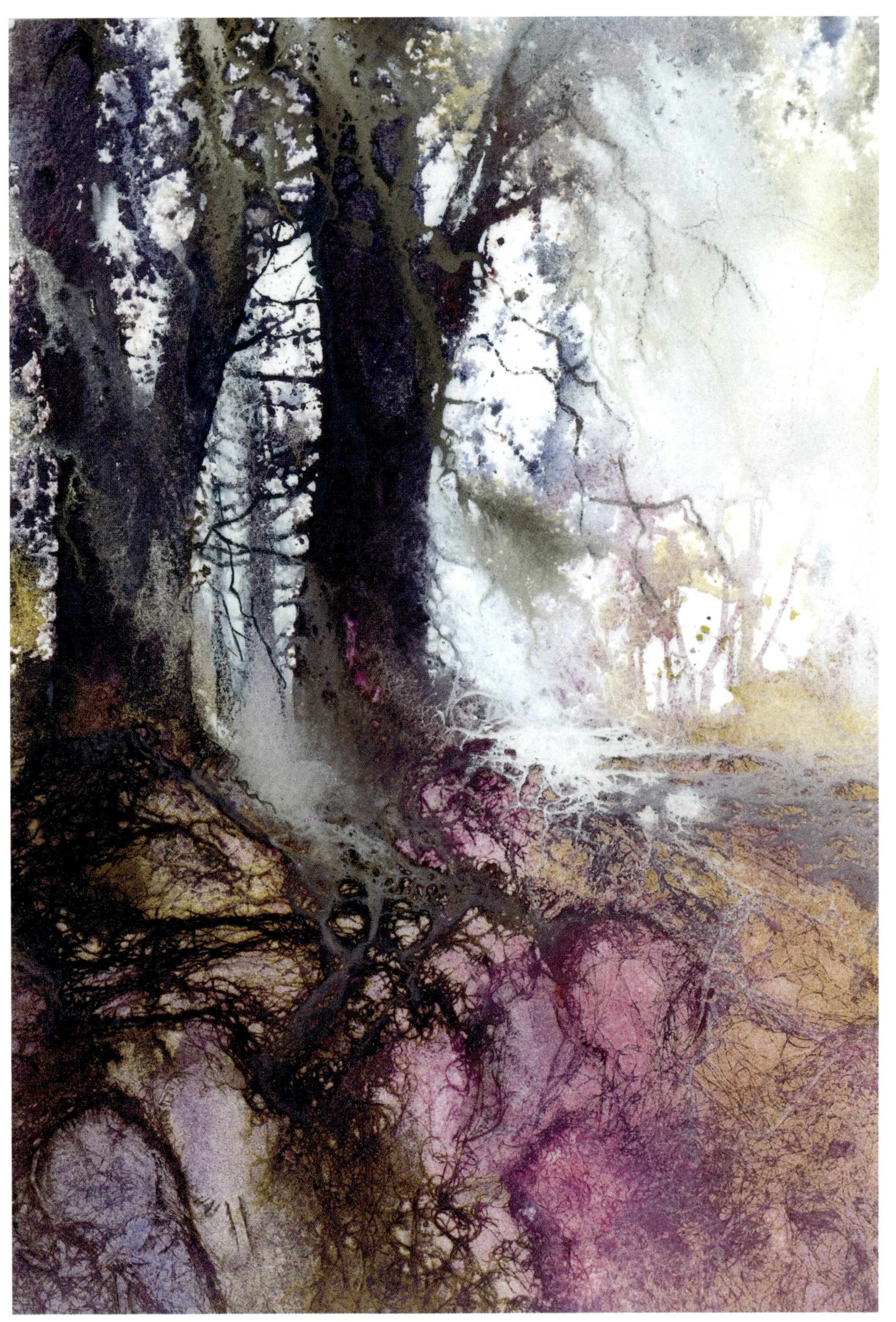

Left: Woodland Fantasy

The silhouette of two dark trees is a recurring theme in my work. Perhaps it is based on a much-loved pair of ash trees that dominated the bottom of the garden when I was a child. It is the first woodland subject I ever painted, and one might speculate about what the trees subconsciously represent. The adult version shown here is a celebration of texture, both seen and imagined. The two trees are representational, but where they grow into the ground a network of more whimsical, root-like textures weaves a tangled web over a cyclamen-pink ground.

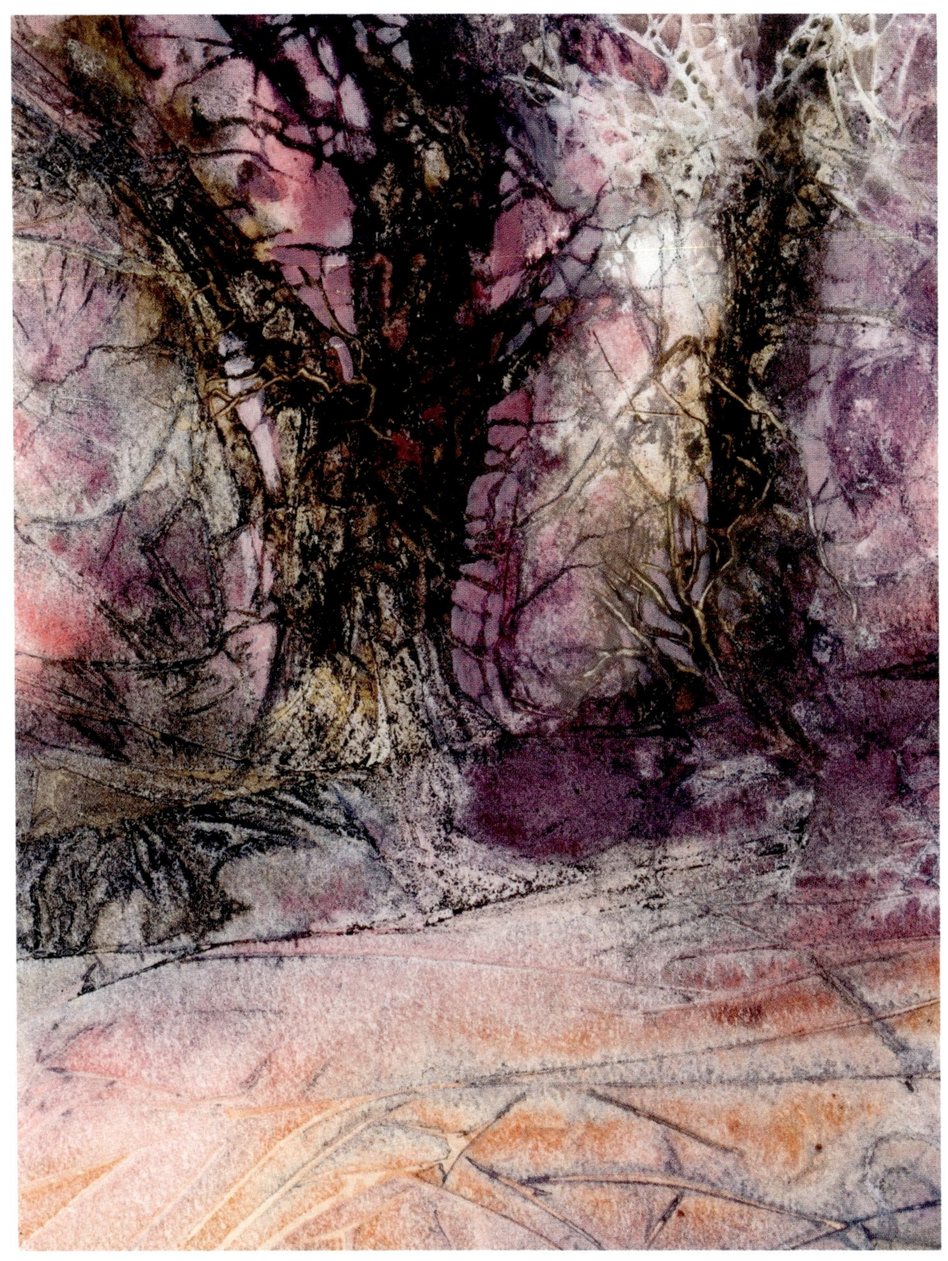

Above: Through Rose-tinted Woods

These twin trees and their background were developed out of an initial abstracted pattern in which different shades of watercolour and ink were applied and then broken into geometric shapes by laying crumpled tissue paper on top. Once the tissue was removed, I delineated the tree shapes using opaque gouache in the negative spaces between the main trunk and boughs, scraping out lines to retain the decorative, mosaic, branch-like pattern. Quinacridone Magenta, French Ultramarine, Brown Madder and Sepia helped build an atmospheric, exaggerated rose-coloured theme.

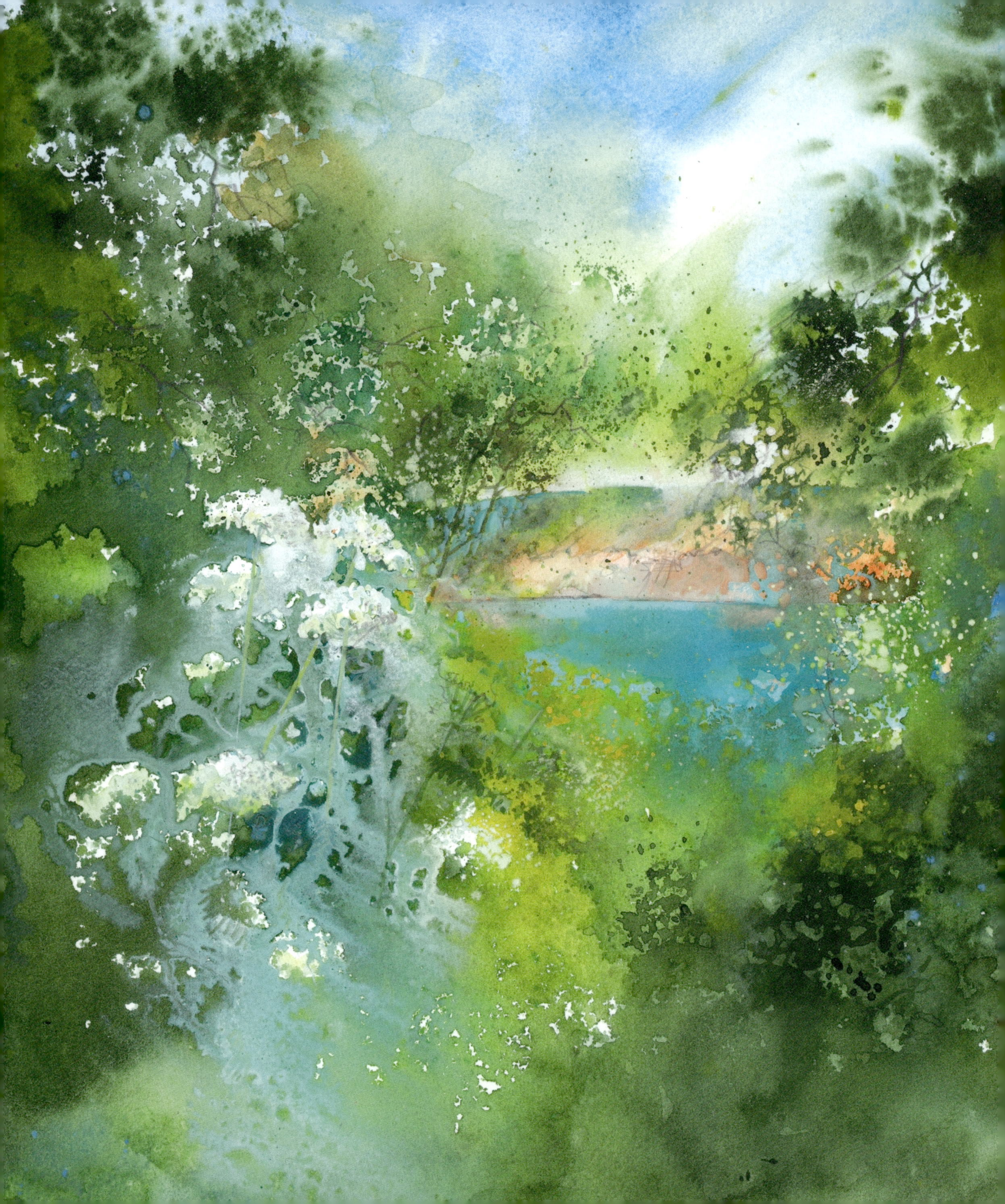

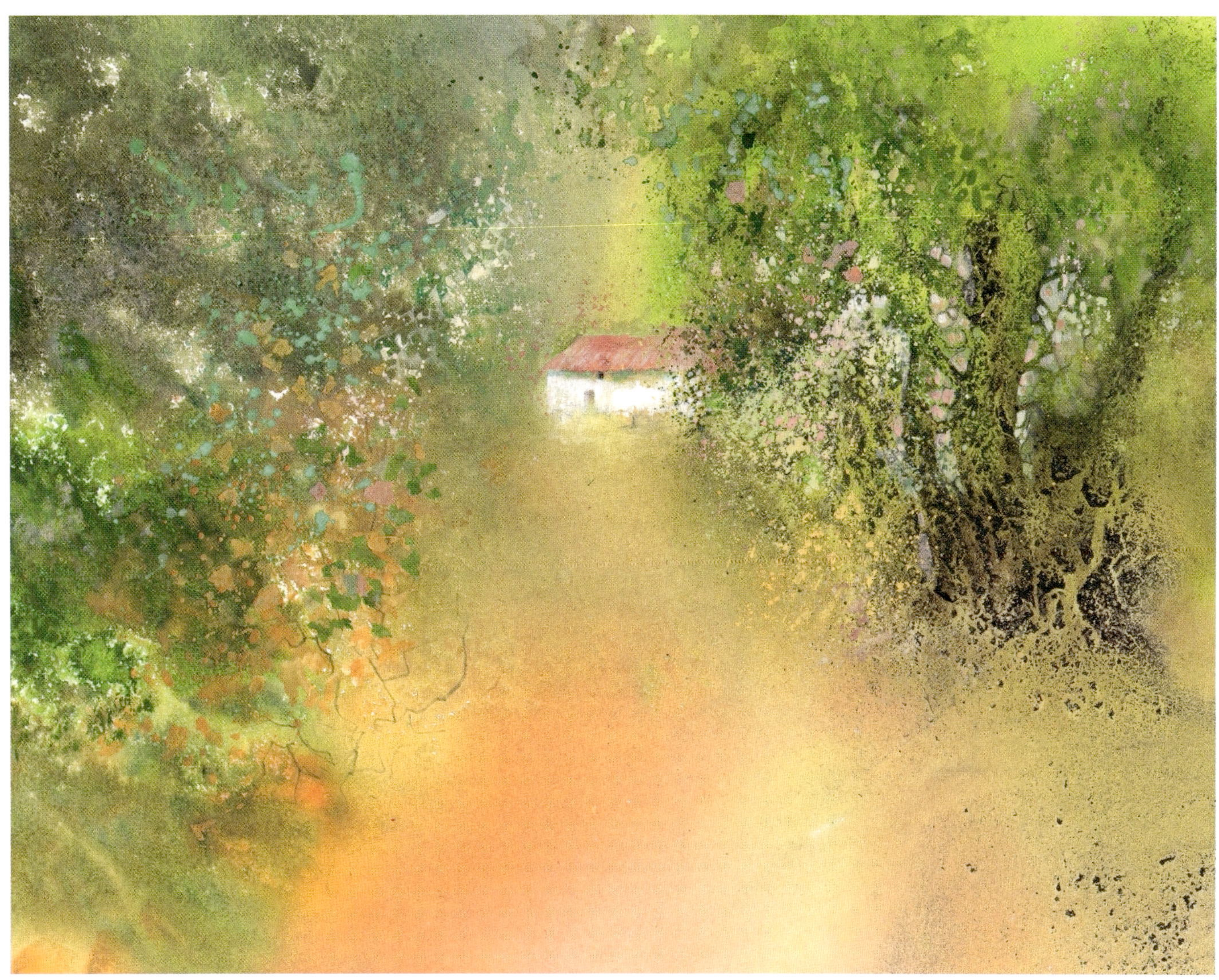

Left: Estuary Glimpse

The woodland walks along the coastal paths near my home provide cameo glimpses of the estuary captured through gaps in the trees. On this calm summer day, the sea was a flat duck pond of turquoise, echoed by hints of blue in the clifftop beyond. Lacy white hogweed mingled with the frills and filigree of foliage. I left the leaves unidentified, preferring a more harmonious, ambiguous blend of greens that was more to do with joyous mark-making than any particular species.

Above: Fairy Tale Wood

We unexpectedly came across this dreamlike, whitewashed cottage in a dusty wooded coppice on a mountain walk in Morocco. It nestled quietly in its surroundings of olive and fig trees that seemed to shimmer in the heat. I decided to be enigmatic about the leaf type, being more immersed in the slightly surreal, fairy-tale quality of the scene. I left the foreground very plain to contrast the dappled and freckled textures elsewhere. Sometimes you need to be selective to emphasize a point.

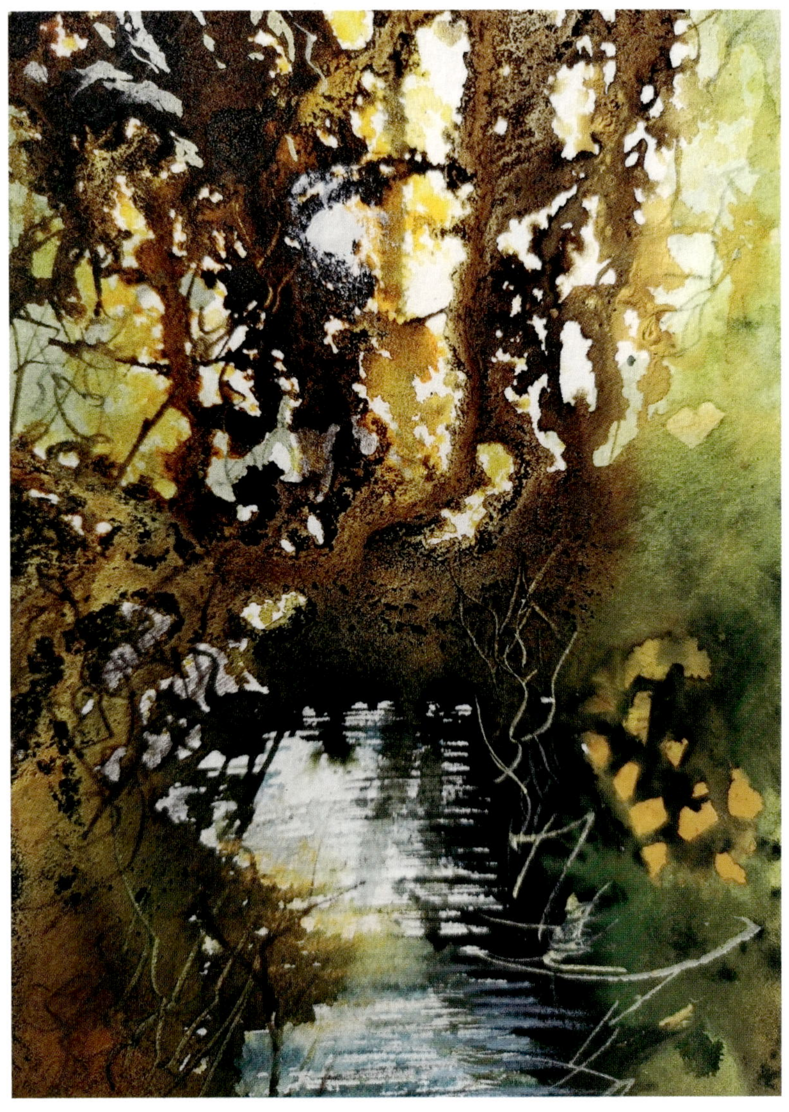

Above: The River's Song

Water among trees is a perfect marriage of elements. Woods can be dark and shady
places, where the only pale areas are the patches of light sky through the canopy above.
In paintings, the introduction of a further zone of shining light opens new possibilities
for composition. A stream or river can be like an illuminated pathway curving or
leading straight towards or beyond the surrounding trees. Reflections break up this
track of light into interesting patterns. In my sketch I contrasted the crenelated,
ragged tree textures with the more horizontal and linear pattern of the stream.

Right: Going with the Flow

Boulders force this river into curved, zig-zag
shapes that lead the eye through the artwork.
This painting was made on a surface that
had been painted with gesso over a previous
version. I like the idea that there is a hidden
story beneath the flowing waters. The gesso
brushmarks altered the way the paint reacted,
especially where the river drifted through.
Granulation medium was added to ink and
white paint in this area, and I let it decide where
it wanted to flow. There is no point arguing with
a river! The resulting texture was quite unique.

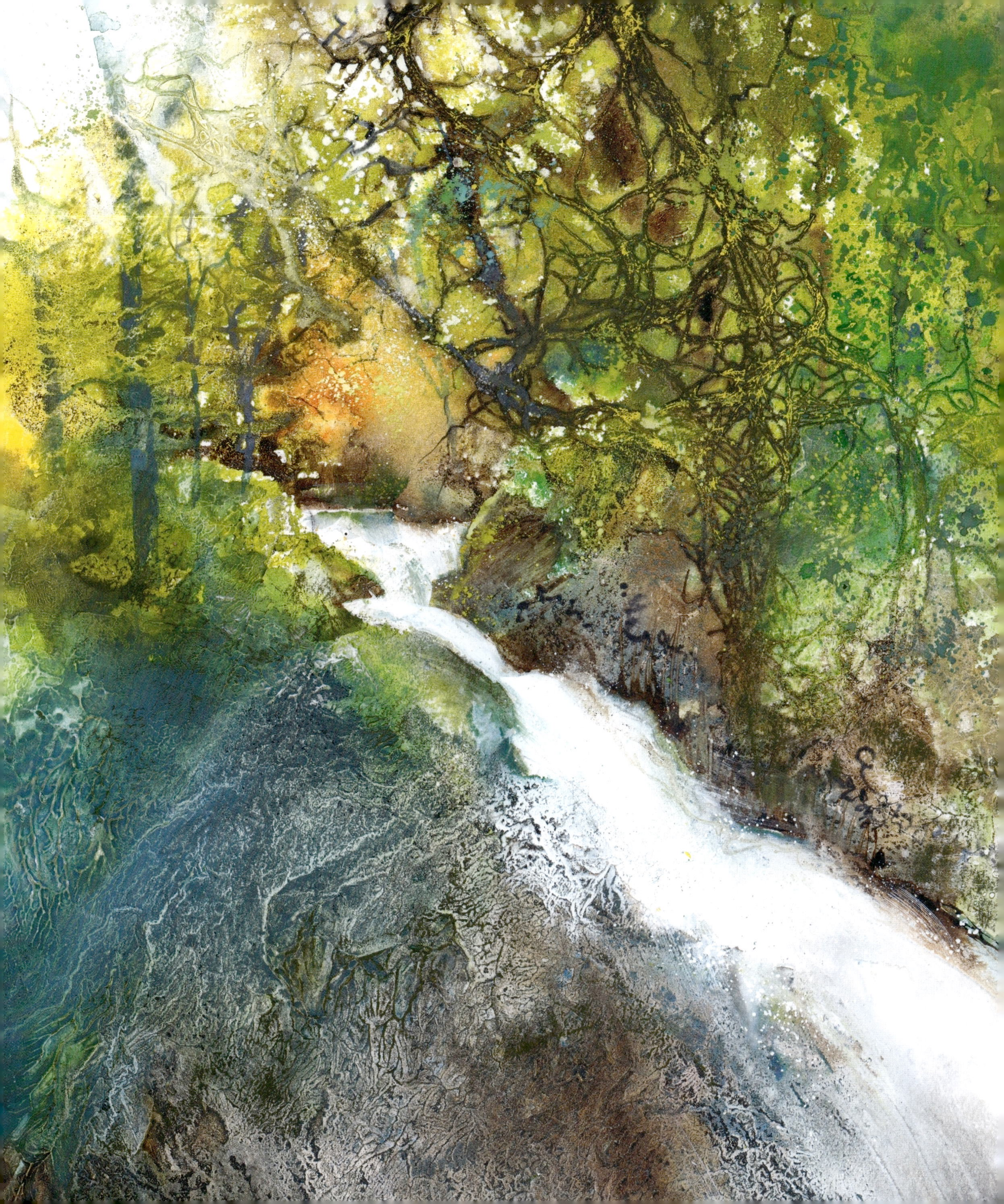

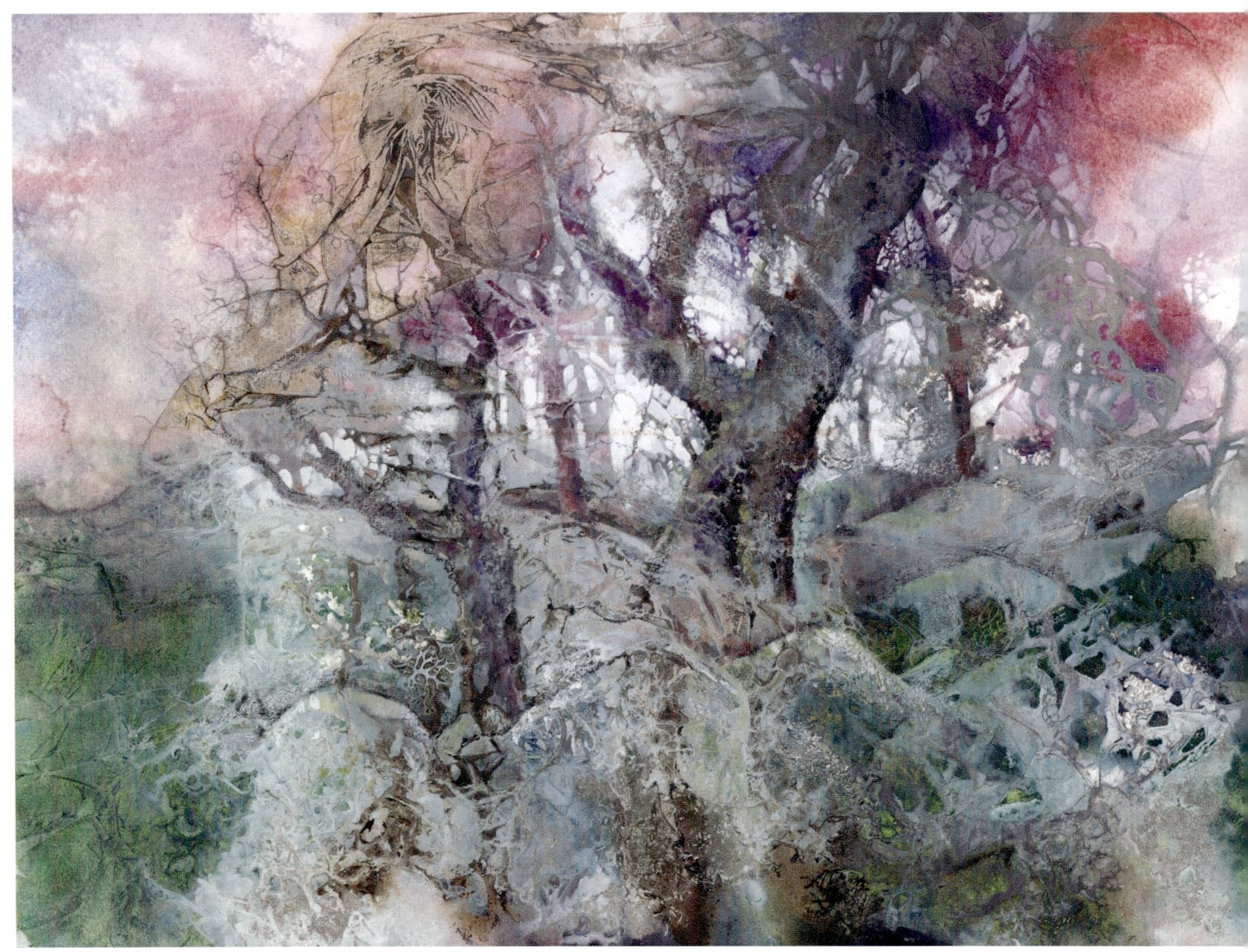

Above: Ancient Oak Grove

These mystical, ancient oak trees bend their gnarled limbs out of huge rocks. Moss, lichen and ferns festoon the branches and drip like stalactites. It is an other-worldly place surrounded by myth and moorland. The feral woods are pixie-led by day, but Wisht Hounds visit on lonely nights in search of prey.

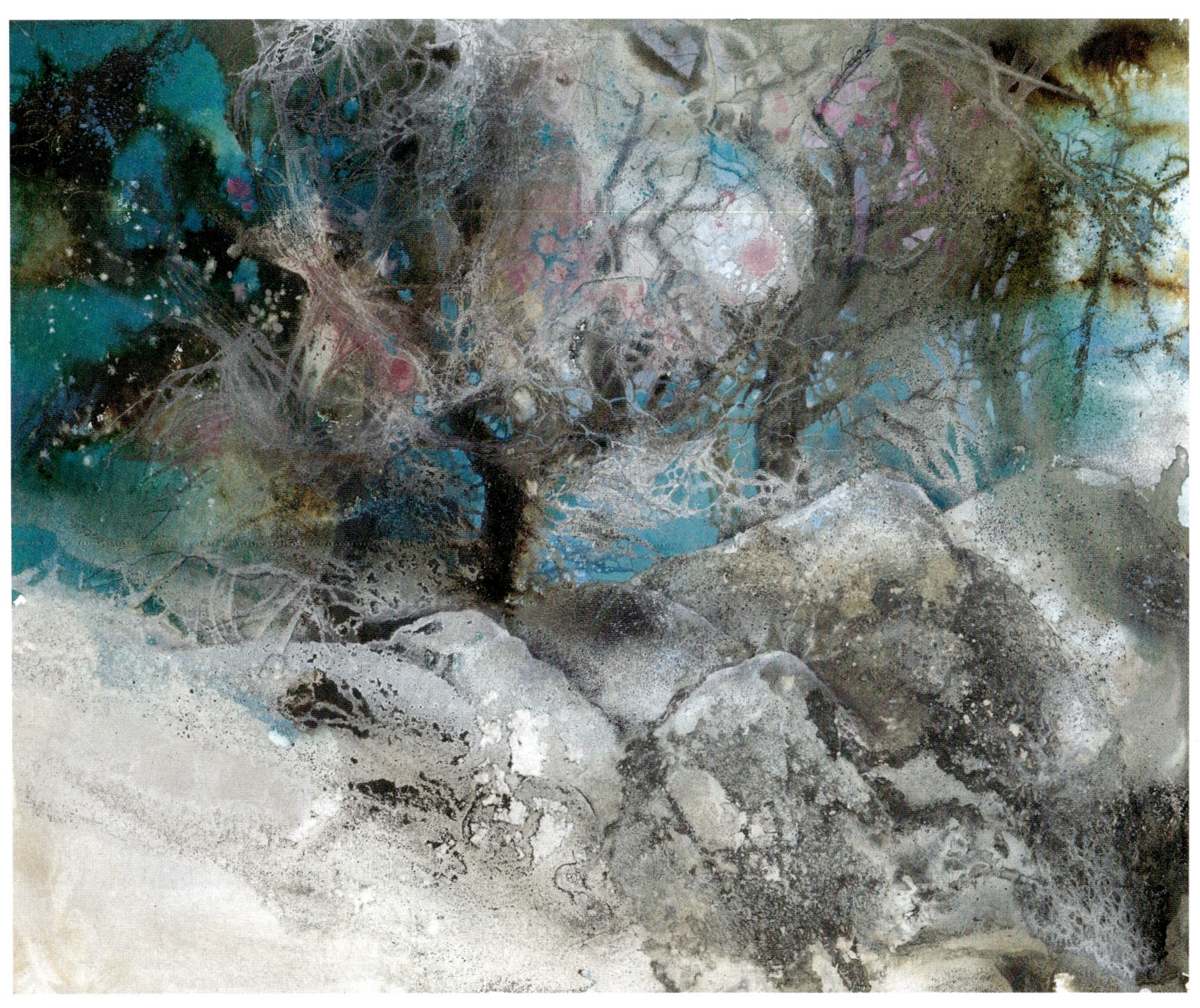

Above: Rhododendron Forest

I made two different kinds of water-based paints using bought pigments and shimmering rock gathered from this site. Both types were ground in a mortar and pestle with a little added gum arabic to bind them.

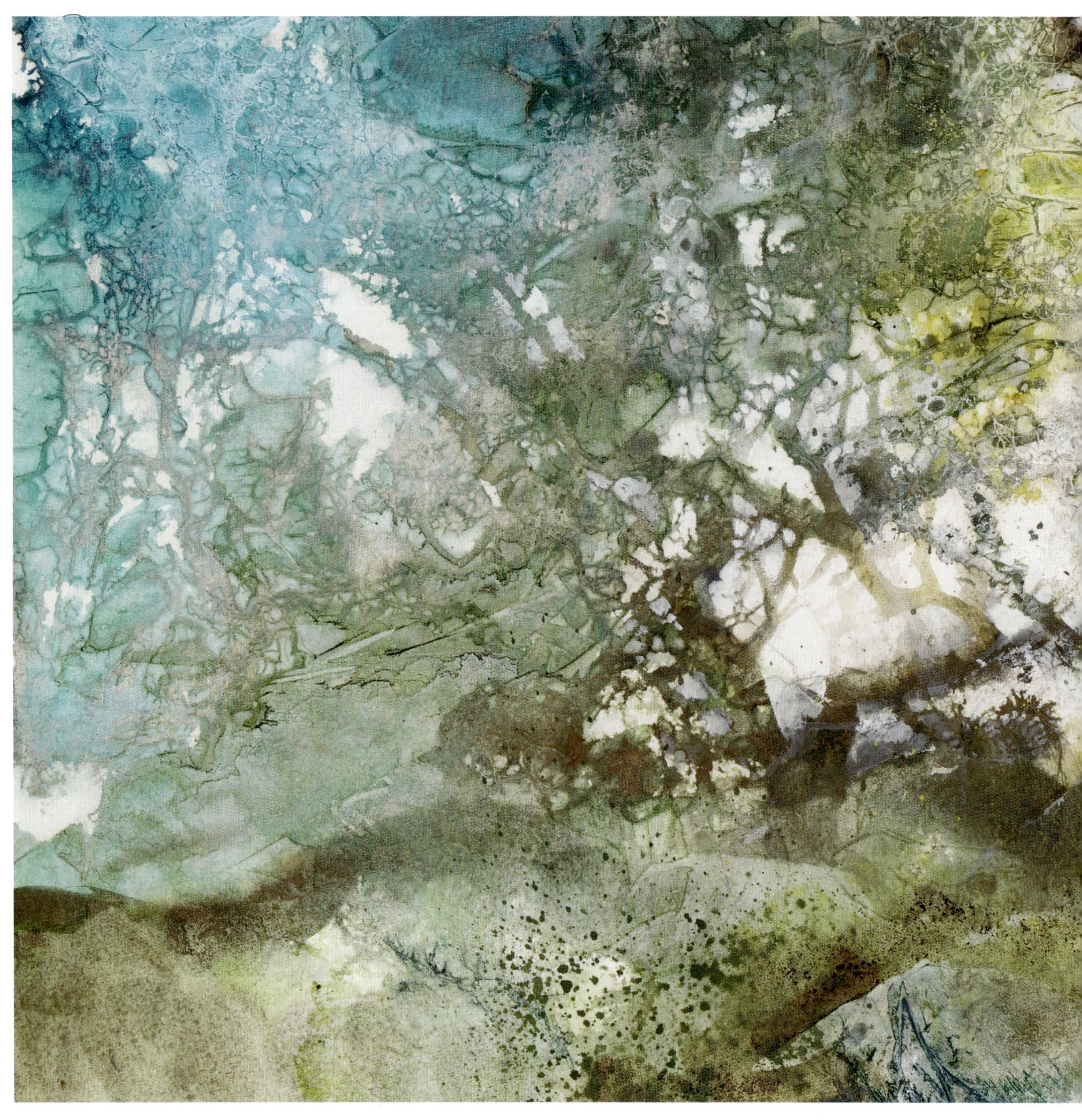

Above: The Wild Wood

Watercolour and ink on paper.

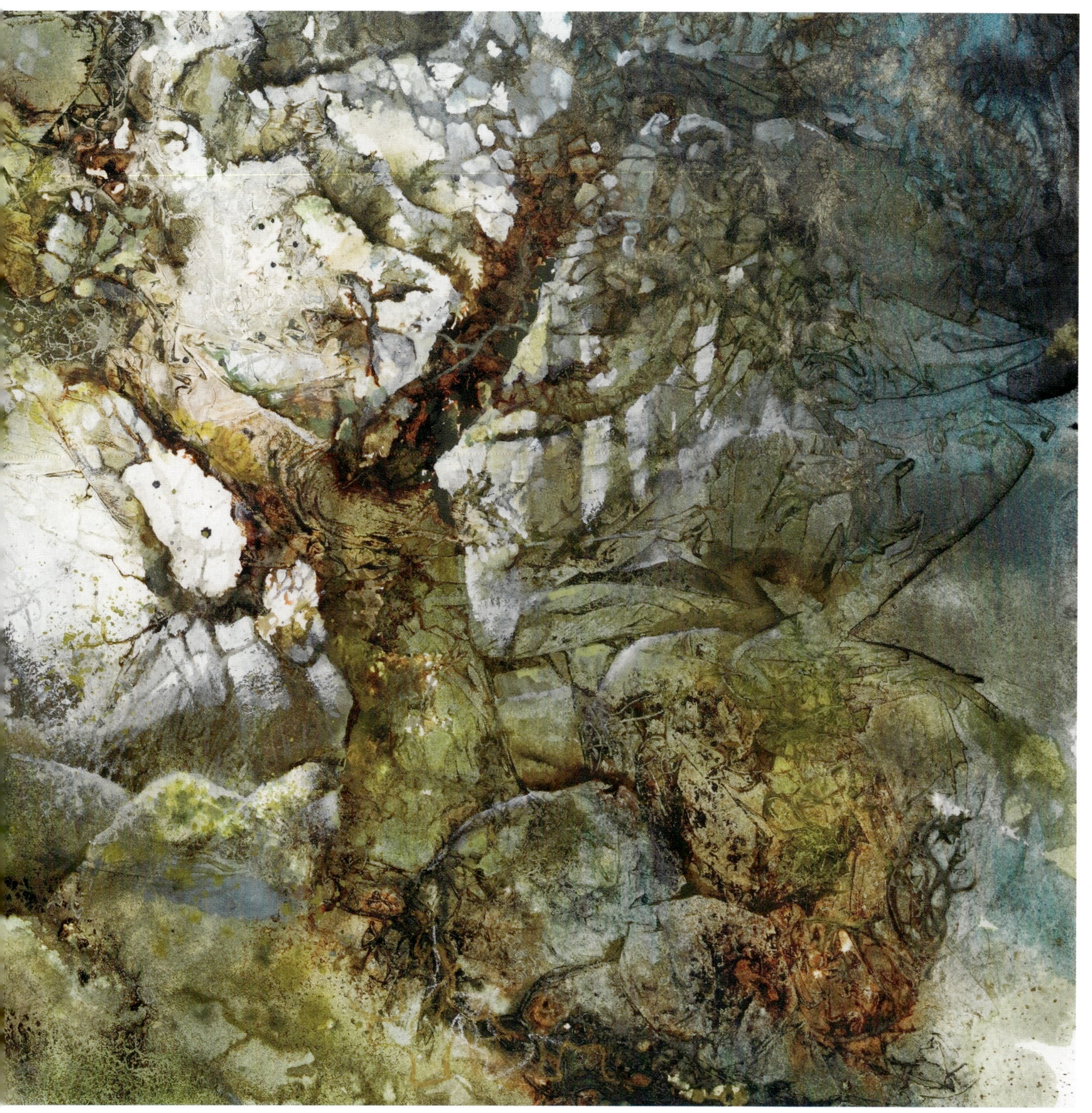

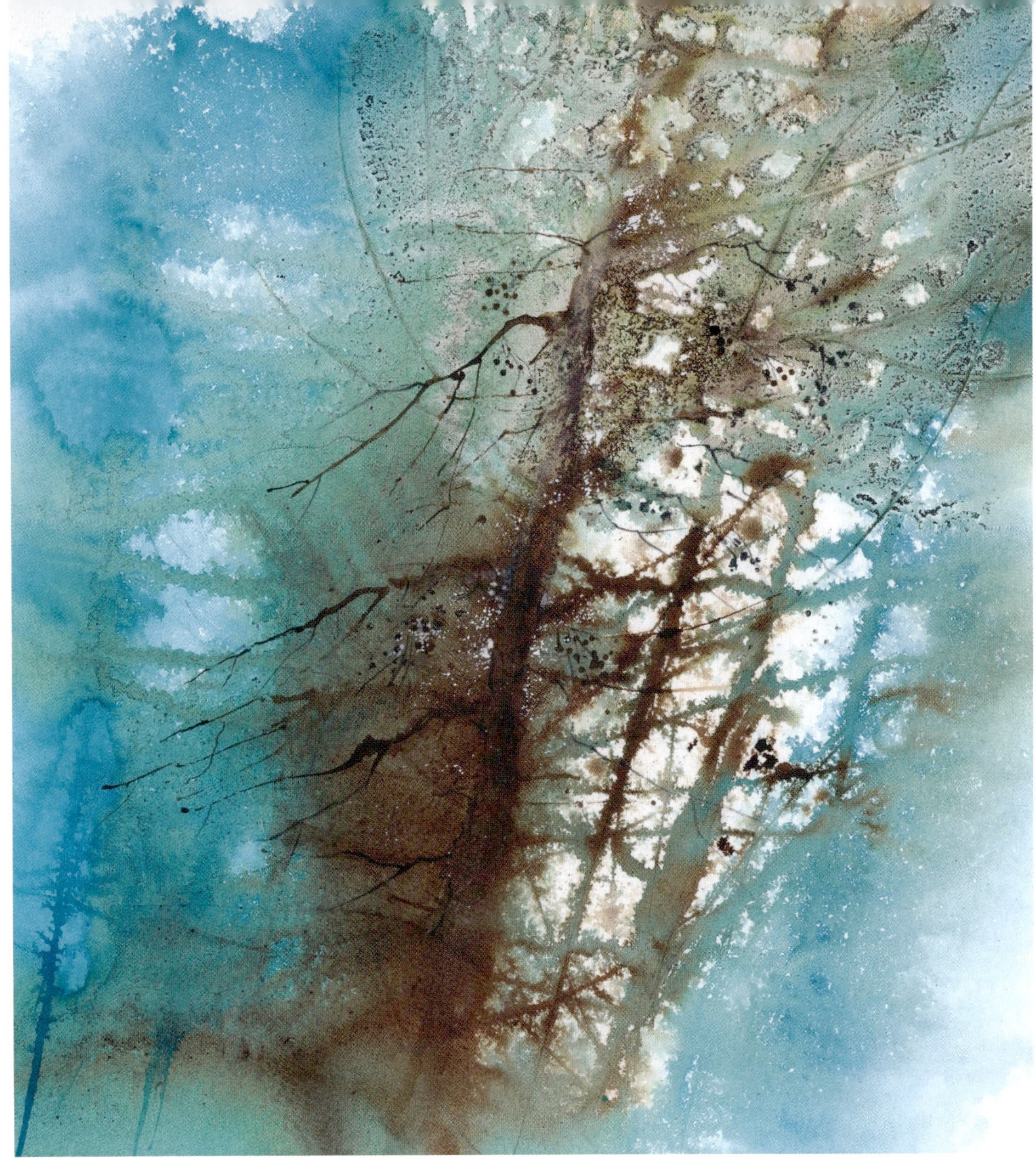

Above: Evergreens

Most conifers like spruce, fir and pine are evergreen, but the larch can be deciduous and shed leaves. My experiment looks at the general habit of such trees in an abstracted interpretation where each element merges to become blurred patterns that merely remind and insinuate. I flooded watercolour into water-sprayed paper, and dribbled sepia ink into this painted fretwork, which left white shapes where the paper was dry. I used a twig to drag ink sideways to suggest the growth habit of the trees. When dry, I added crisp dark circles to represent small cones, like expressive punctuation marks to make you pause and look.

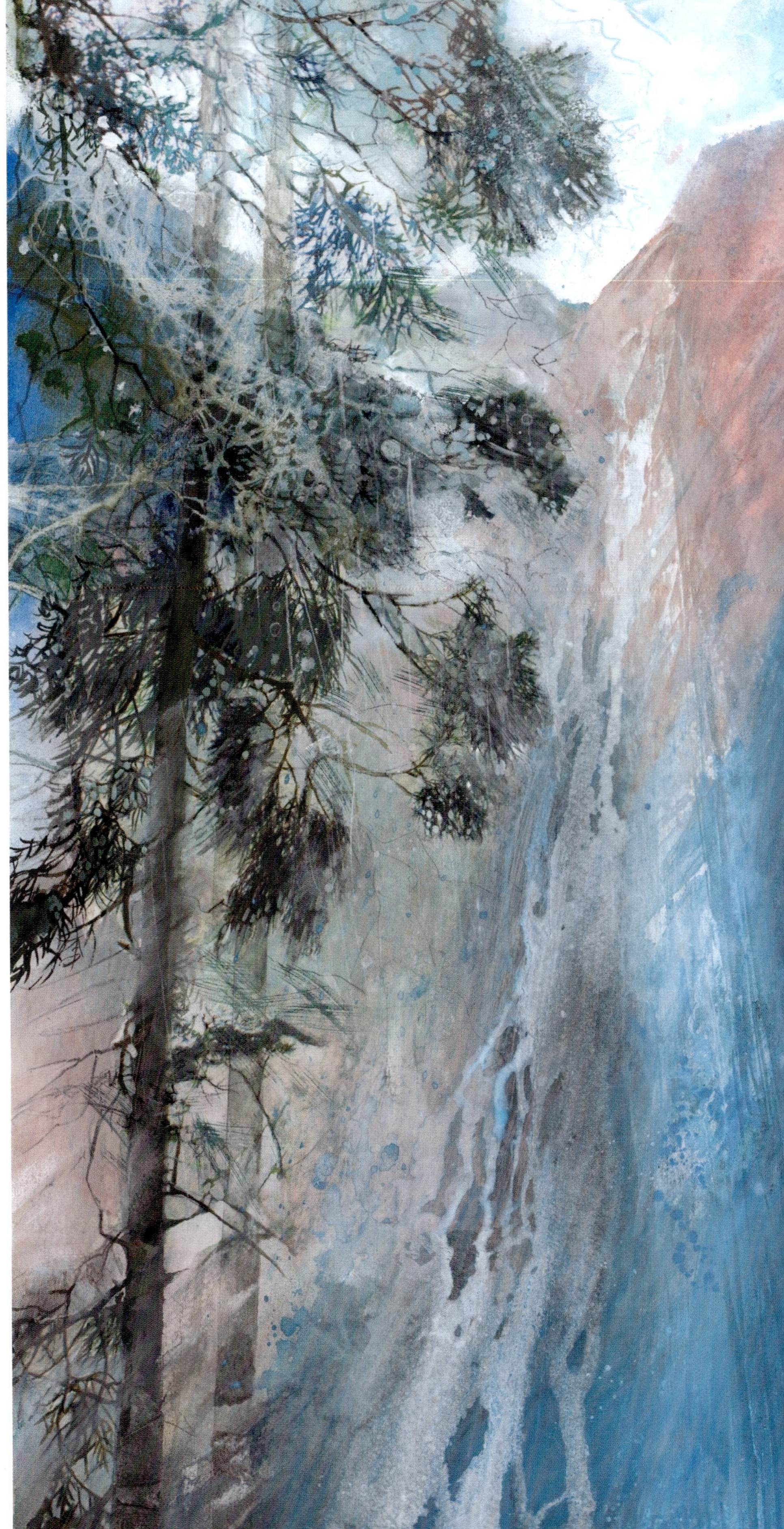

Right: Mountain Pine

Viewed through a showery veil, the silvered needles of rain echoed vertical, almost parallel trunks of the mountain pines that railroaded upwards, pointing to the sky. A filigree of ferny foliage broke through the formal pattern. Water cascading down the nearby mountainside echoed the soaring design but in softer, dreamlike broken markings. A palette of muted turquoise with dusky pink seemed to capture the mystical, rain-drenched atmosphere.

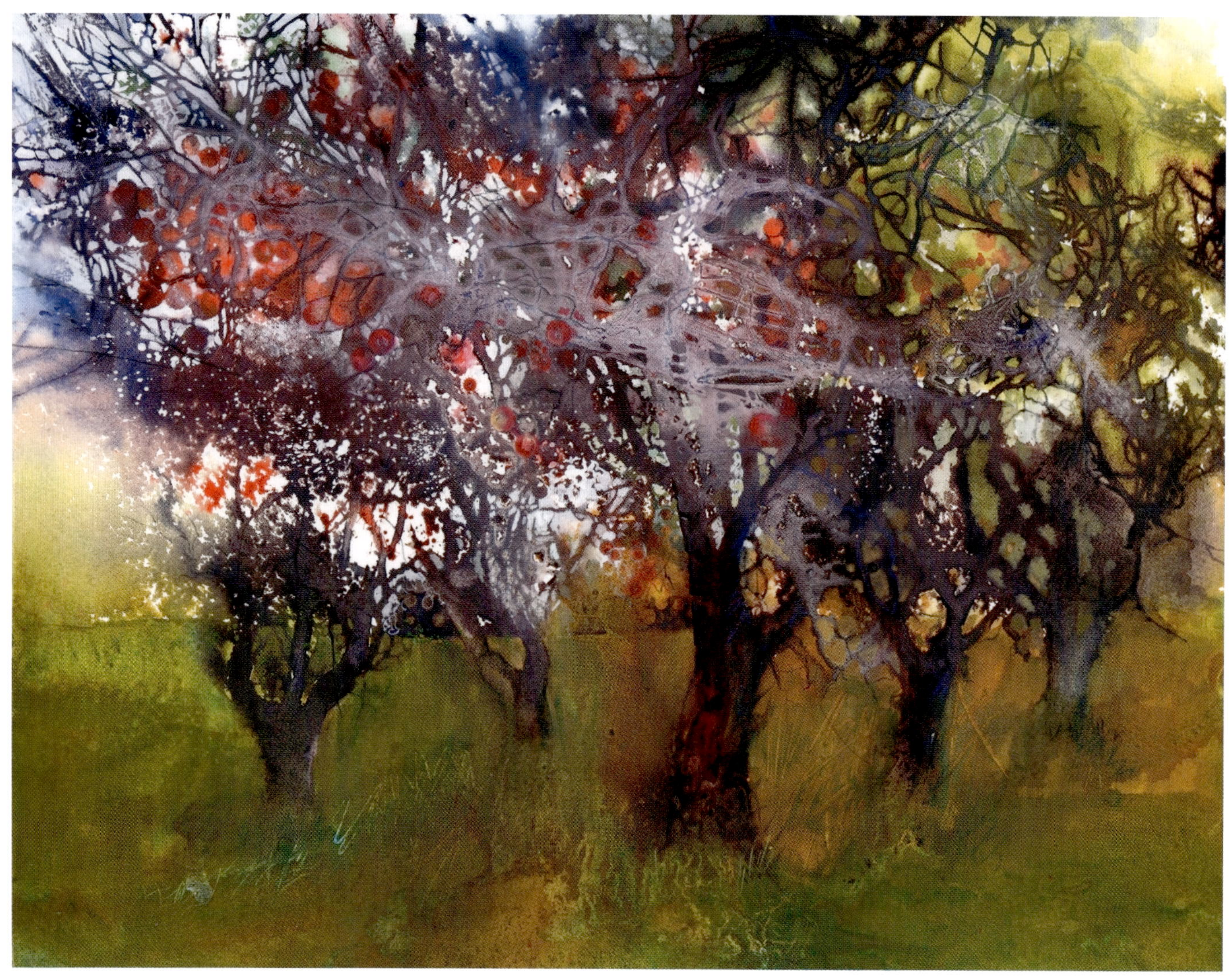

Two painted versions of an orchard were an opportunity to revel in the luscious, decorative patterns that the tangled branches offered. The red and rounded shapes of apples complete the ornamental tapestry effect, like large jewels threaded through, offering temptation. The crown of each tree has joined together in a wild dance, while the trunks remain separate. The foreground grasses were kept plain to offset the busy chaos of the fruit trees.

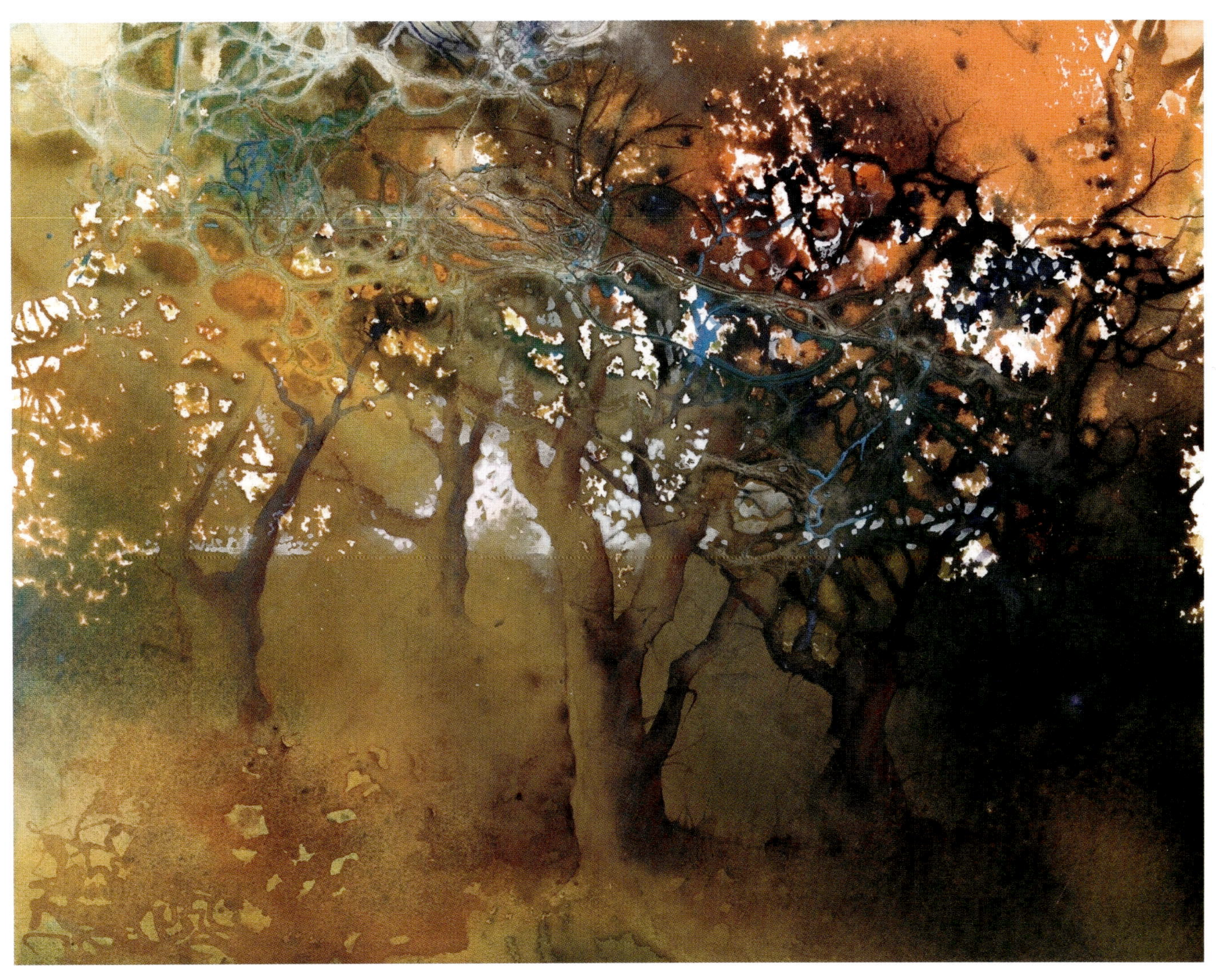

This interpretation uses different hues to give a golden autumnal glow. The background colour is shared by the tree trunks, which creates a harmonious atmosphere. I added purple ovals into the tangled area to suggest plums and introduced a hint of this colour into the branches. Note how the trunks blend softly into the ground so that they appear to grow out of it. Leaving a hard, contrasting edge can make them look separate, as if about to topple over.

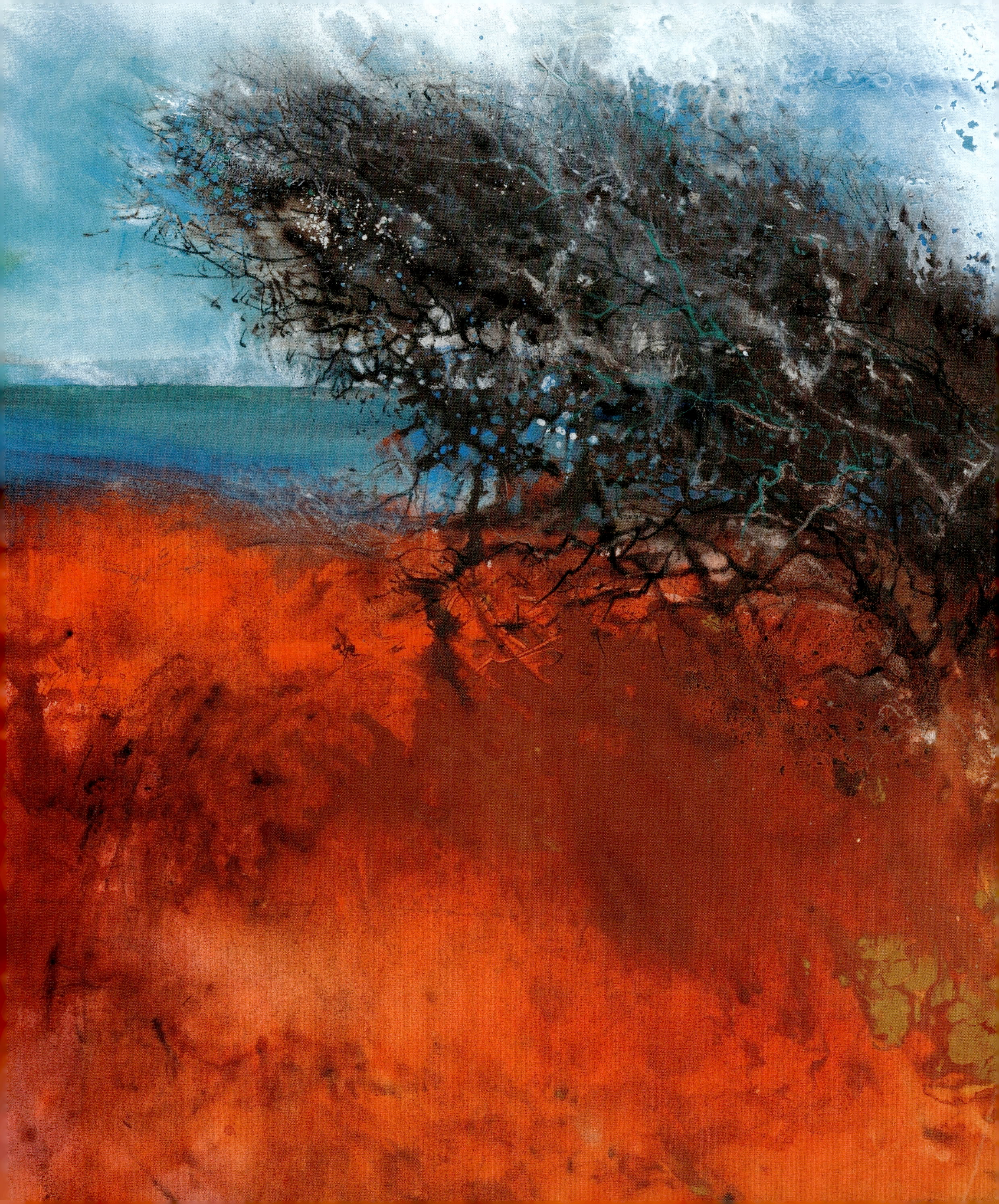

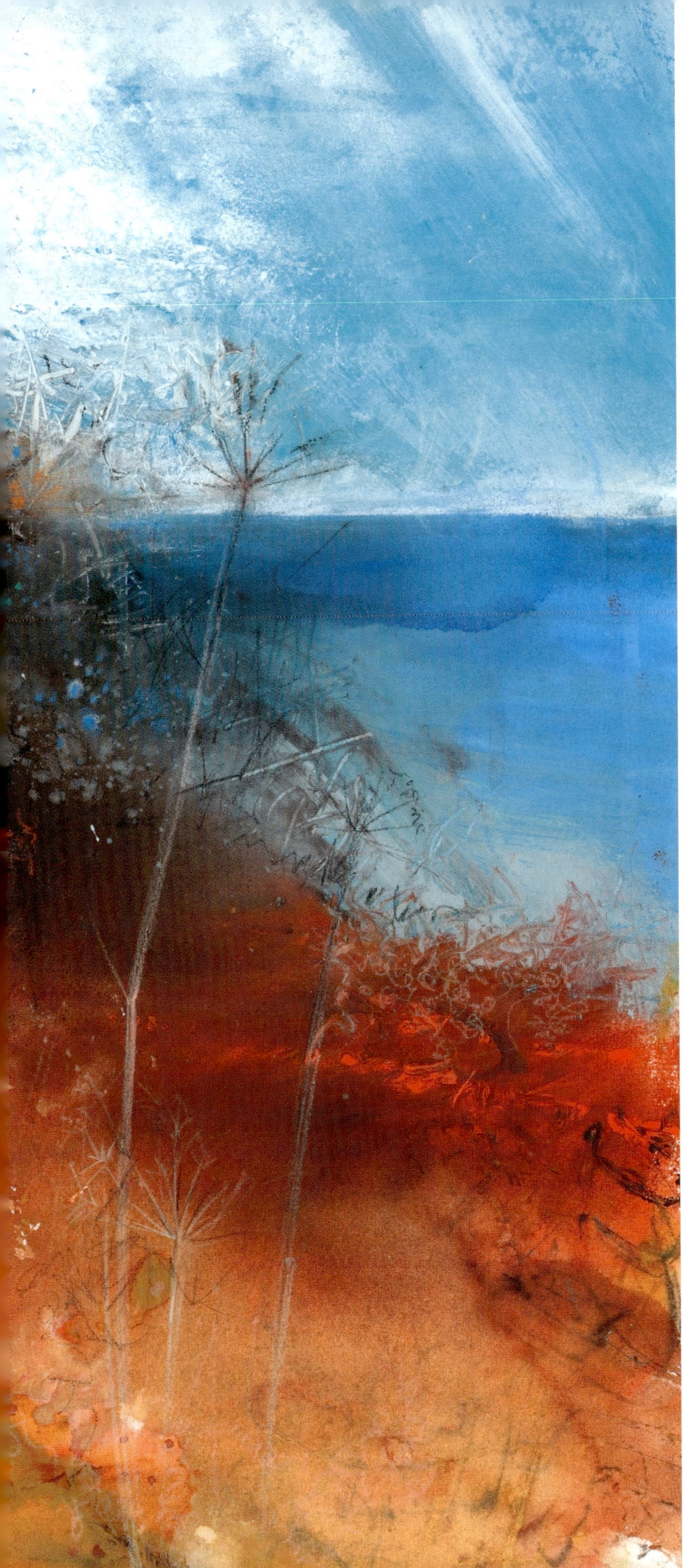

Left: Windswept Hawthorn

Salty winds and rocky soil make the clifftops a poor environment for trees to grow. Solitary, misshapen thorn trees pepper the windswept paths. Carved by harsh storms and sculpted into asymmetrical leaning shapes, they imitate those in the landscape around them, or even the waves below. Returning from a wild clifftop walk, I grabbed a full-sized sheet of watercolour paper, wet it, and hastily squeezed watercolour directly on it. Impatient with the restraints of a brush, I used the palms of my hands to smear the paint; scratching it with my nails, dabbing with fingertips, I 'drew' the foreground bracken. The rest of the image was painted with equal enthusiasm and energy with a few more careful details applied at the end.

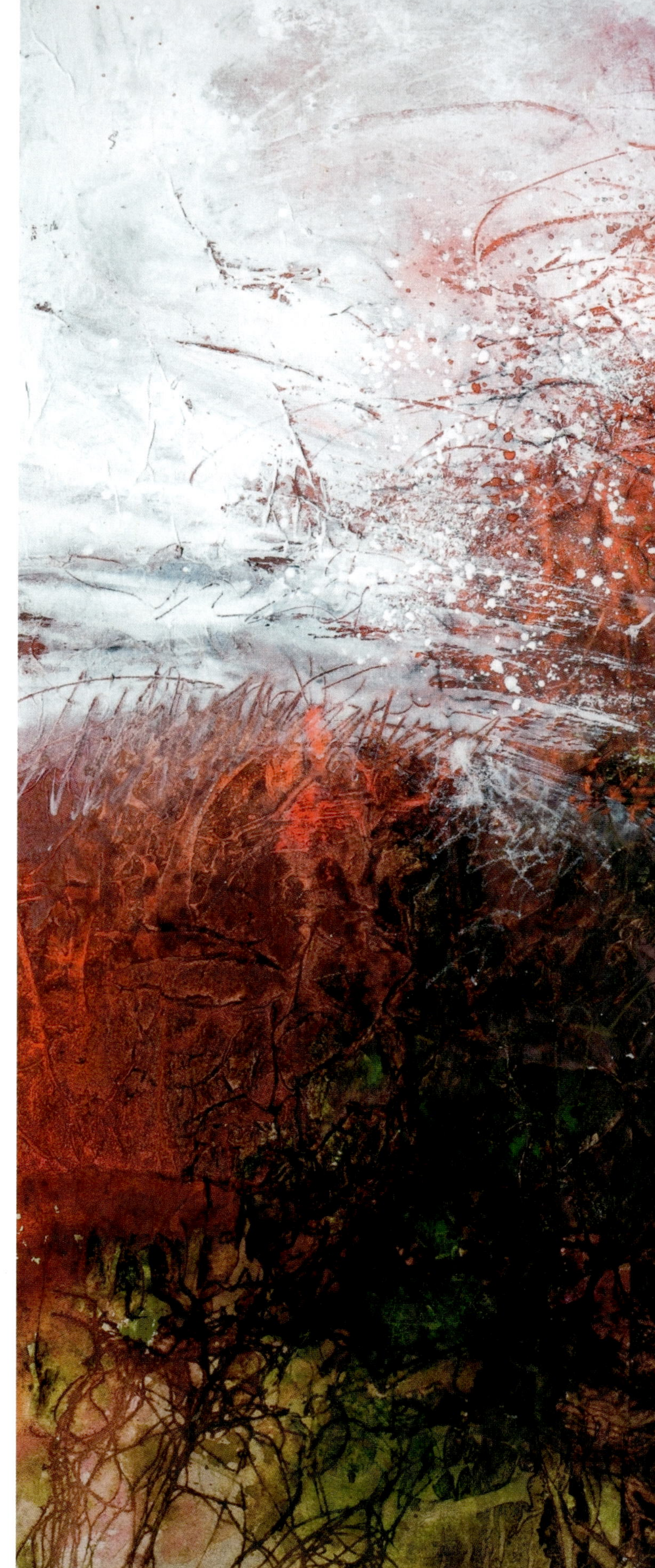

Right: Moorland Hawthorn

*One autumn on Dartmoor, I was drawn to the
particularly vivid scarlets of a ragged hawthorn.
It was a scurrying day of texture and movement.
I used plant materials gathered from the nearby
undergrowth to print a moorland background,
using ink and watercolour, back in the studio. I then
developed the thorn tree's shape as it blew in the gusty
wind, avoiding the temptation to be too literal. After
all, a hawthorn is, in fairy lore, a tree of enchantment,
especially when alone in the landscape. My aim was
to capture some of this magic in my painting.*

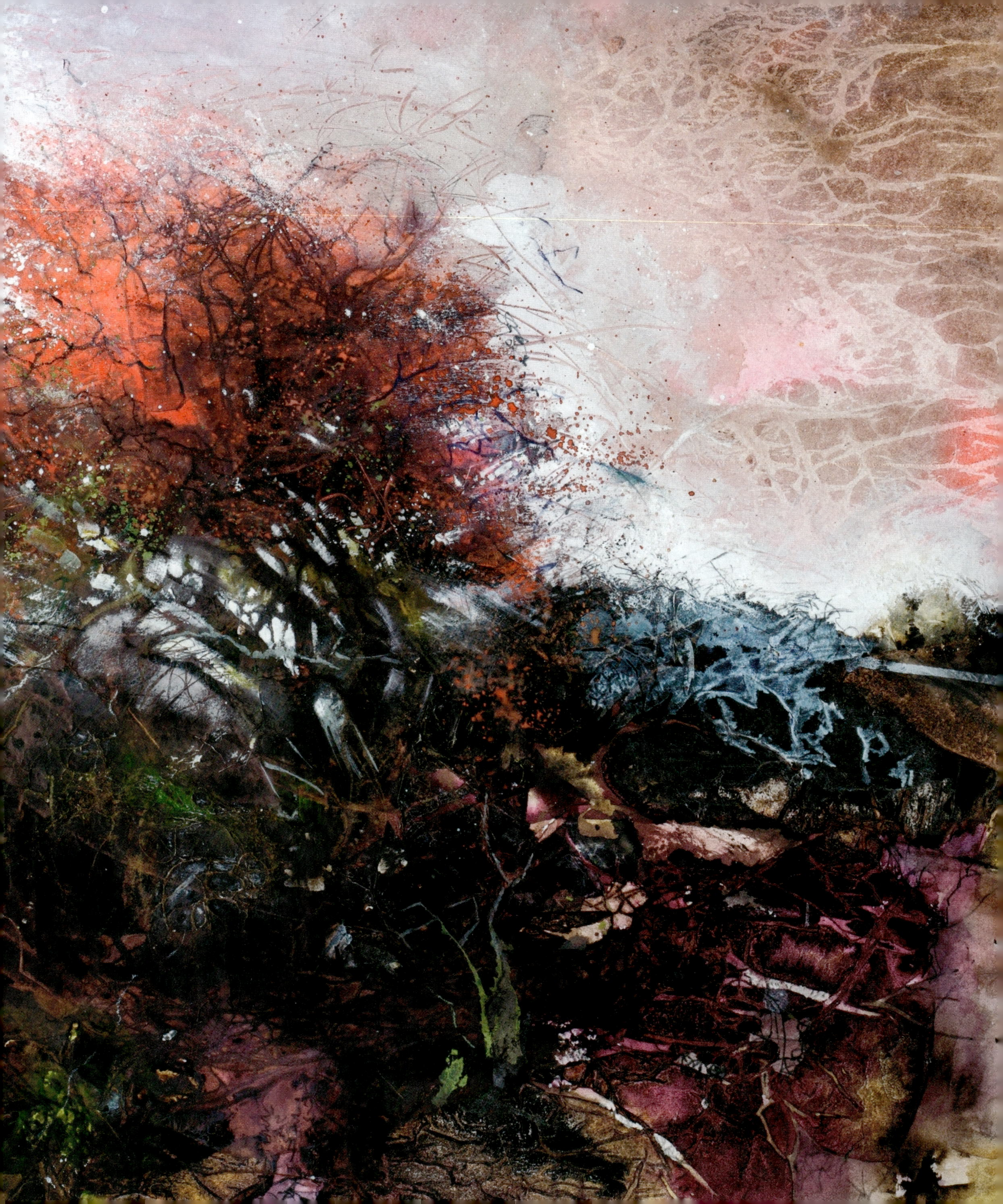

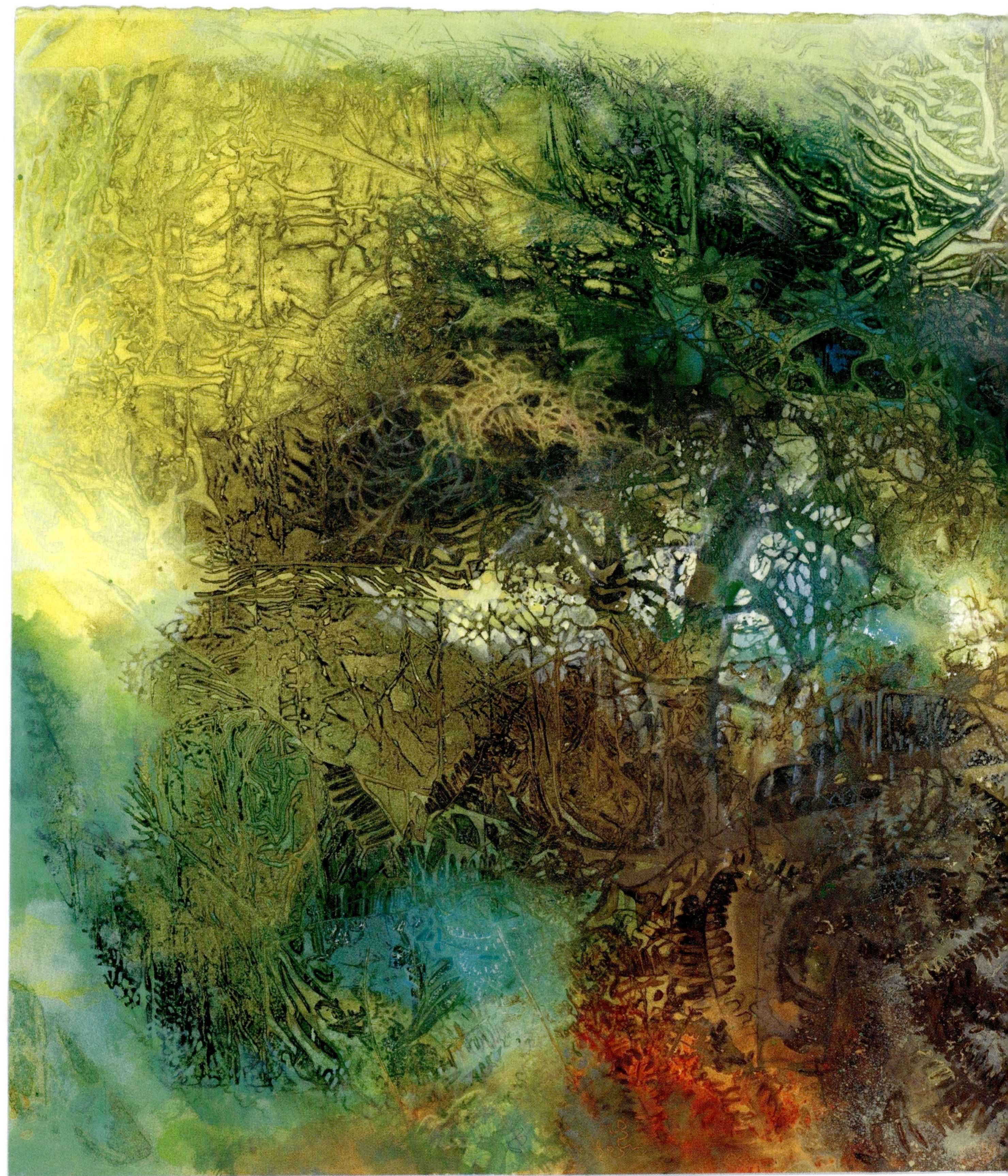

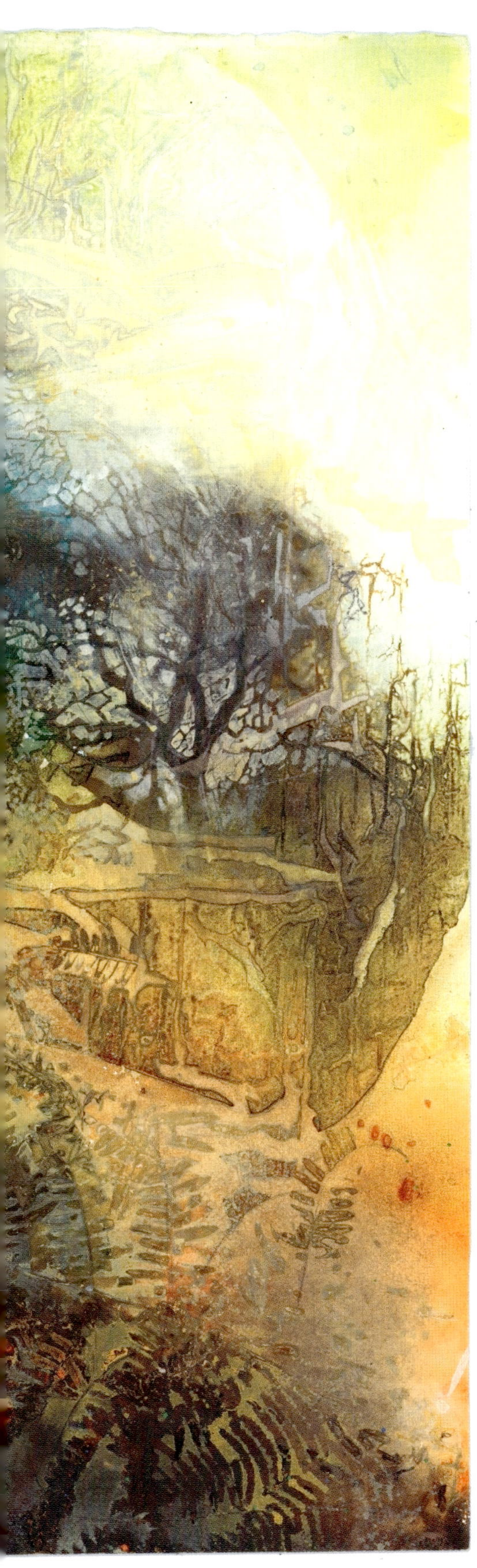

Left: The Tangled Grove

I often play with expressive mark making for its own sake, to encourage an experimental approach. If I like the result I wait until its abstract marks remind me of something seen. Then I coax the subject out of its hiding place. I have done that here using pale gouache to create broken negative shapes that describe trunks, branches, and treetops.

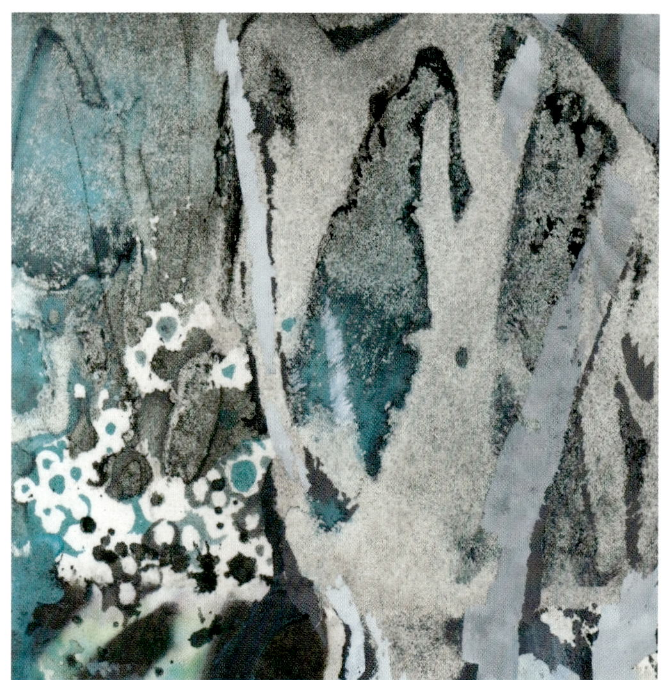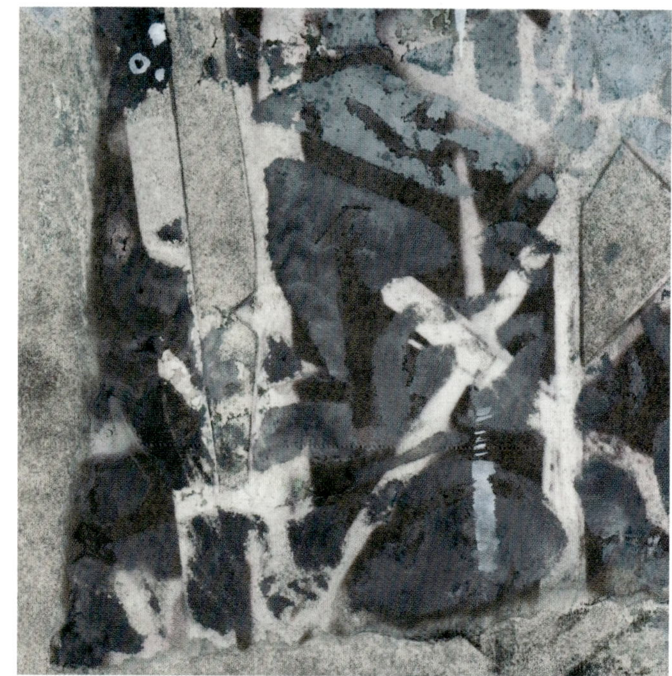

Cropping an image is an abstraction in which marks can be seen for their own merit. Doing this is a useful stage in learning to develop more abstracted work and give ideas for further non-pictorial images. Using monochrome is a good starting point as removing colour is another way of displacing actuality. I particularly like the sections shown here and the way that my fanciful marks still insist on being arborescent.

Right: The Bare Winter Bones

Some abstract artists depend on the visual world as a starting point for ideas although the result may not be realistic. Other abstract artists aim to capture emotions and spiritual experience rather than physical reality through their use of gestural marks, colour and shape. If I were to give my work a label, I would call it 'towards abstraction' as it contains elements of the above, while retaining a representational presence of the natural world. This image contains photographic collage of hogweeds placed upside down, painted over, washed out and worked into until the forms became increasingly abstracted. I did not set out to paint 'trees', but the pale shapes that formed themselves do give that enigmatic illusion.

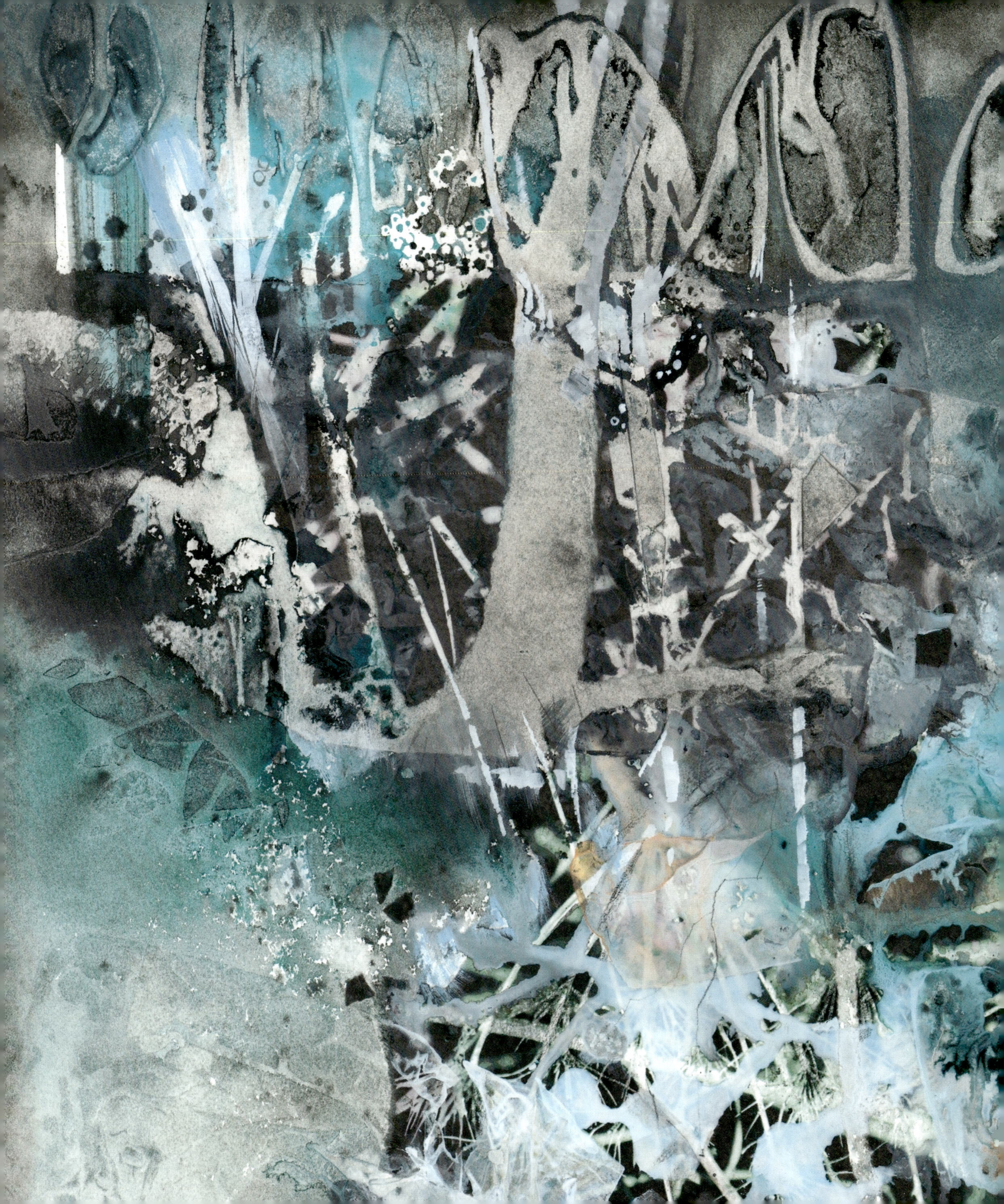

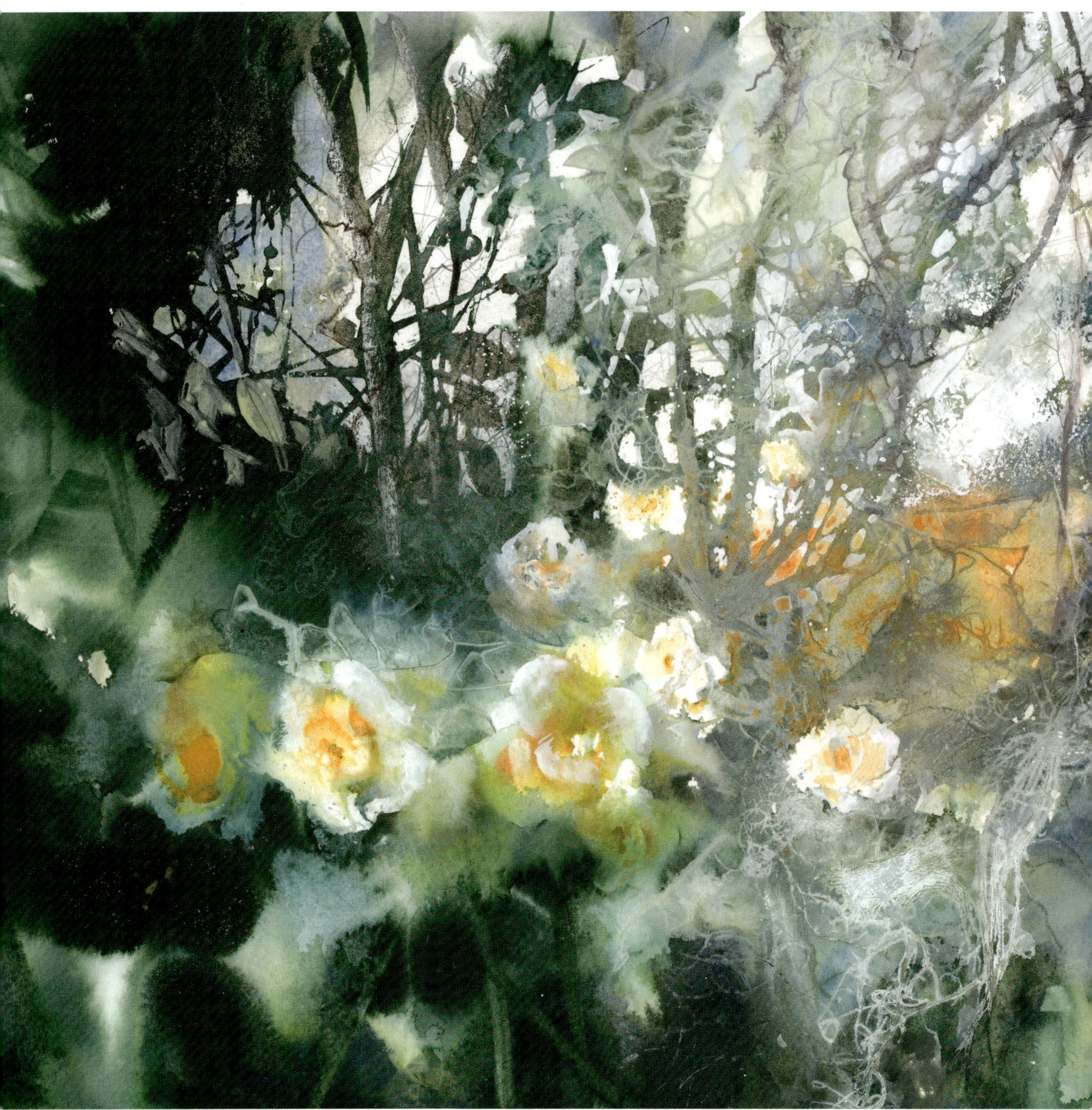

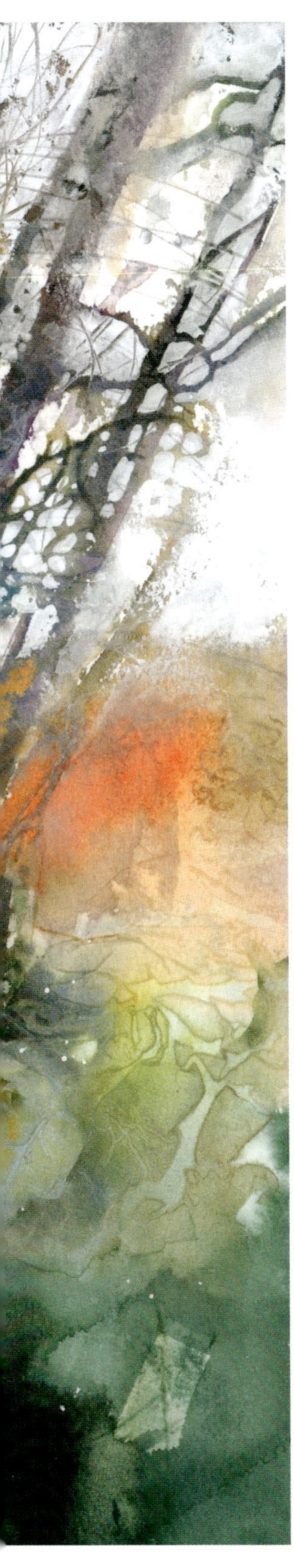

Through the seasons

A personal project

I live in Devon, where we have several acres of beautiful, wooded garden. It is a nature reserve; a wild, magical wilderness where woodland flowers cover the ground or scramble in treetops. In spring the moorhen visits the tree-lined ponds to raise her chicks. In summer the woods become an oasis in which to hide away. Quintets of Canada geese fly overhead in autumn, squirrels hoard supplies of nuts and deer hide in secret corners. Bats and owls navigate through wintry trees at dusk. It is an enchanting place, and I decided to make a project of recording it through each season, using paintings and words in whatever way I wished. The poems do not necessarily illustrate the images that accompany them and vice versa. The intention is to generate a flavour and sense of the different seasons and enjoy every moment of doing so.

I believe that artists need goals to stay motivated. Developing a personal project is a great way to do this. While exploring a theme with passion, you can learn new ways of thinking and as you strengthen your voice and skills, you also enrich your life. Your project might involve keeping a visual diary, compiling a sequence of related drawings, or collaborating with another artist. You could concentrate on a particular tree, exploring all aspects of it. The woodland is your playground. Being creative is an opportunity to be self-indulgent – only then can you truly express what you feel.

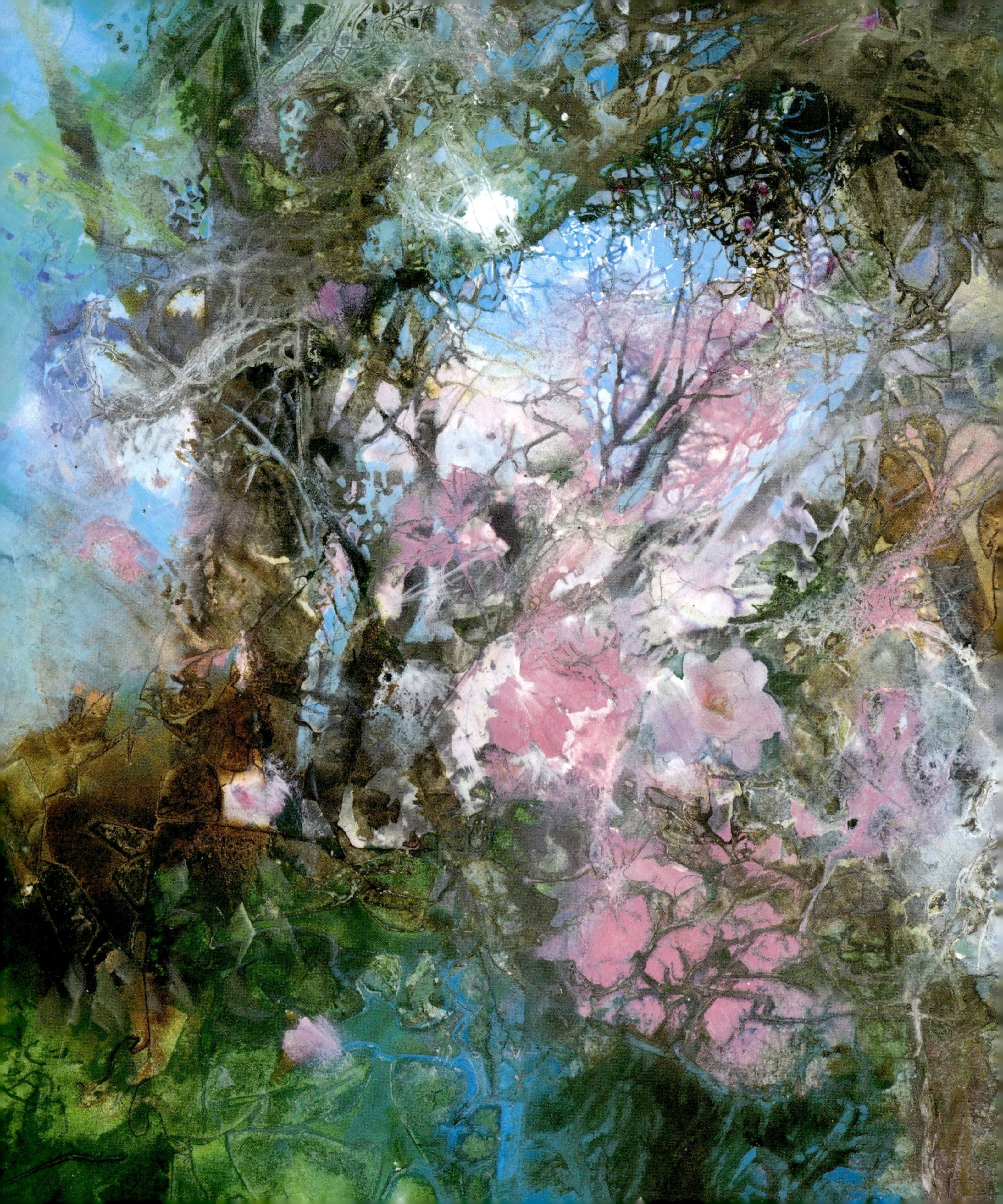

Spring

There are hundreds of camellias growing in our garden from late November to May, but it is always a surprise to see them clambering 20m (65½ft) into trees in early spring, long before the primroses have woken from their pillows of moss. One magical evening the moon shone through tangled labyrinths of twigs illuminating tissue-paper twists of flowers, whose silky flush of pink fused with the twilit sky. Camellia varieties have names like 'Moonshadow', 'Ballet in Pink', 'Dream Weaver', 'April Kiss', 'Pink Snow' and 'Anticipation'. On that night, I was certainly full of anticipation about how the spring woodland garden would unfold.

Spring rushed in this year with a shimmer of green quickly frothing the bare branches of the limes and oak. The pond grew noisy as tiny froglets abandoned the tadpole dullness of the muddy pond edge to croak and croon through sedges, ignoring the warnings of the anti-social moorhen. Wild garlic spiced our salads and red campion sweetened our shady garden views. Ferns unfurled like question marks, fingering the air, testing it to see if the time had come for the bluebells to venture out of their hiding places and ring brightly in the wood. The daffodils hosted a party to liven up a dark hedge. Yellow flags unfurled in triumph, while the horse chestnut held on with tight fists to its candles, not ready yet to light up the celebration.

Left: The Moon Dreams of Camellias

Collage and water-based mediums.

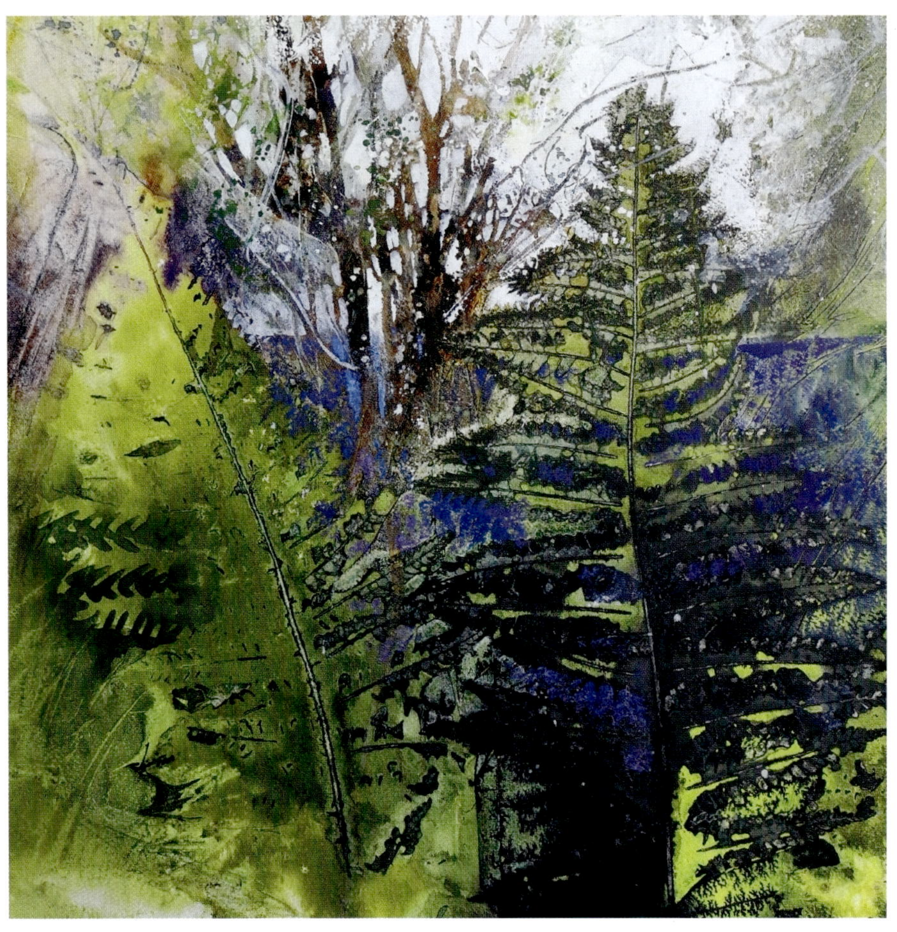

Above: Ferny Bluebell Wood

There are ferns everywhere. Curled tightly or spreading their fingers out wide
to display incredible patterns. I used some to make prints into paint and ink,
then painted in between the negative shapes with Cobalt Blue warmed with
Quinacridone Magenta to suggest the bluebells that turn woods to ocean.

Right: Narcissi

One late afternoon I noticed light piercing
the dark, tangled mat of this shady area,
shooting starry spears of light towards the
floral constellations of narcissi below. I rushed
out greedily to grab the moment, slashing
watercolour and ink onto paper, contrasting
plain washes with decorative texture. I
instinctively borrowed the maroons of nearby
purple hellebores to complement the greens.
This outside work was quick and spontaneous
although I added some details once back inside.

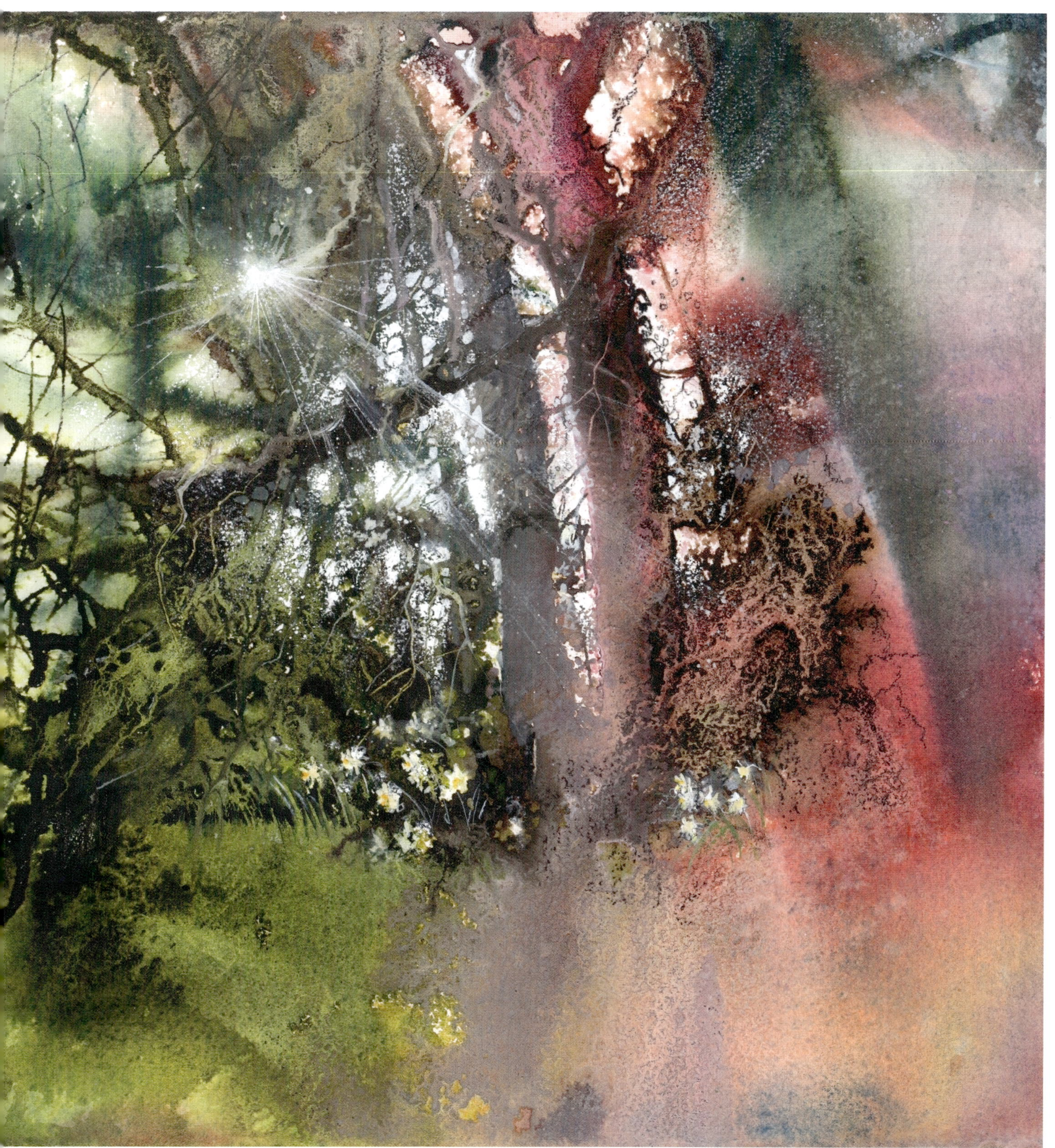

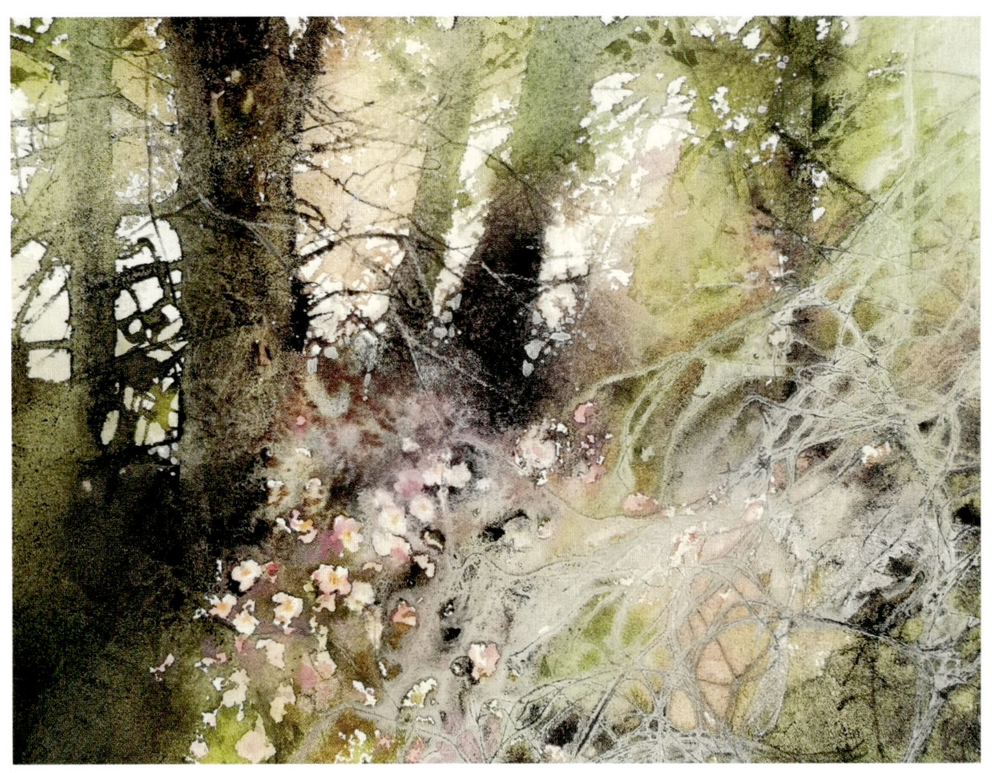

Spring Fanfare

It's a festival of birdsong
It's an April jubilee
It's a party for the primrose
A celebration for the tree
It's a scatter of pink petal
It's a flutter of leaf and wing
Let us fanfare our welcome –
To the arrival of spring.

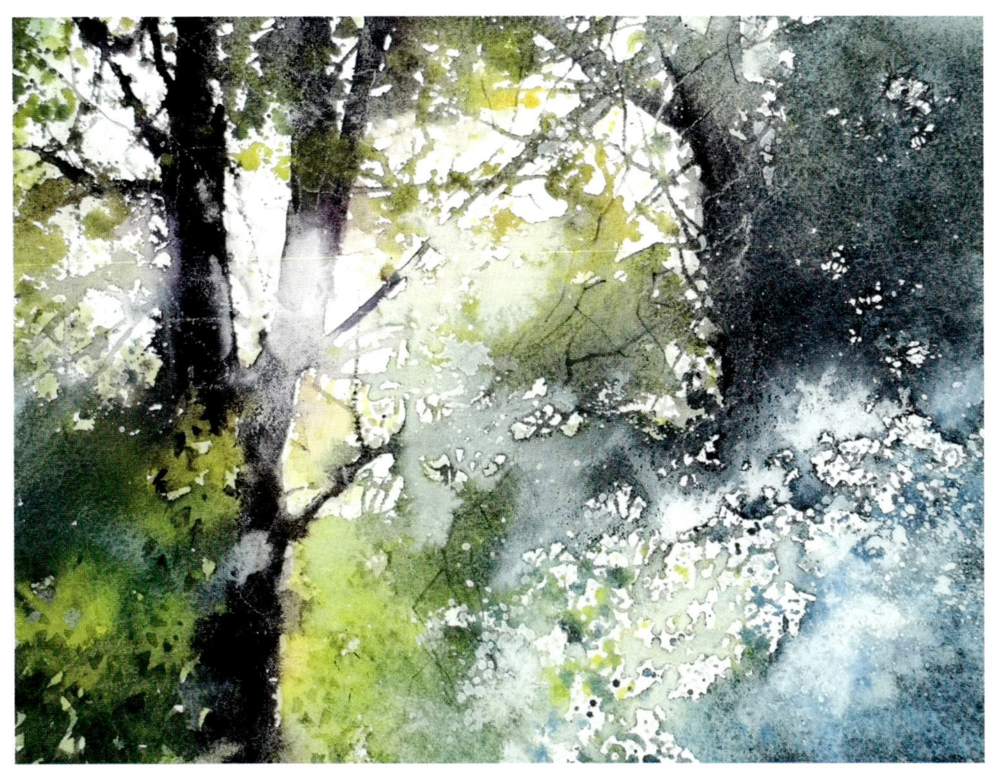

Beneath My Feet

Above my woodland-shaded face
A breeze plucks and kisses
Each lip-glossed, scarlet treat
From the tree's embrace.
Rubies glow on brown earth's skin
Wild cherries smile as they lie
Where stars of garlic used to shine
And scent this aromatic place:

The savoury and sweet
Fallen beneath my feet.

: Robin's Nest

*There is a raised bank between our garden and the woodland, where daffodils dance
and hellebores huddle. I was clearing some winter debris and exposed a mossy robin's
nest, complete with five milky-pale, oval eggs. Aghast at disturbing it, I quickly
replaced the dead bracken and watched for a week until I was certain that it had
been abandoned. I sat beneath the earthy embankment to paint the intricacies of
the fine filigree work, lined with tiny feathery lichens and moss, surrounded by leaf
skeletons and sticks. The entwined and knitted weavings of the nest immediately cast
a spell that made me paint in a dreamlike trance. The opal treasure of the eggs had
hypnotized me until I was unaware of time passing. In the autumn I was drawn back
to see if the nest was still buried in its cradle of ferns – but no trace of it was left.*

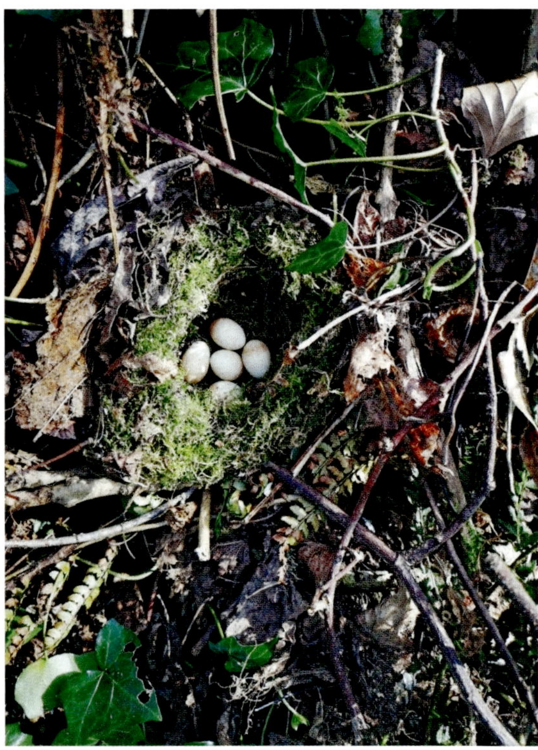
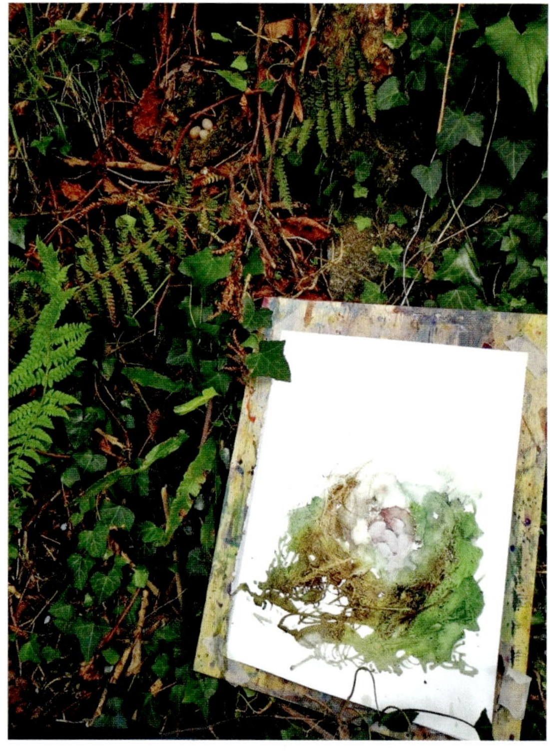

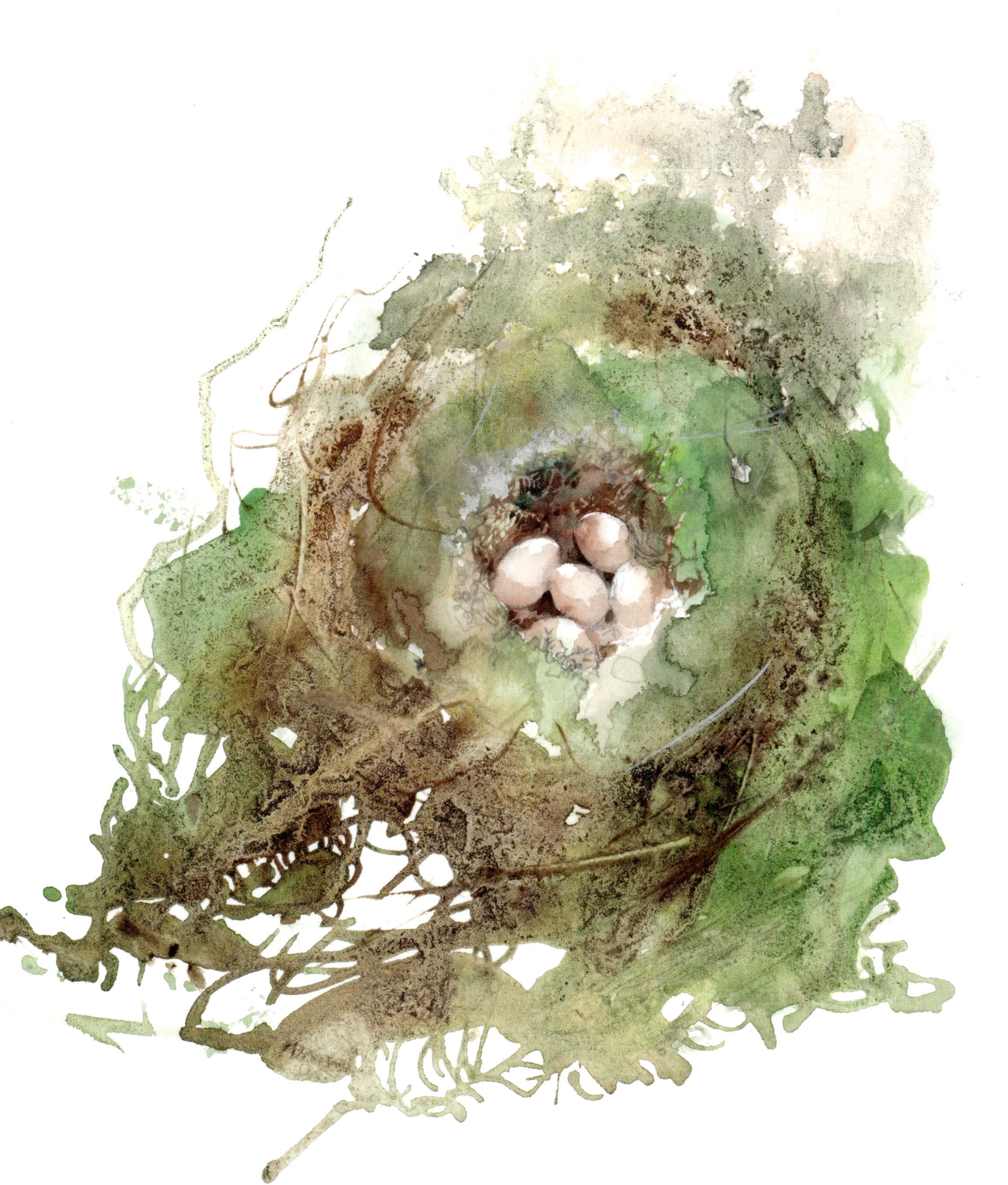

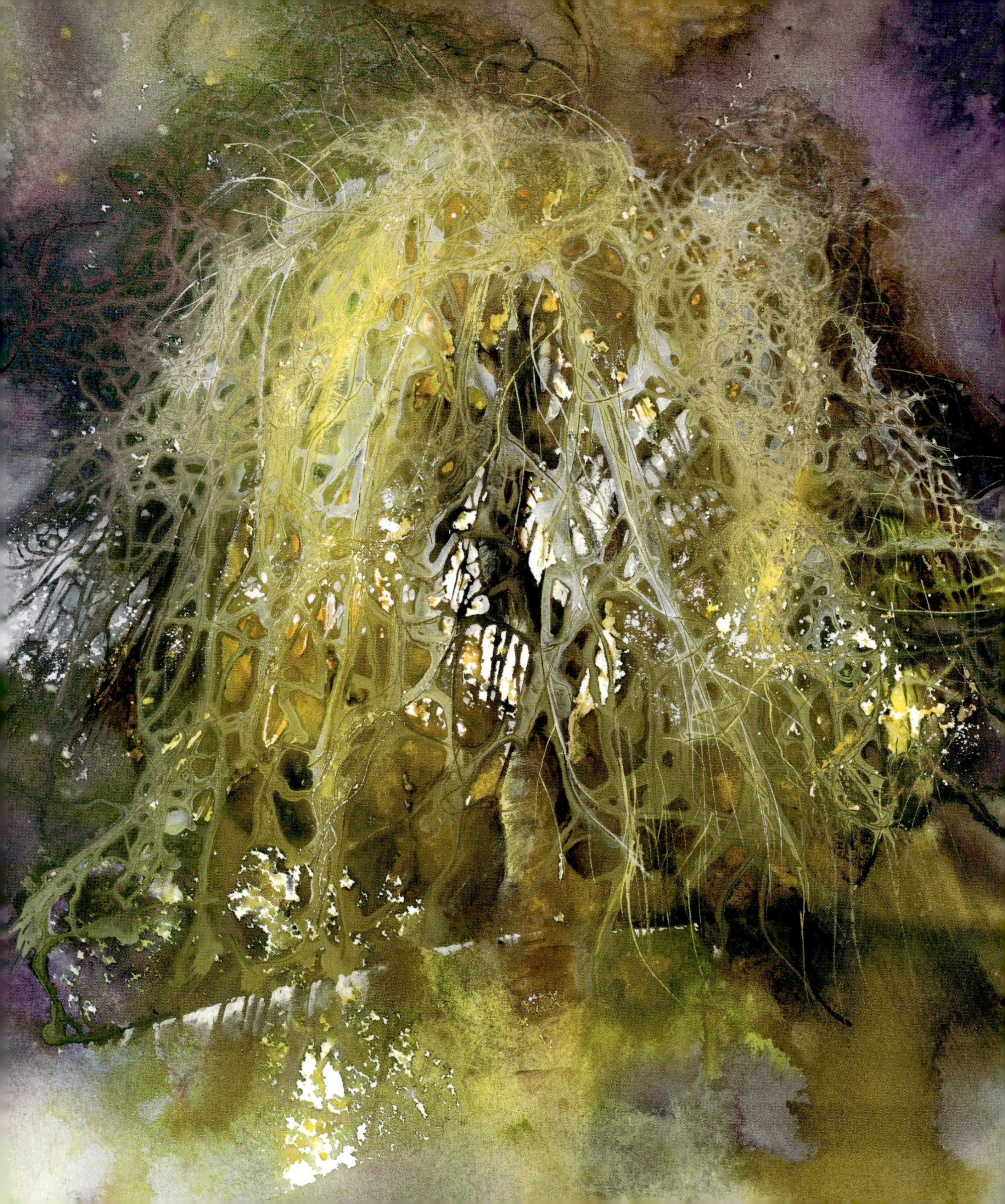

The Willow Weeps

Slivers of lemon gold light:
Sharp-nosed fish twins
caught on the lines
of fine arching branches.
They weep over the brook
with a halo of midges,
like cloud-shoals of bait.
They wait;
these slender yellow willow leaves,
that yearn to be free of the hook
which ties them to their tree;
a breath of air to set them free
to float on backs and swirl and play,
as the river waltzes them away.

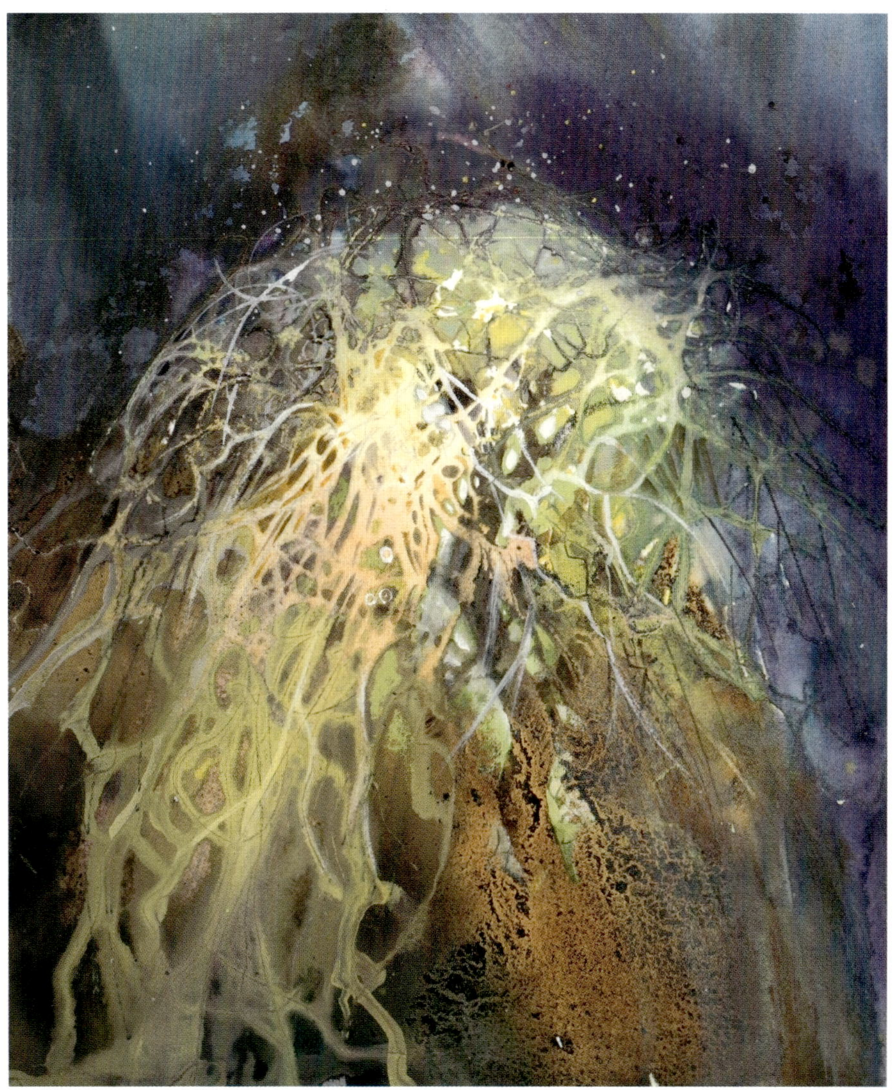

Above: Bad Hair Day

Left: Weeping Willow

*The trailing veil of branches that define the weeping willow is still bare this
spring but will become a hiding place when summer leaves adorn it. Last
autumn, I was inspired to write a poem as I watched the last two leaves fall
from a slender overhanging stem into the brook, where they swam, like fish,
through our meadow beyond.*

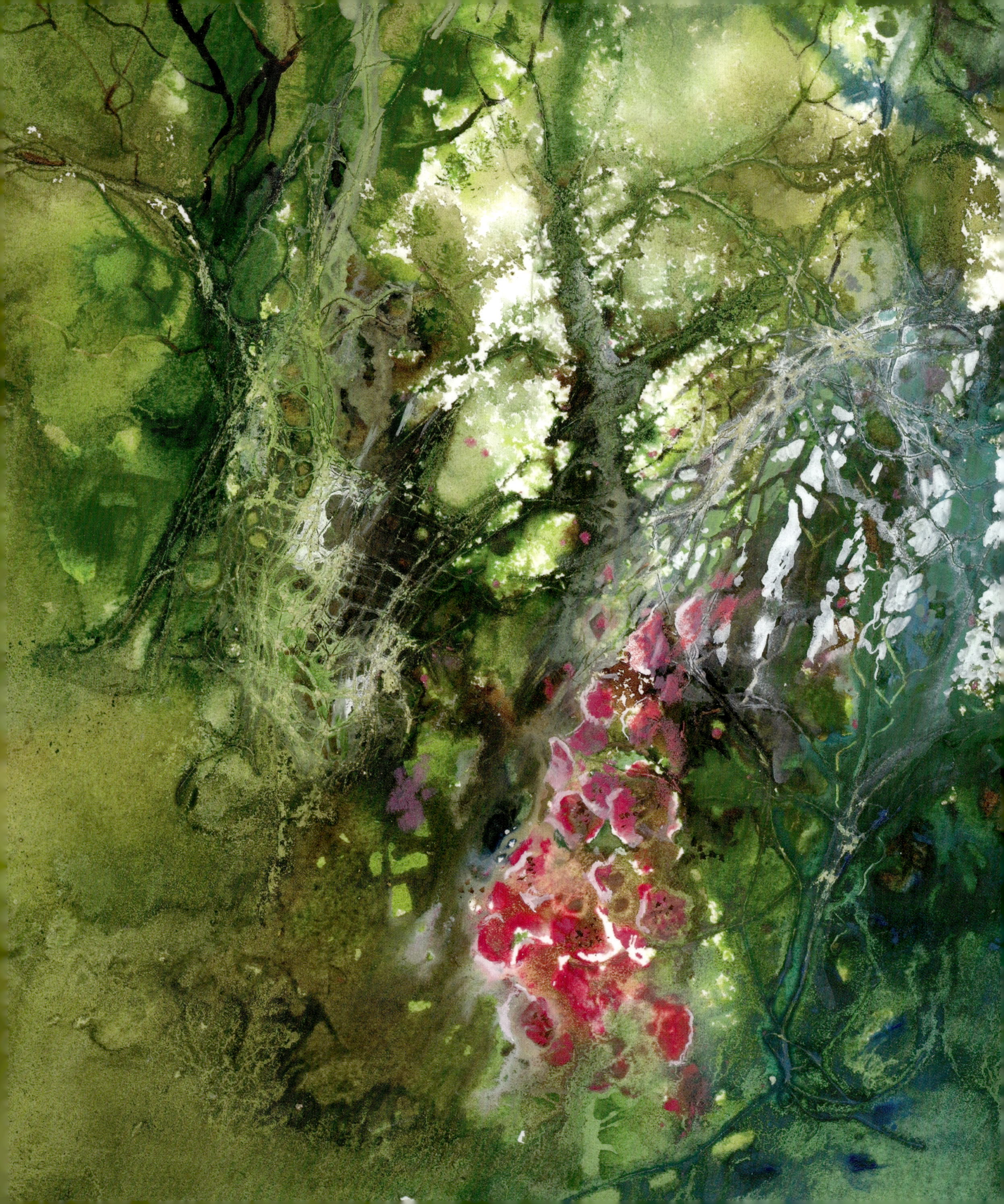

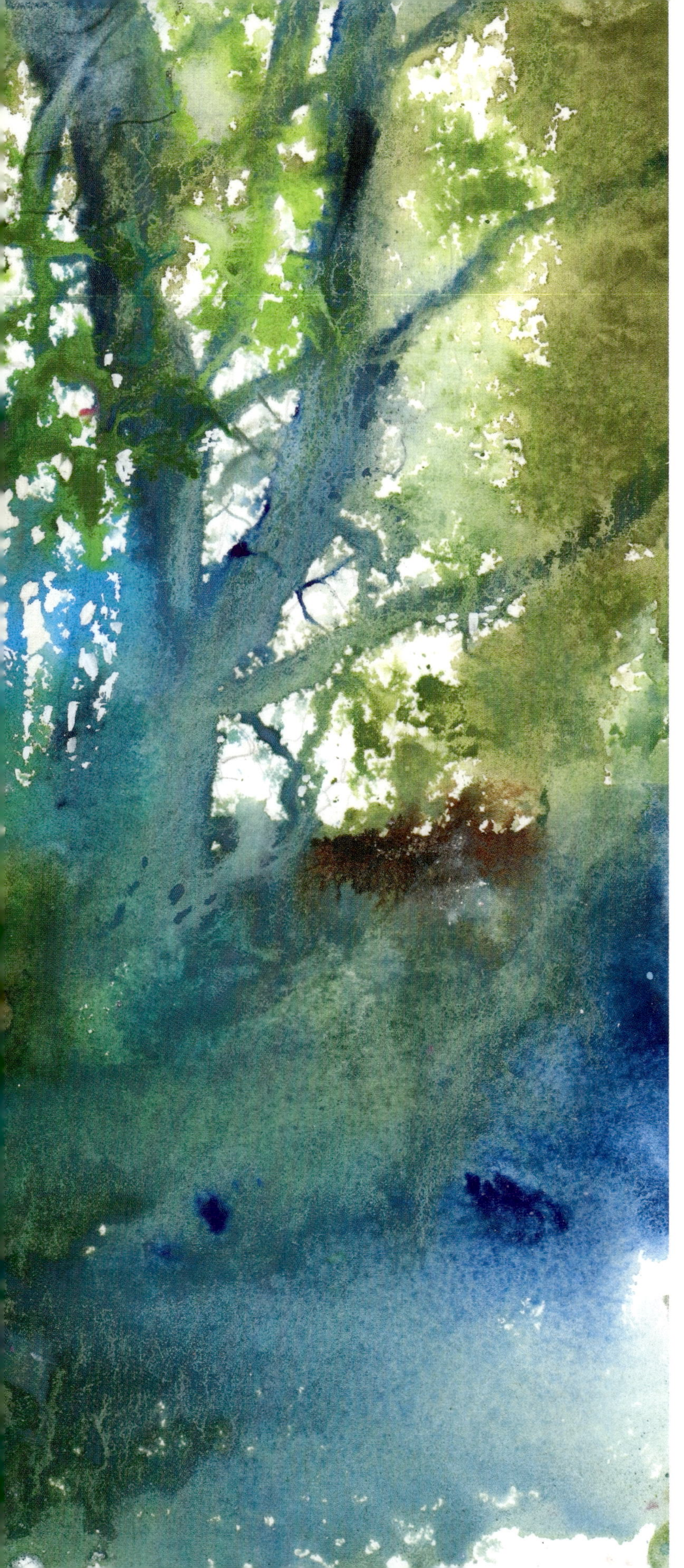

Summer

It is a hot summer and as the garden dries and struggles, the woodland spaces become places to retreat to as the temperature continues to rise. It is cool under the limes and cherry trees and the hazel fringe along the hedge blocks out the sultry sun. At noon the waterlilies awake in the willow pond but still float sleepily over the water, basking and sunbathing. Dragon- and damselflies dart and zig-zag a lightning-quick path over and around the ponds. Sometimes they hesitate to stare at me with magnified, jewel-like eyes. Midge clouds flicker over the pond, sparkling like fireflies at dusk. The woods are humming. The honeybees swarm. The hives are full and buzz for attention. But the hammock, strung between the trunks of the oak and the sycamore, also beckons.

I write and muse. I paint under the leafy crown of trees. Thunder threatens. It is claustrophobic among the dense foliage of the wood. And the green. Oh, tedious green. You can call it jade and chartreuse; you can term it verdigris; you can christen it prasine or malachite, chrysoprase or smaragdite – but it will remain, in spite of its name, just murderous, boring green!

Left: The Faerie Foxglove Path

An ancient fern-lined track runs past our garden to a bluebell wood beyond. Each time I walk there it has mysteriously metamorphosed. In March it is dripping with primroses. These are quickly replaced with a white tidal wave of lacy wild garlic. Before its lingering scent has faded, the spires of foxgloves appear, as if conjured by faerie incantation. The light had an eerie quality one midsummer eve, and I photographed the flowers. In the resulting images, black trees had been transformed to turquoise-blue – methinks, by elfin hand.

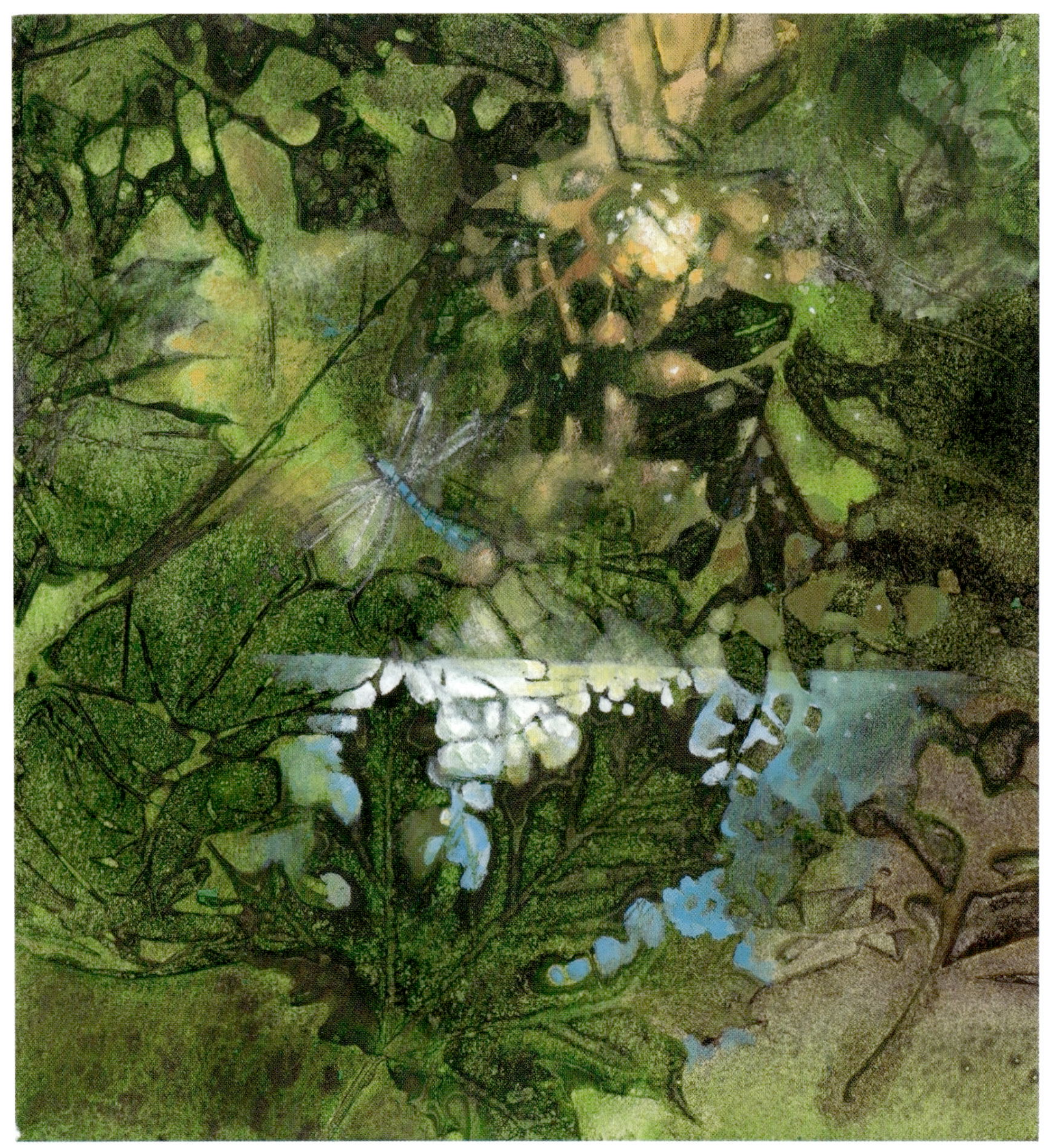

Mosaic Pond

Damselfly:

electric spark,

shooting

a shard

of neon blue,

towards the shattered

mirror-pool.

It hides

and glides

within the glade:

a scattered dance

of glittered light,

and verdant

leaves with

playful shade.

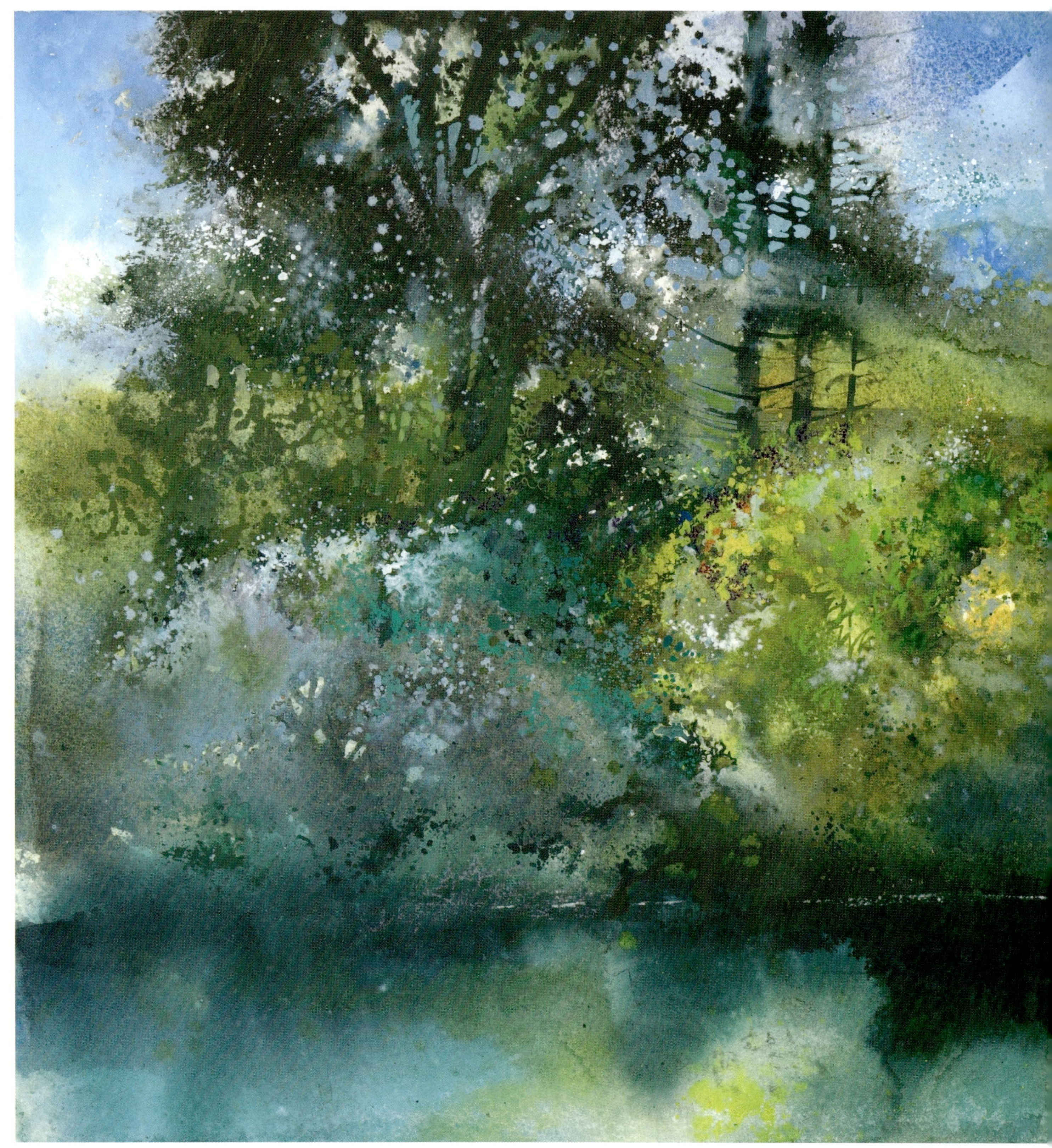

The Secret

Listen.

The willowy wind is whispering tales
that spread in ripples across flat water.
There are secrets deep in the garden,
in this woven wilderness, stitched together
by chiming birds that flit over
and under, through and between,
the weft and warp of branches.
Threaded with silken filaments,
a mischievous, teasing light
swings and sideways slides.

Wait.

There's a mystery in the secret pond
at the centre of our wooded garden,
above hidden gold of silent fish,
where dark trees hang upside down.
Blurred shapes unravel and travel
towards a frayed, uncharted world,
where only wild birds dare enter.
They sing a song of vernal equinox;
when night and day, tree with tree,
water with land join hands.

But look

how a breeze has bravely blown aside
the curtained leaves at each ragged hem of
the sequinned pool. See how water curls
beneath, around, below – to show
an island on our pond!
And in the centre of this moated place,
a mottled mallard sits and rests
on feathered nest of opal ovals pale.
She waits to see what further tales
lie in the secret garden isle.

Left: Tree-fringed Pond

The perimeters of our wild pond needed some serious attention before nature
completely strangled the trees with brambles and enthusiastic climbing plants.
The pond appeared to be divided into two parts, with trees overhanging at one end.
Months after we moved here, I noticed a glimmer of light underneath some of the
shrubs and realized to my delight that the water went underneath and around the
side of the neglected trees – that they were in fact hiding an undiscovered island!

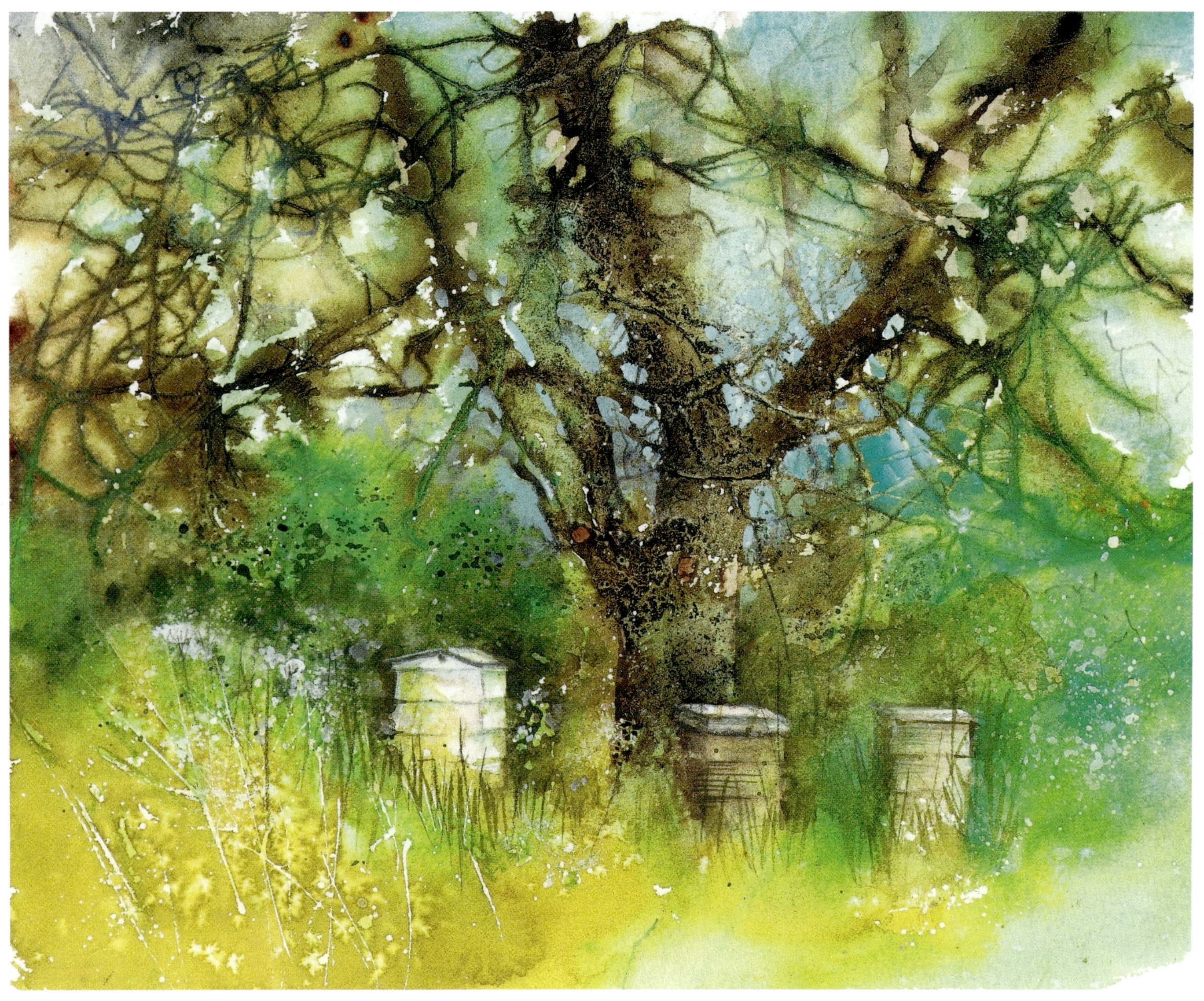

Above: Under the Web of the Walnut Tree

It is almost a relief to insert some geometric shapes into my paintings of the constantly free-flowing organic patterns of nature. My husband's beehives offer that perfect contrast and focal point, under the trees in dark wild corners. The hives also help give a sense of scale to the large walnut tree.

Right: Time for Reflection

It is not often that I paint man-made subjects, but in the context of our garden's domesticated woods it felt appropriate to illustrate the human interaction with nature that is important to our well-being. Here, we are lucky to be able to enjoy freely the sense of being connected with woodland and seize any opportunity to enjoy the extraordinary therapeutic value of trees and water.

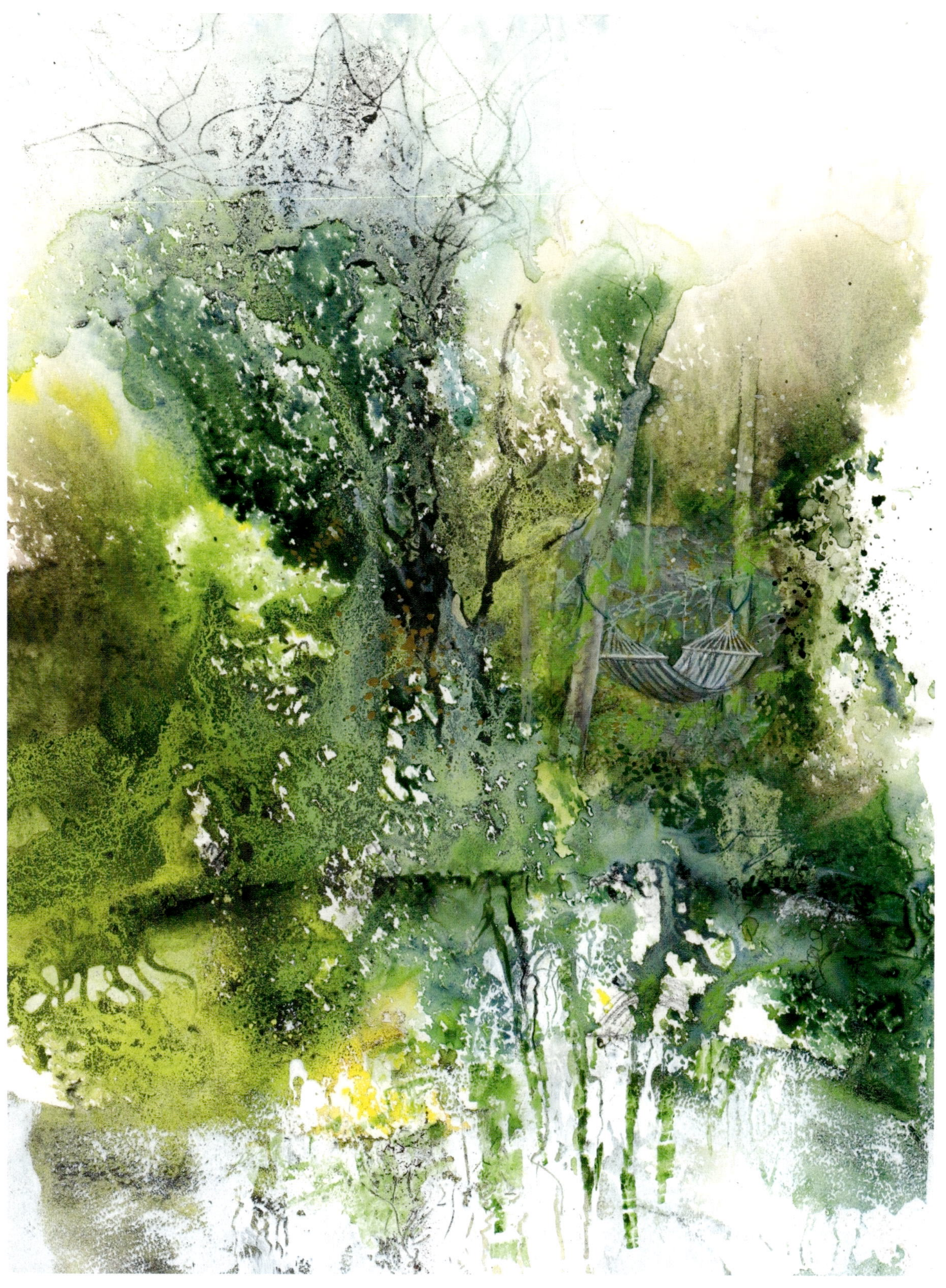

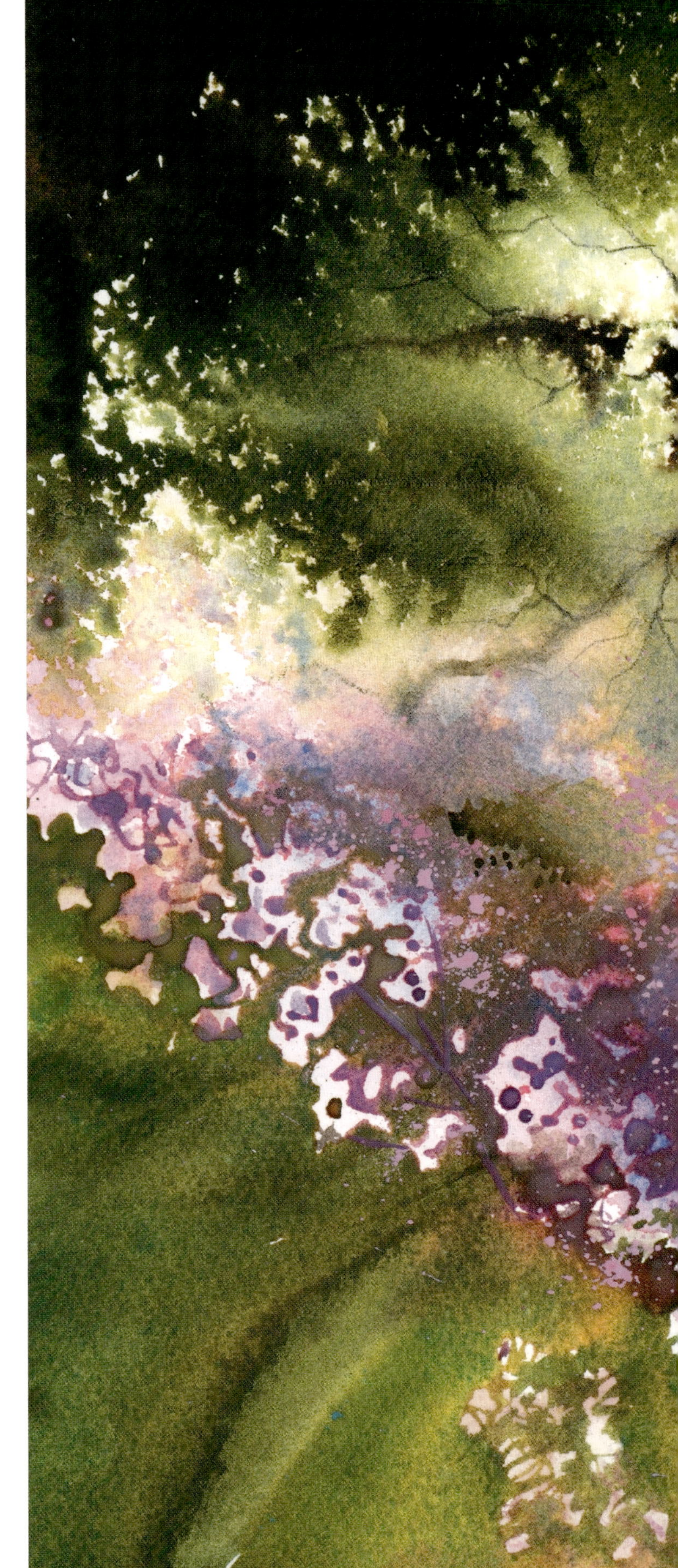

Right: Hydrangeas

Mountains of hydrangeas tower at the woodland edge where light filters through. They grow in every hue from permanent magenta and opera pink to cerulean blue and ultramarine. Some are magnificently sculpted doilies, while others are tightly crocheted domes. They fade and change to papery shadows as another three months roll past; just as the summer itself is already becoming a memory. But the mophead and lacecap flowers are still joyful, intricately meshed collections that sprinkle and punctuate the greens of the forest. In fact, these are already tinged with warmth as if the colour from the fading mauve petals has seeped and stained the woodland surroundings. I make no attempt to replicate the skilful floral patterns that nature has designed. Instead, I paint loosely, with a sense of light-hearted relief, the effervescent confetti confections that are illuminated by shimmering light.

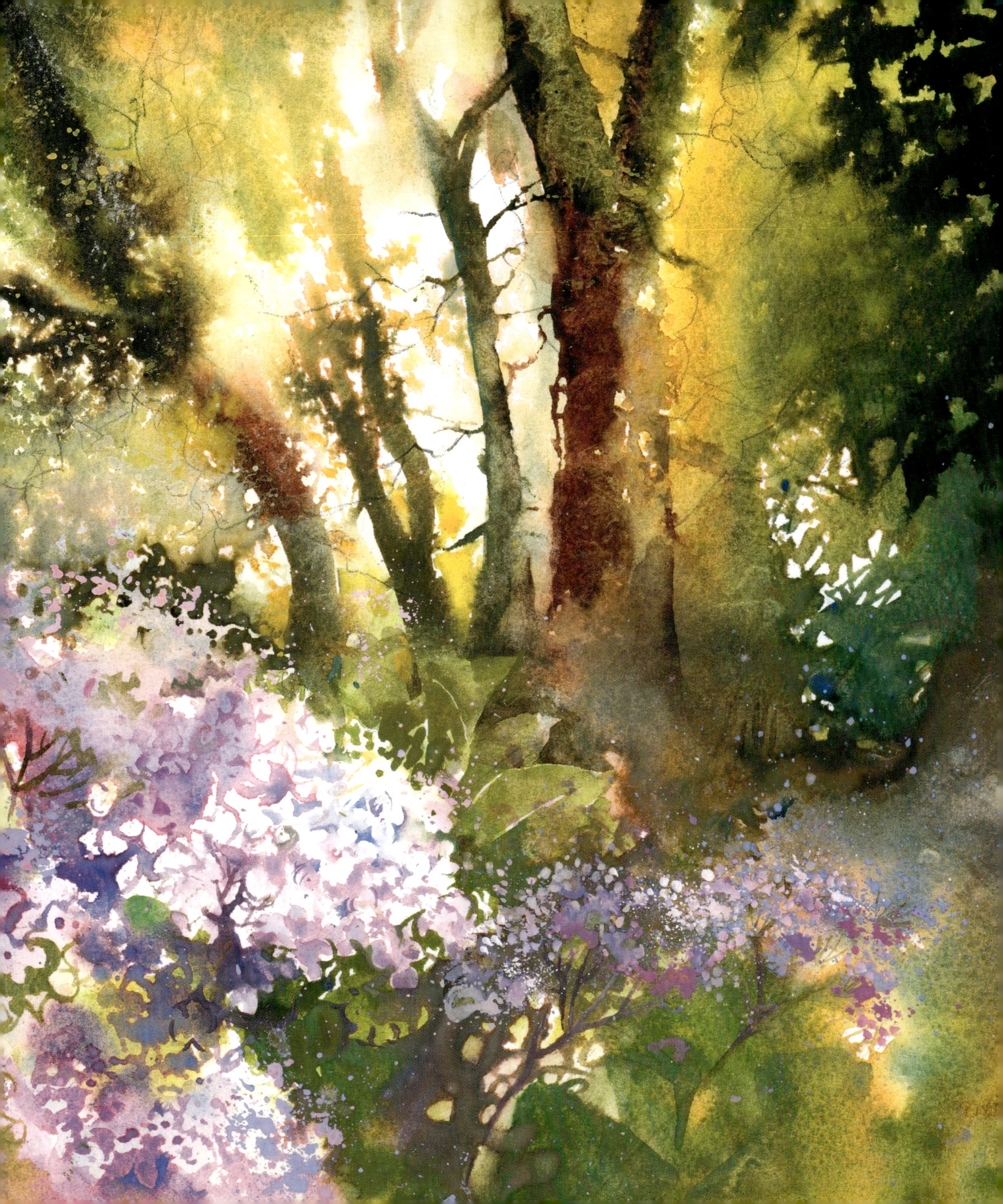

Autumn

I love all the phases of autumn in the wood and watch the garden change daily as trees begin their seasonal rituals. There is an air of excitement and activity as foliage begins to colour and swirl in abandoned acceptance as the year flies by. Later, when many leaves have fallen, spreading networks of branches become visible in the empty gaps. The designs that twig and bough weave together are so beautiful and intricate. They make me forget their prosaic, everyday identity and I allow myself to get tangled in their decorative but essential abstract woodland maps.

The natural world is built from exquisite structures produced by nature called fractals. They are seen in the rivers, the tributaries of water flowing through sand, in seaweeds and seashells. In the woodland they are in each fern, leaf, tree and lichen. Research has shown that stress might be reduced by up to 60 per cent purely by looking at these miraculous patterns, where each tiny piece is a never-ending copy of the bigger whole. A fern is made of progressively smaller, fern-shaped sections. They are repeated at an ever-decreasing scale, just as a branch divides and replicates itself.

There is something immensely poetic about these natural patterns and as I gaze into the branches of our wood, as the sinking sun is caught in its net, I lose myself in the complexities – and stand in awe.

Right: Sundown in Tangly Wood

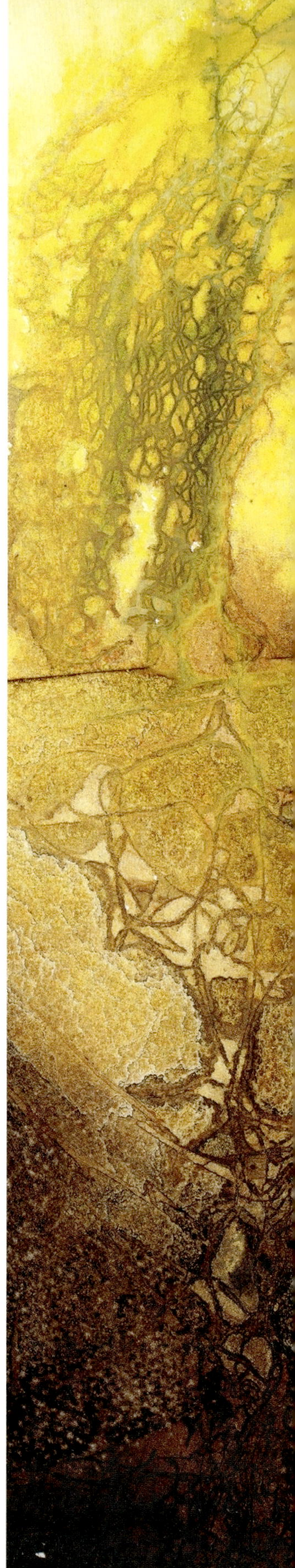

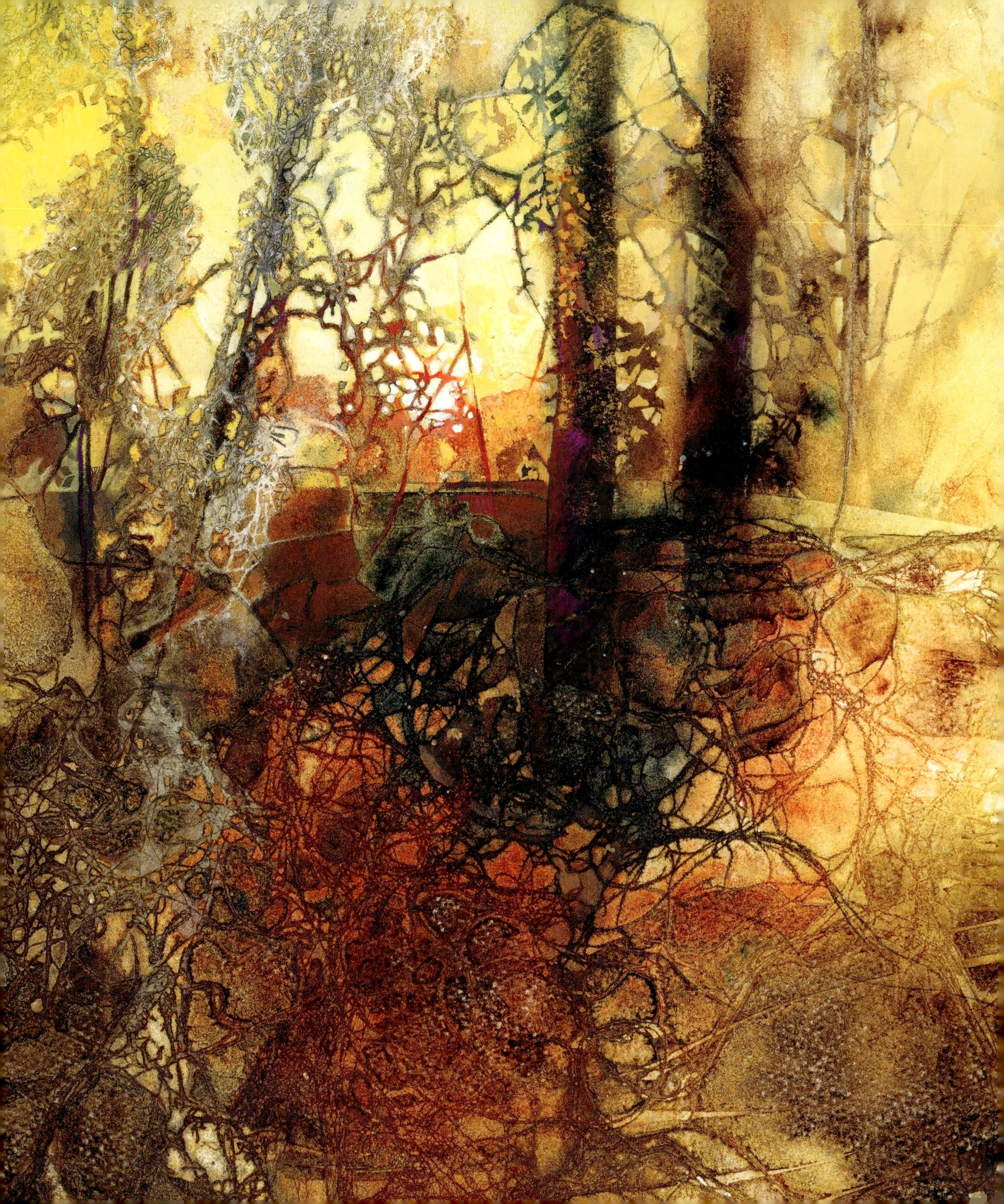

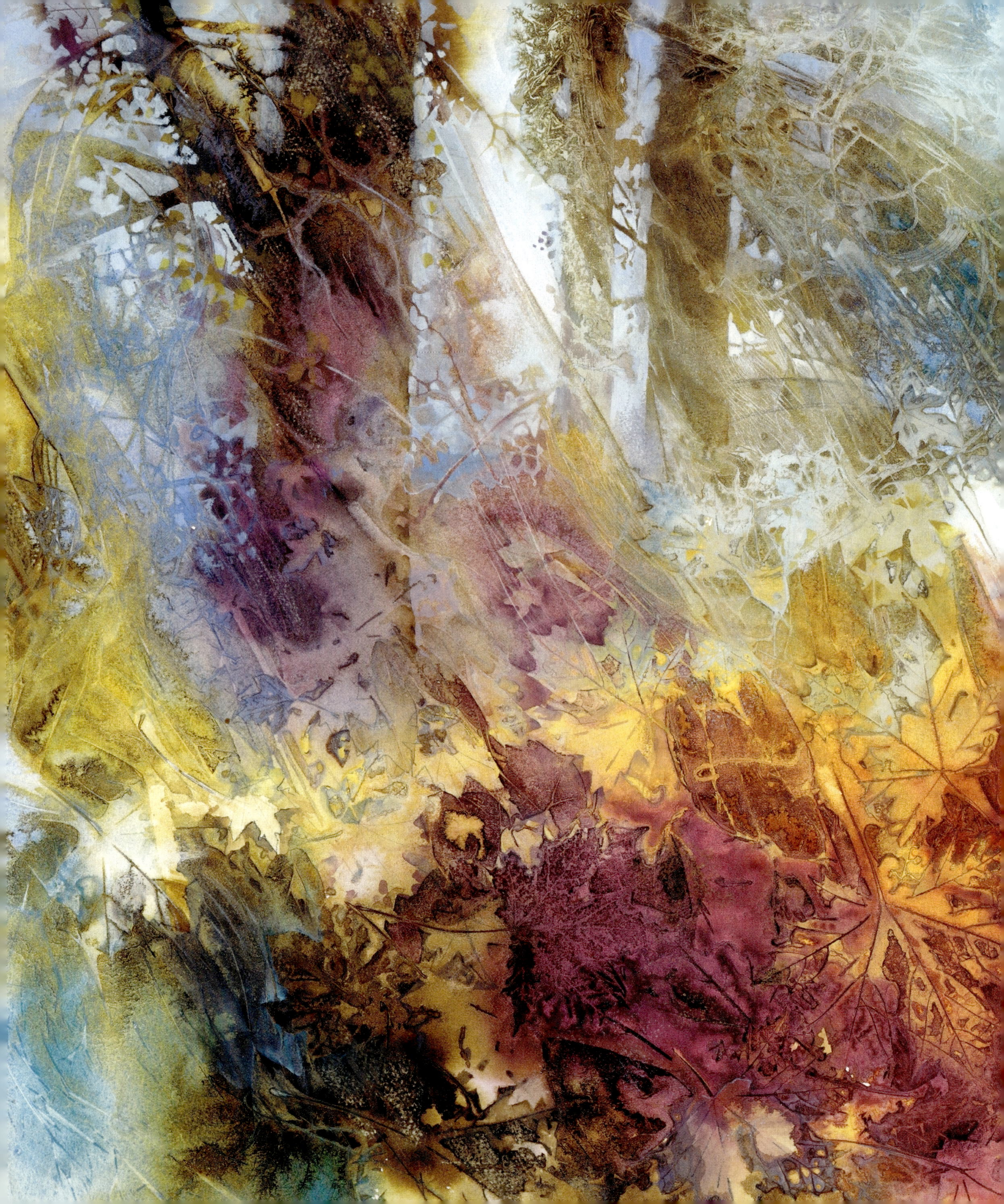

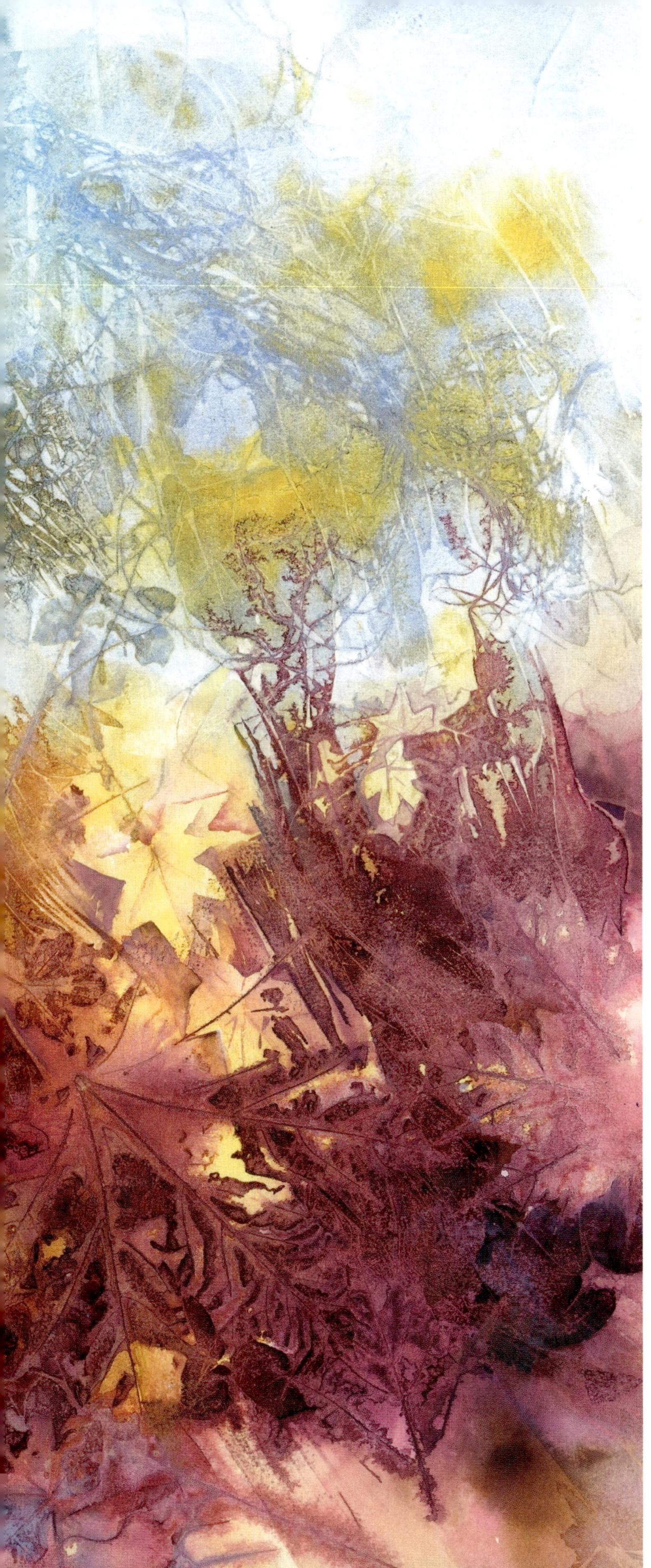

Dance of Leaves

Leaves flicker,
　　flurry, flutter,
　　　crackle, hurry,
　　　stutter,
　　　　gyrate, rotate,
　　　shiver and quiver.

Wind falls.
Leaves pause.

Then
　swirl and twirl,
　　cartwheel and whirl,
　　　spin, waltz, and sing,
　　'Let the autumn reel
begin'.

Left: Leaf Fall

This watercolour was made by pressing autumn leaves into paint to create abstracted leaf prints and background colour. Opaque gouache was used afterwards, to paint negative shapes between the trees and define them. This was scratched through to create diagonal lines indicative of sweeping movement.

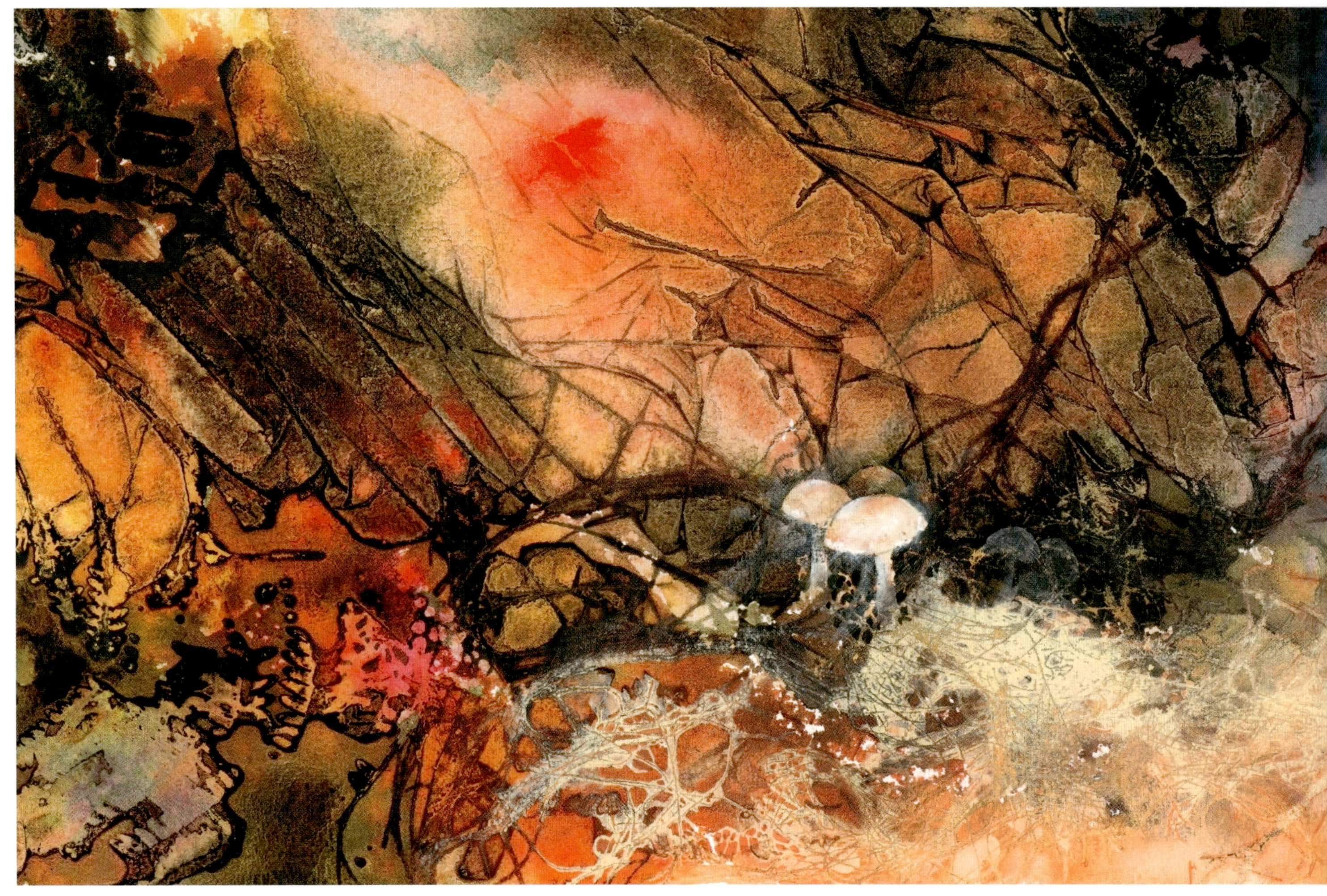

In autumn my eye is drawn to the ground where vibrant leaves nestle with windfallen fruits, seeds, mushrooms and toadstools, acorns, sycamore keys, walnuts and pinecones. Some of these can be used to make ink and the ground where they lie often contains earthy pigment with which to make paint. A simple way of doing this is to use gum arabic or acrylic medium as a binder with finely ground-up clay, earth or soft stone. Water can be added to create your preferred consistency. In *The Woodland Floor* I used ink made from inkcap mushrooms combined with diluted watercolour to create a printed background using materials gathered from site. In *Magic Mushrooms* I incorporated photographic print, which created an interesting tension between my imagined magical memory of the scene and its actuality.

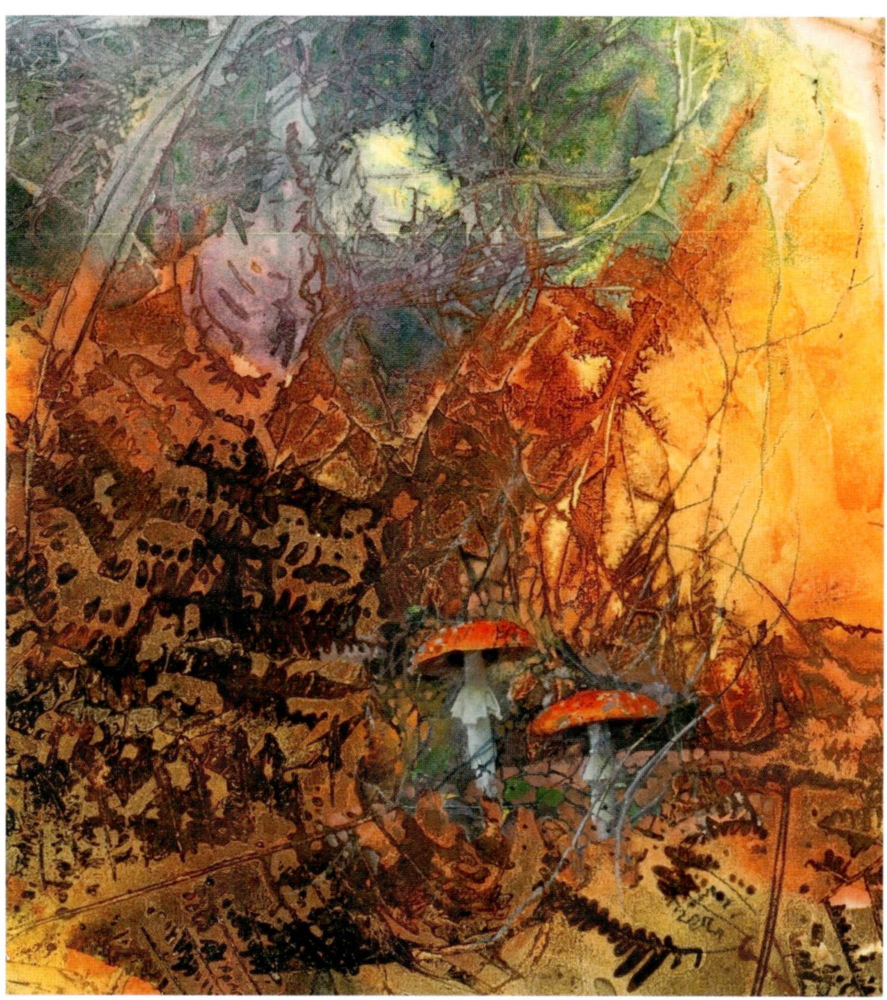

Left: The Woodland Floor

Right: Magic Mushrooms

This autumn has been a fungi festival. Overnight, toadstools and mushrooms appeared throughout the grounds. There were many shapeless brown varieties, but also delicate pale clusters of angel's bonnets. On a stroll in nearby birch woods, I announced, 'My life's ambition is to find fly agaric toadstools!' I had never seen this hallucinogenic, scarlet species with its white markings, that Alice encountered in Wonderland. They are the stuff of fairy tales. Five minutes later the path forked. It climbed steeply uphill to the right, and the left was narrow and overgrown. I turned left and walked a few metres over loops of bramble. My husband was just saying 'I think we should turn back', when my eye was caught by flashes of ladybird red – a whole troupe of perfect fly agarics in all shapes and sizes. Amazing!

Enjoying the wood in autumn and absorbing the rich, rusty hues of bracken, I watched a squirrel collecting cobnuts. I was thinking about how the trees played host to many creatures when I noticed a pheasant perched on a branch. His gold and chestnut mottled breast and tail feathers matched the forest floor, but his teal-blue head coordinated with the cool background of the trees. With no time for a sketch, I photographed him quickly before he could take flight. In my studio I experimented with two different ways of capturing what I had seen.

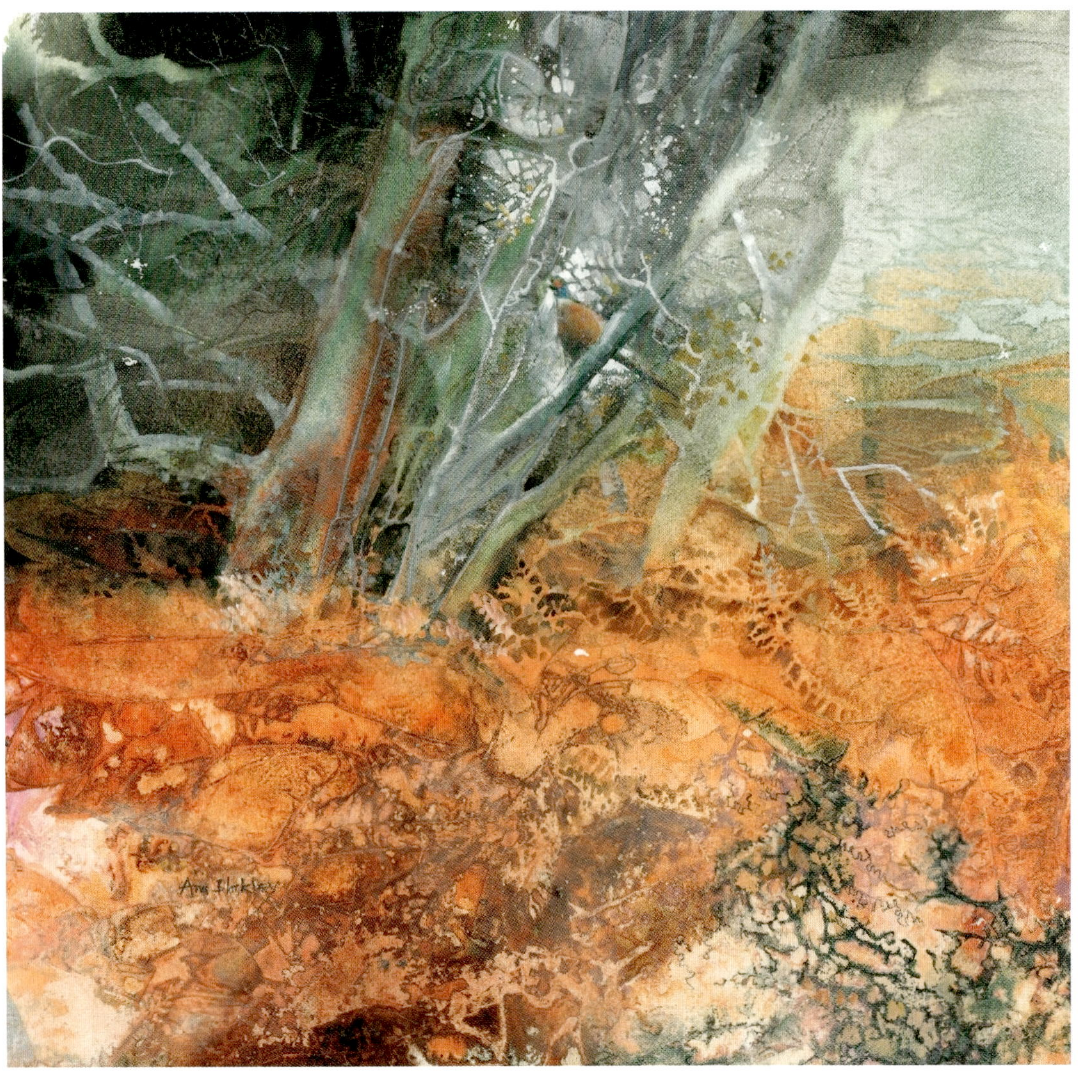

Left: Of Pheasant and Bracken

This first version has a painted foreground, texturized using dead bracken gathered from the scene. The aim was to achieve fern-like shapes. The result was not as pronounced as I had hoped but I still felt I had established a connection with the experience. I collaged a piece of my photographed pheasant onto the background, then painted over to blend it in.

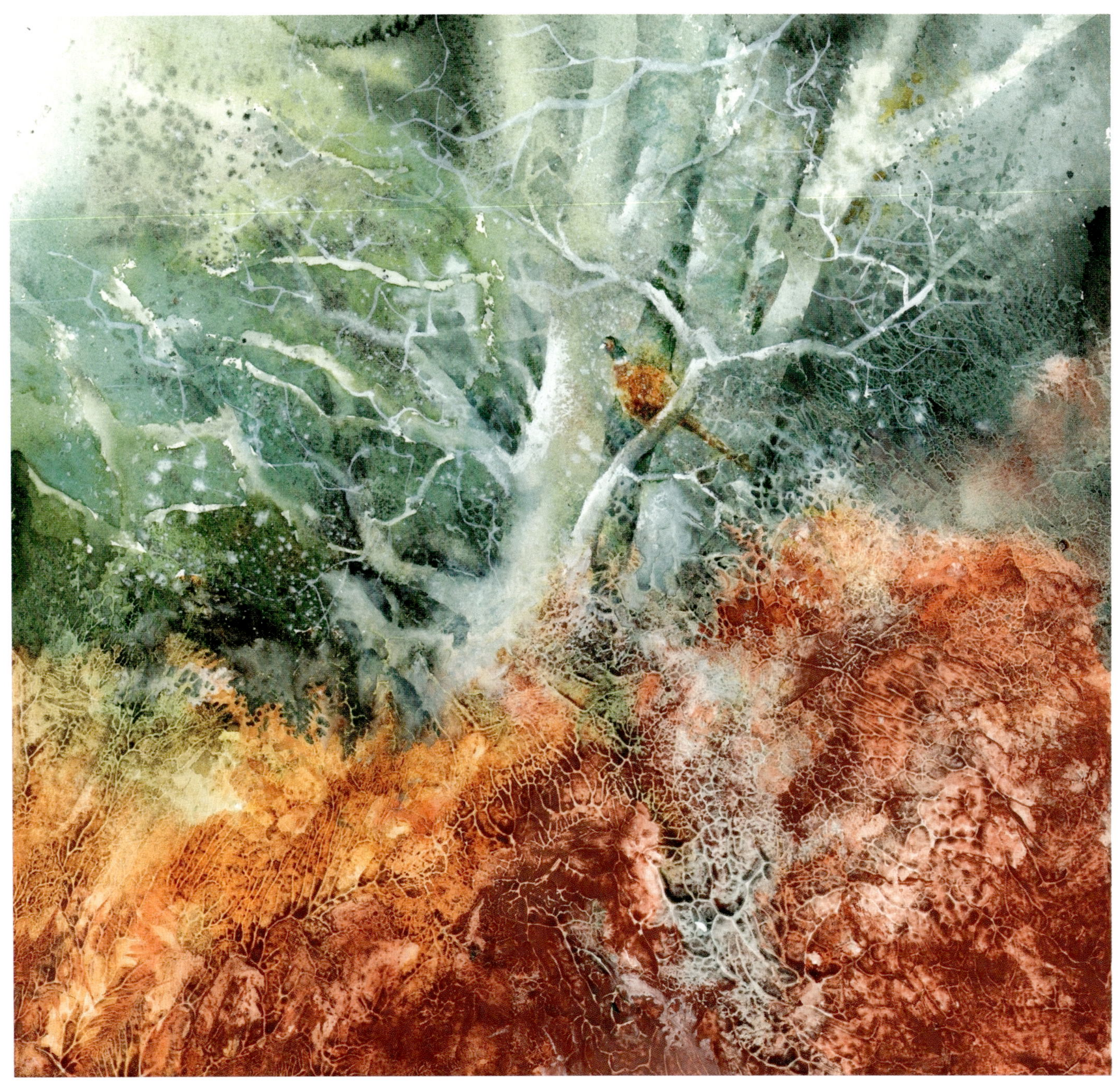

Above: Woodland Watch

I began the second version by preparing handmade watercolour paper with gesso, pulling it into a raised texture as described on page 32. The effect suggested crumpled bracken without being too pedantic. The top half was largely left uncovered so that a layer of watercolour behaved normally there. The bird was also painted in by hand. Thicker colour was applied on top of the dry gesso and some of the pigment wiped away to emphasize the markings.

There are many myths and folklores surrounding brambles. They used to be hung above cattle shed doorways with ivy and rowan which are both protective charms. It is said to be unwise to pick blackberries after Michaelmas Day because that is when the Devil casts his spit on them. Thickets of thorns feature in fables of enchantment, symbolizing the challenges we must navigate to reach our goals.

I adore the old fairy tales and especially the dark, disturbing, 'other-worldly' forest settings where they often take place. They are magical realms of adventure where transformation can happen. In these allegories, woods represent ideas of exploration, potential danger and being lost. It is both frightening and exciting to be lured into the wood where you may encounter either good or evil. There are witches and wolves in the magic realms of Hansel and Gretel and Red Riding Hood. There is threat but also refuge.

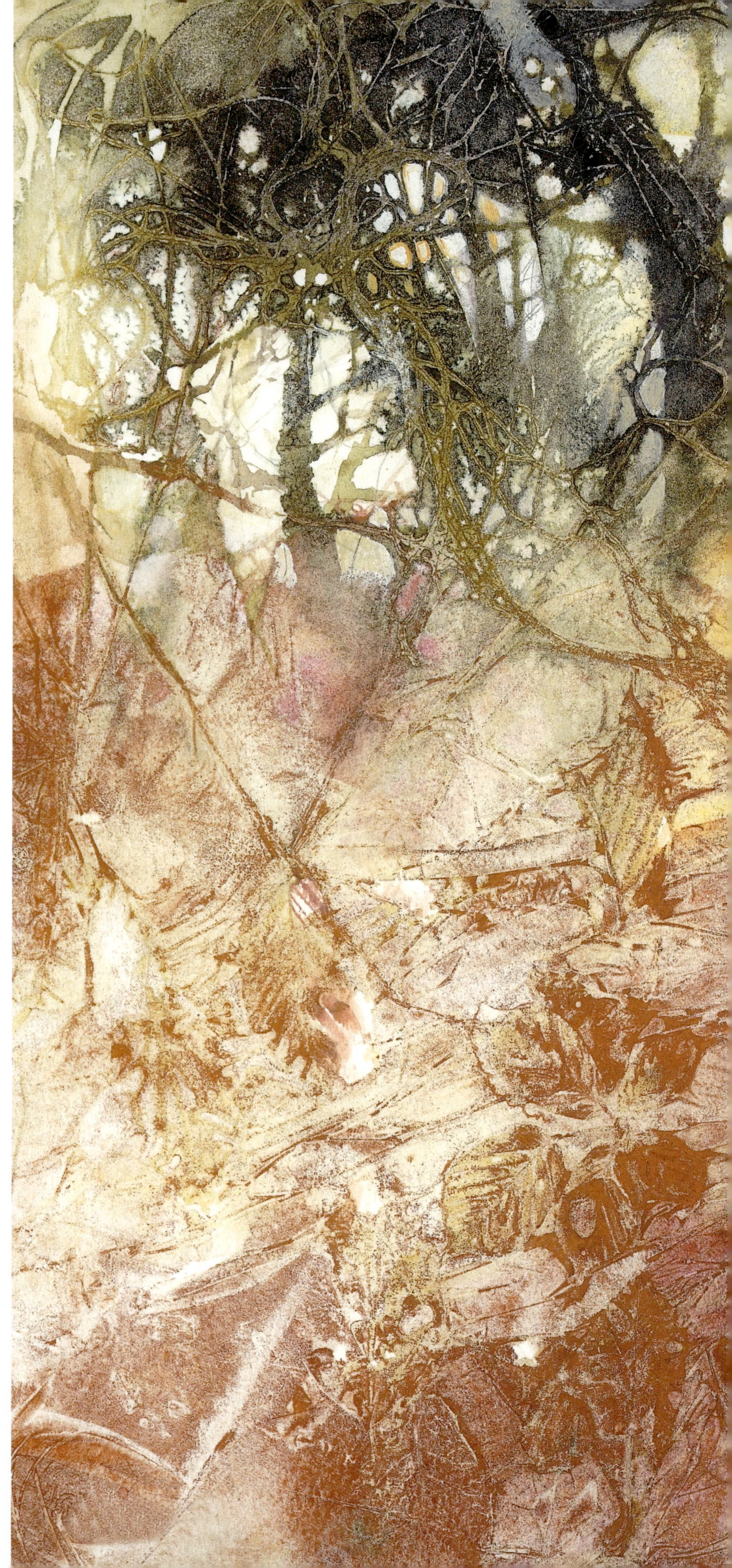

Right: Brambly Hedge

The edges of our woodland garden are a perfect habitat for brambles. As a gardener they annoy me, but as an artist, brambles remain a favourite subject. When portraying nature, it is sometimes a relief to counteract the over-pretty with an edgy, scratchy subject.

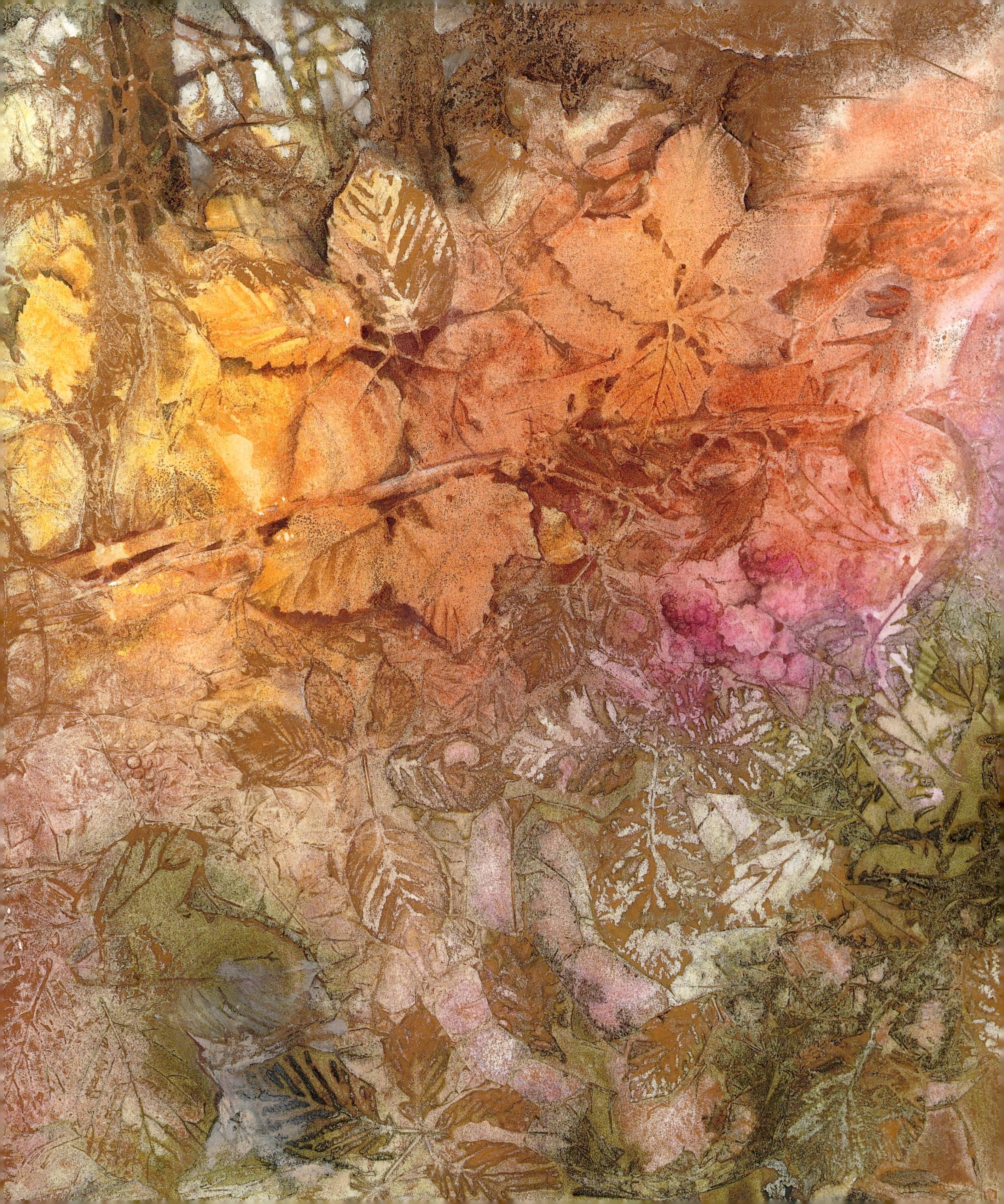

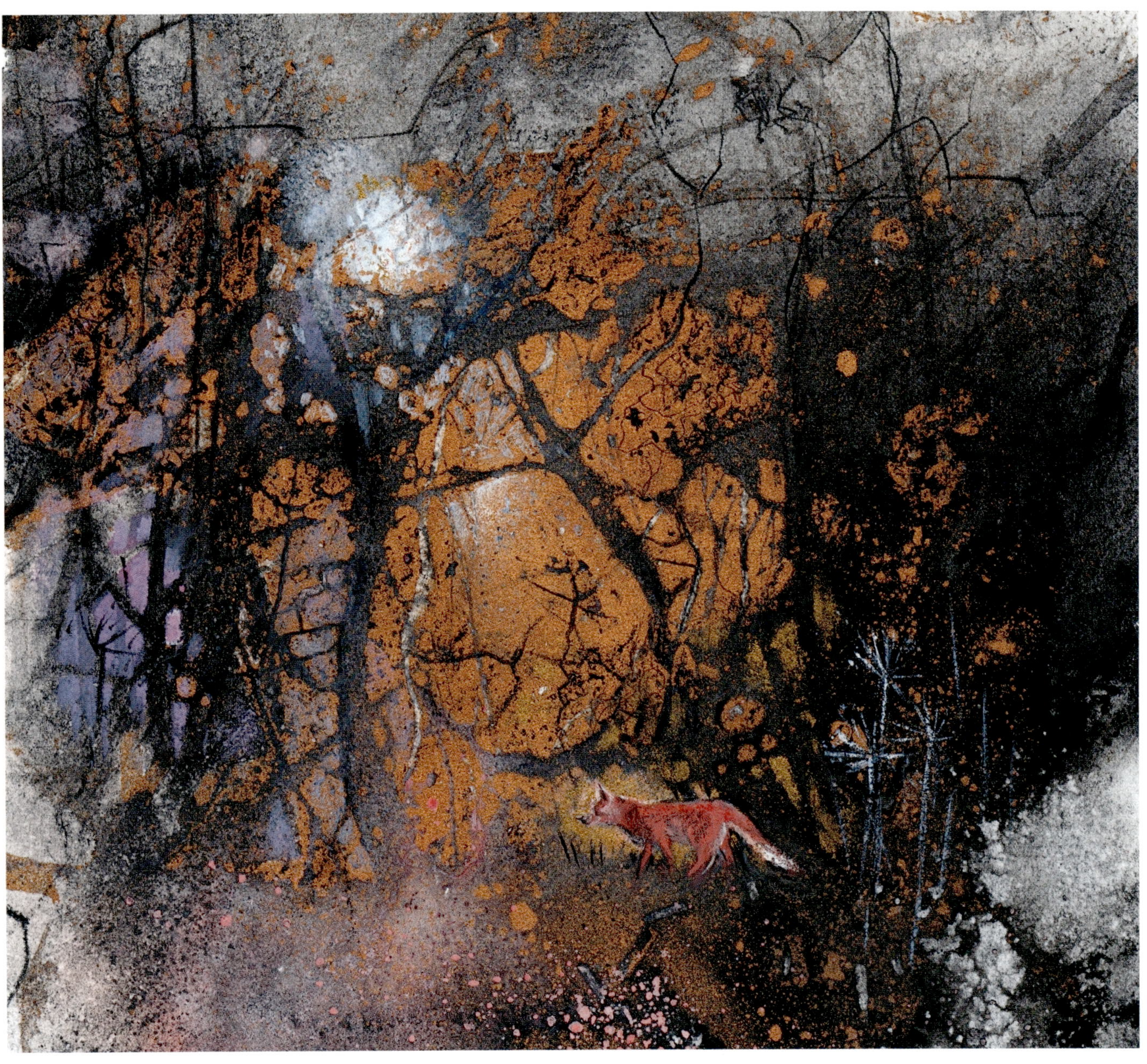

Above: Fox Moon

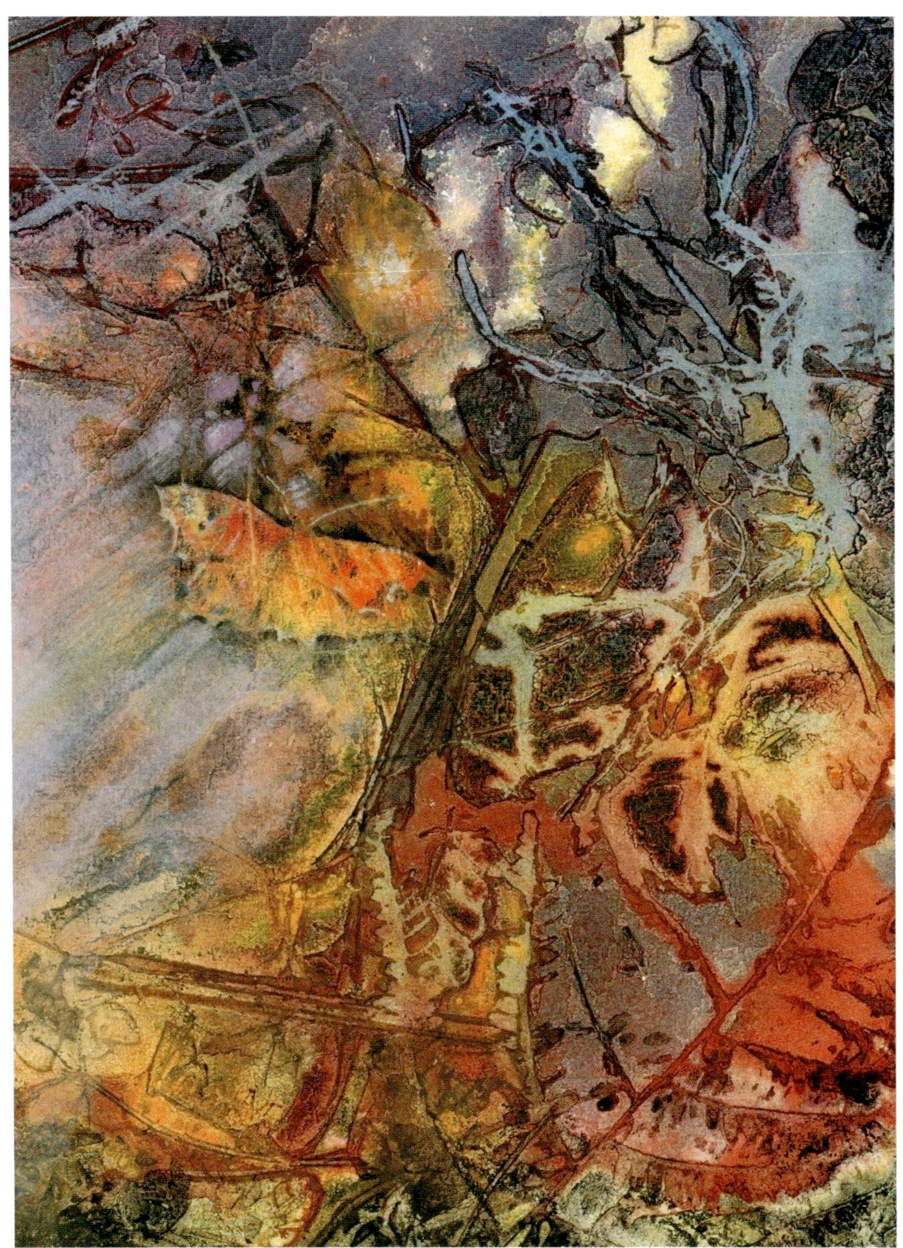

Comma Butterfly

Comma,
leisurely opens and shuts
the pages of her story book,
showing tattooed illustrations –
punctuation marks
on deckle-edged flyleaves –
tales of metamorphosis.

She pauses,
closes her wings
together in prayer –
contemplates and meditates,
hesitates –
then, turns over a new leaf
to quickly flutter by.

Above: Woodland Butterfly

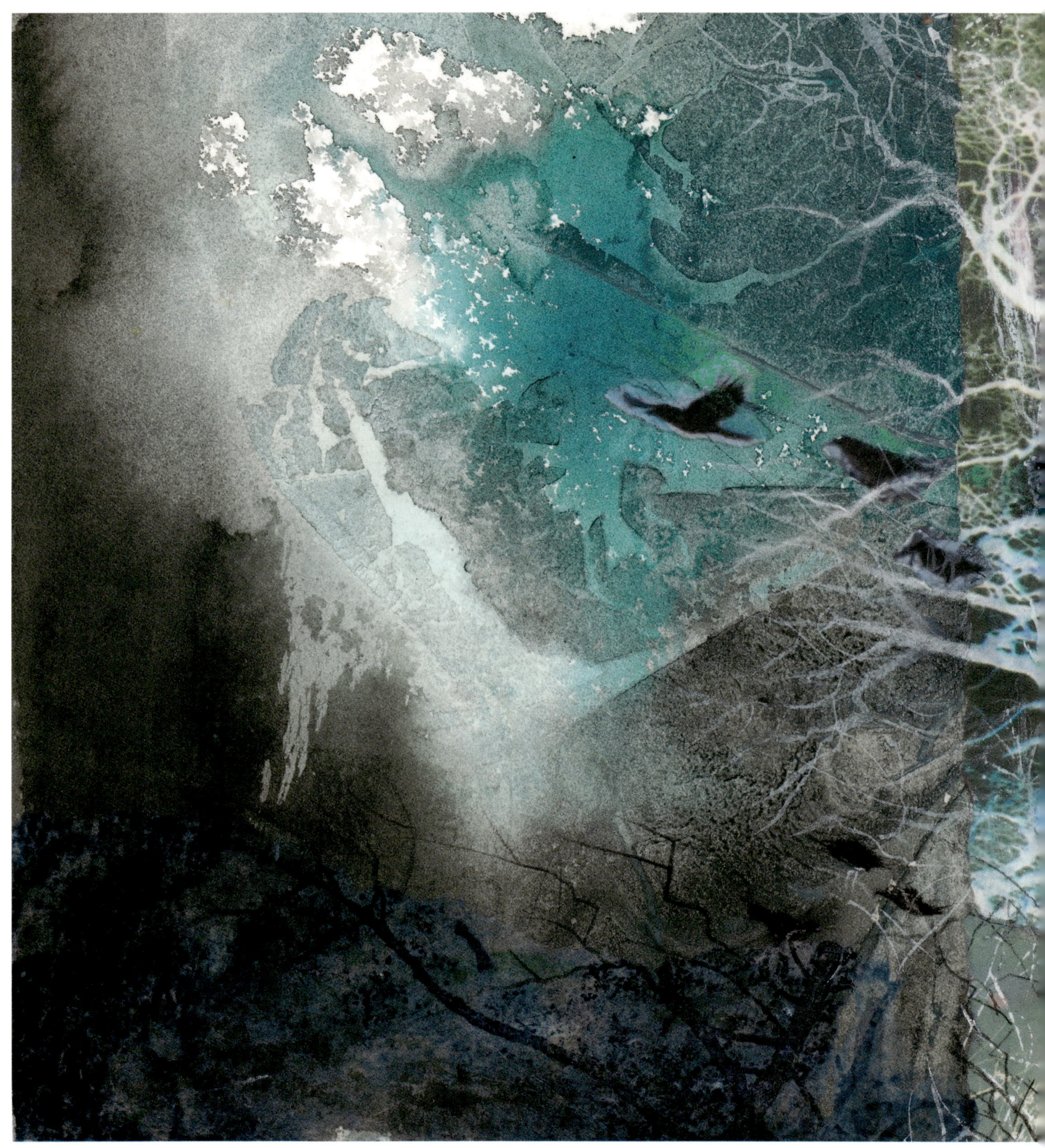

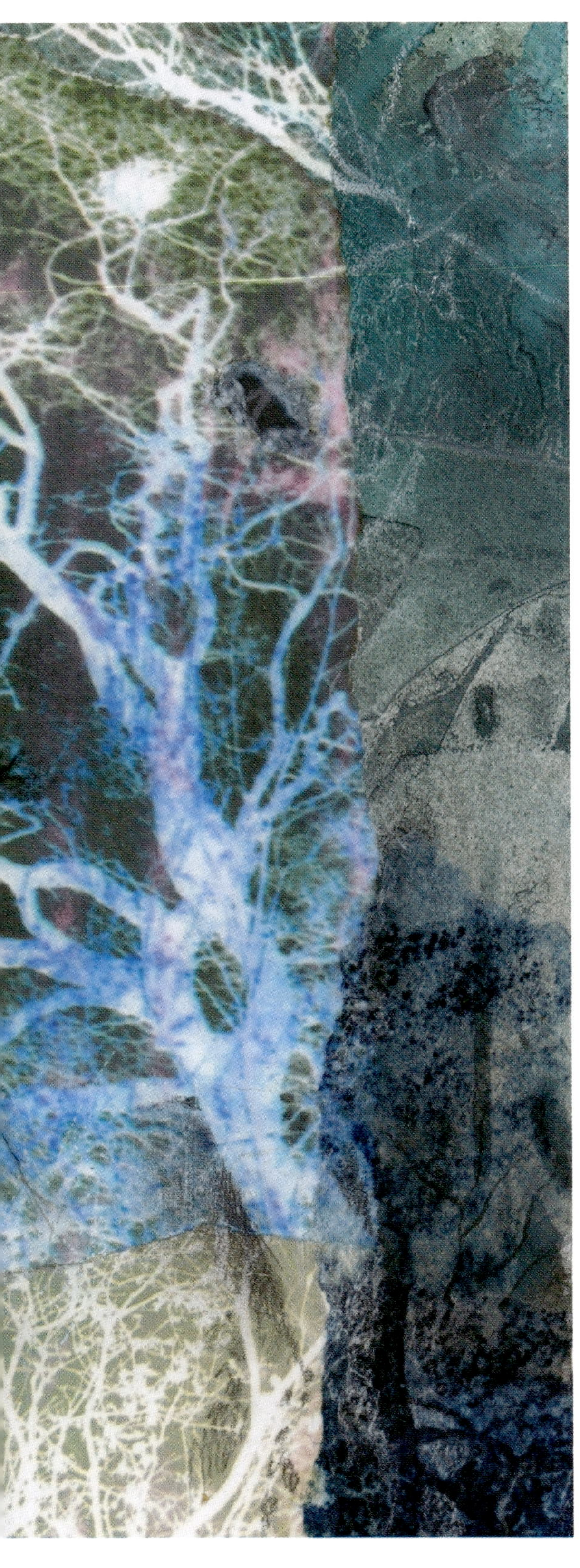

Winter

As Rooks Roost

Tree skeletons shake
the moon-chilled night,
rattling brittle fingers in
the haunted light.
Ashen bones stalk
the woodland edge,
scribing ghostly memoirs
as rooks roost and dream.

Left: As Rooks Roost

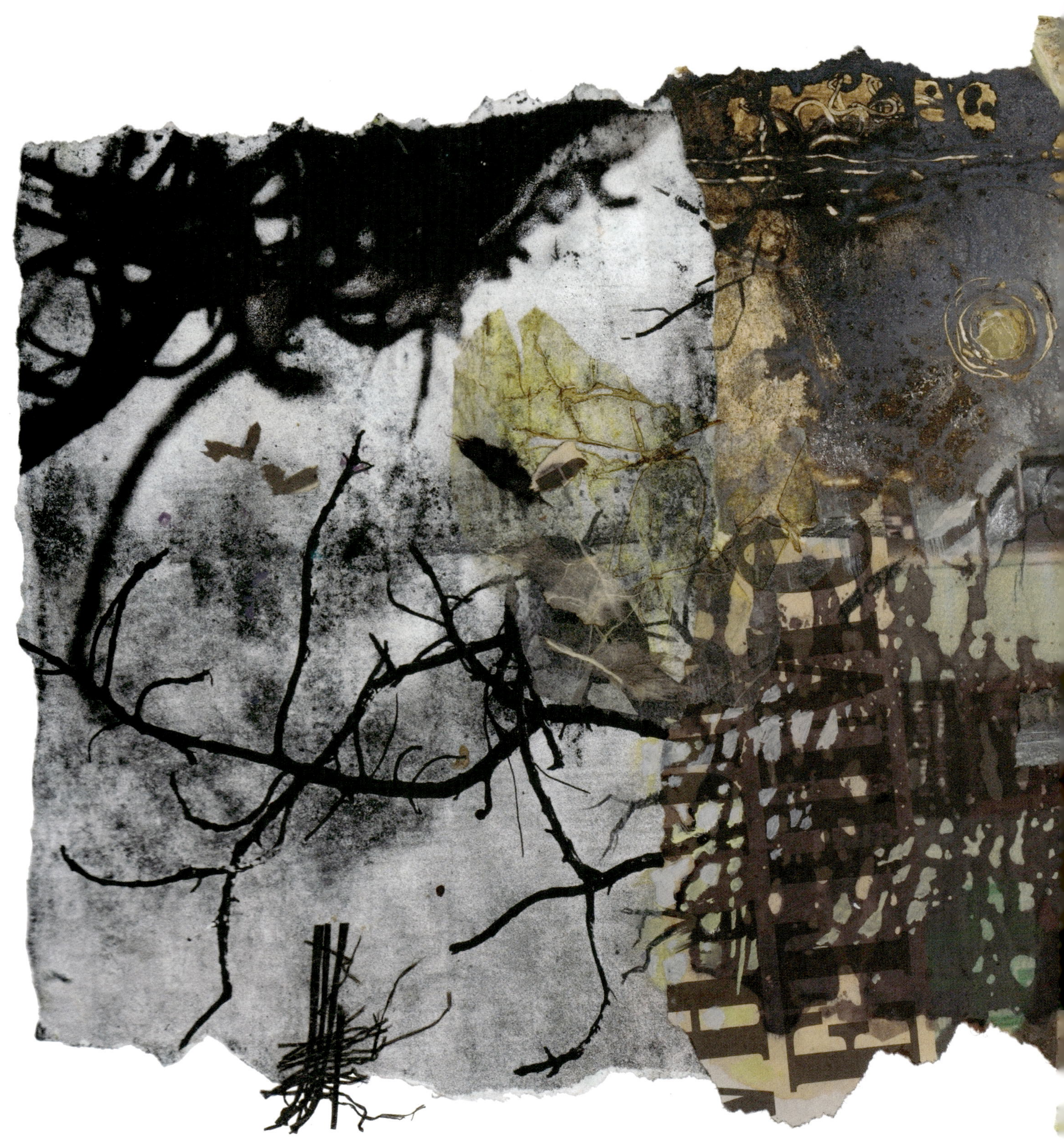

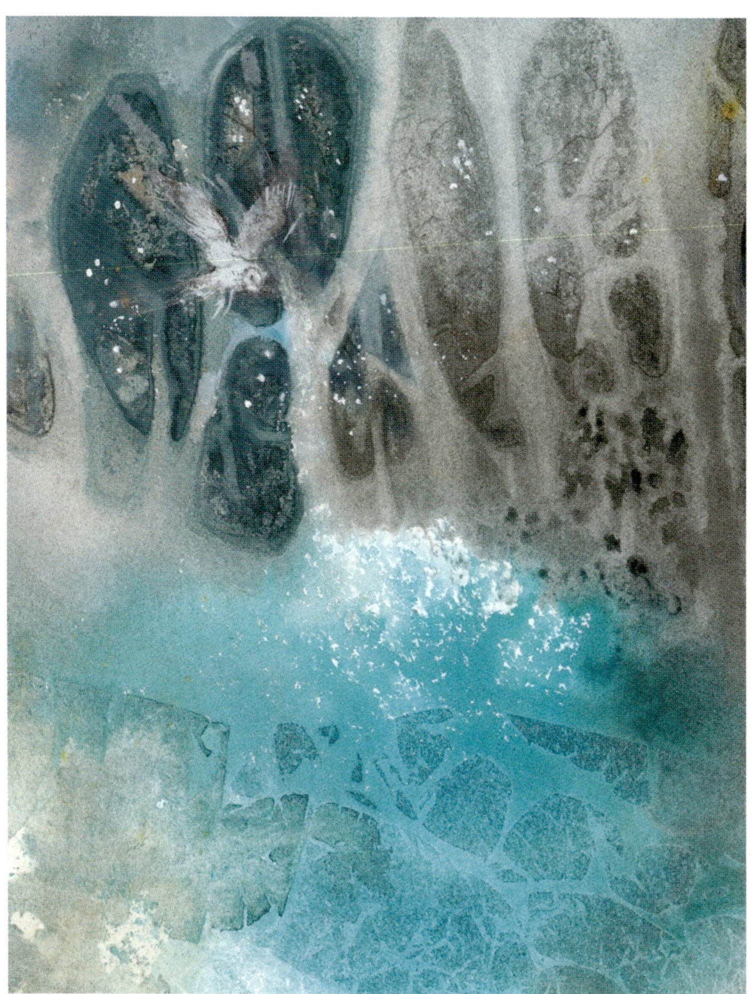

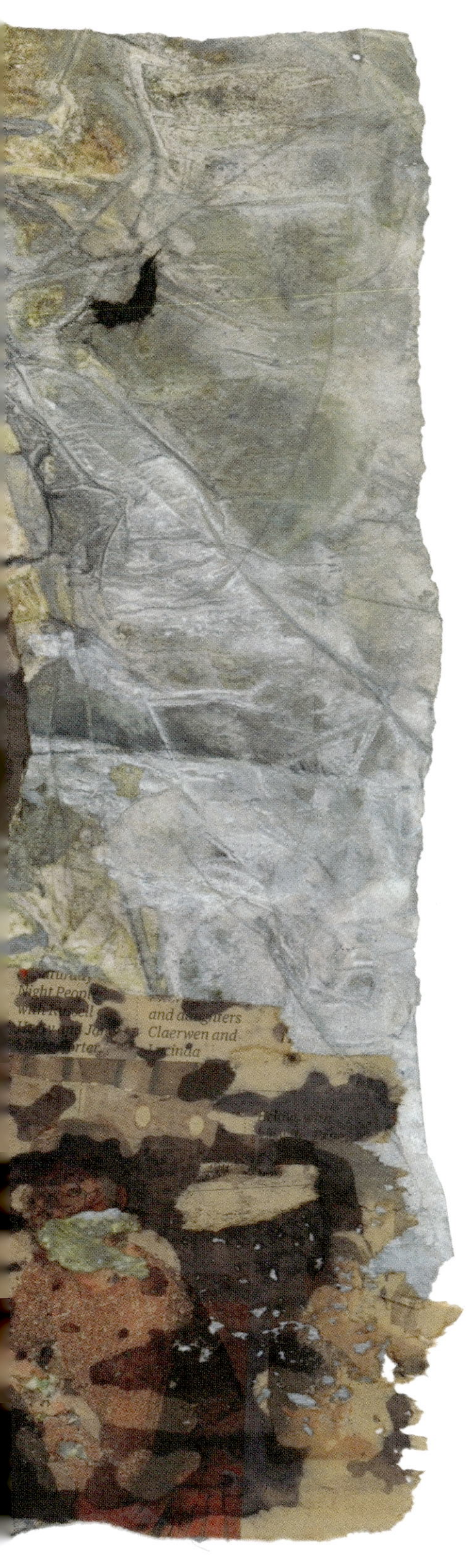

Above: The Night Owl

Watercolour. Looking at tree patterns with an abstract eye.

Left: Shadow Bats

Collage of printed, painted paper, with fabric scraps.

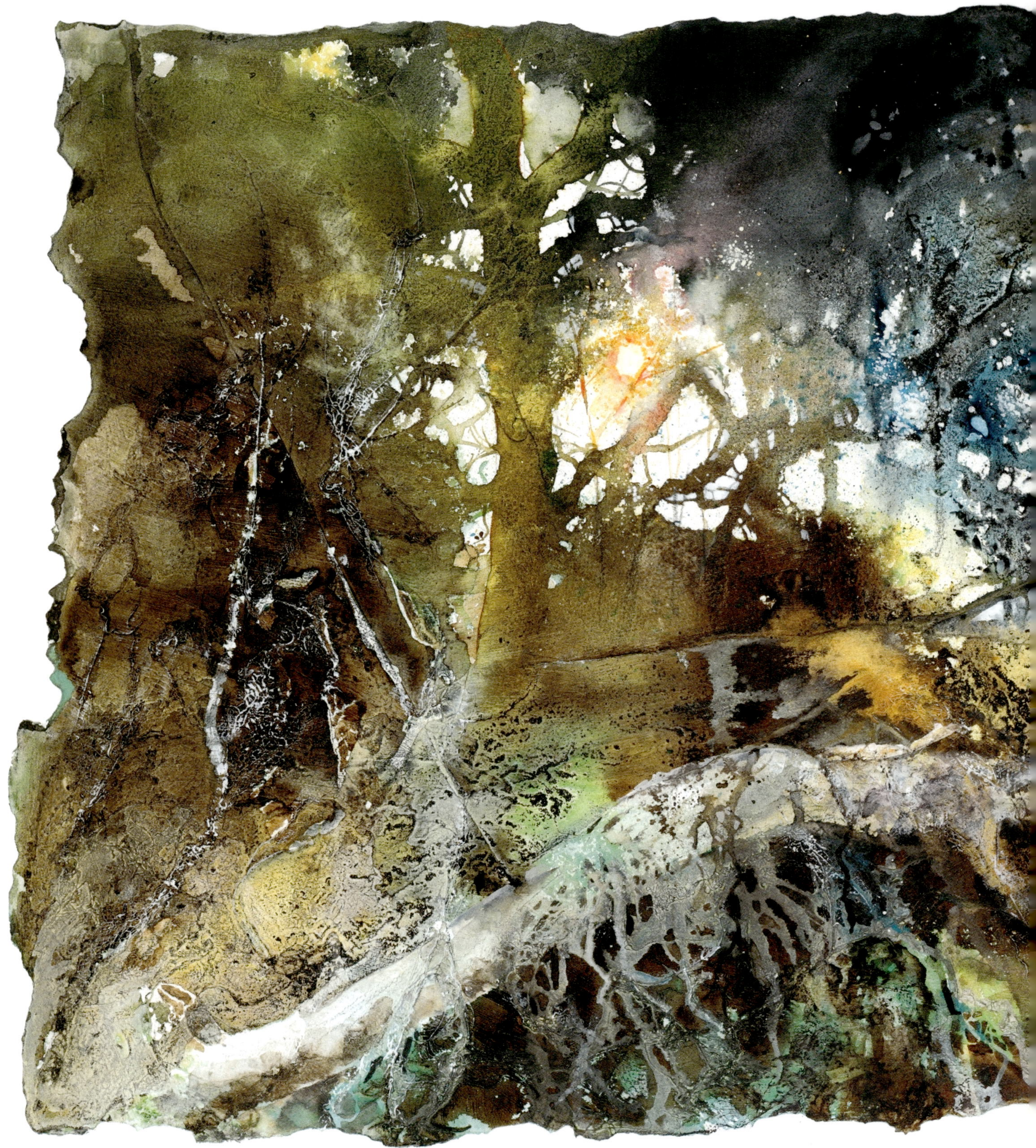

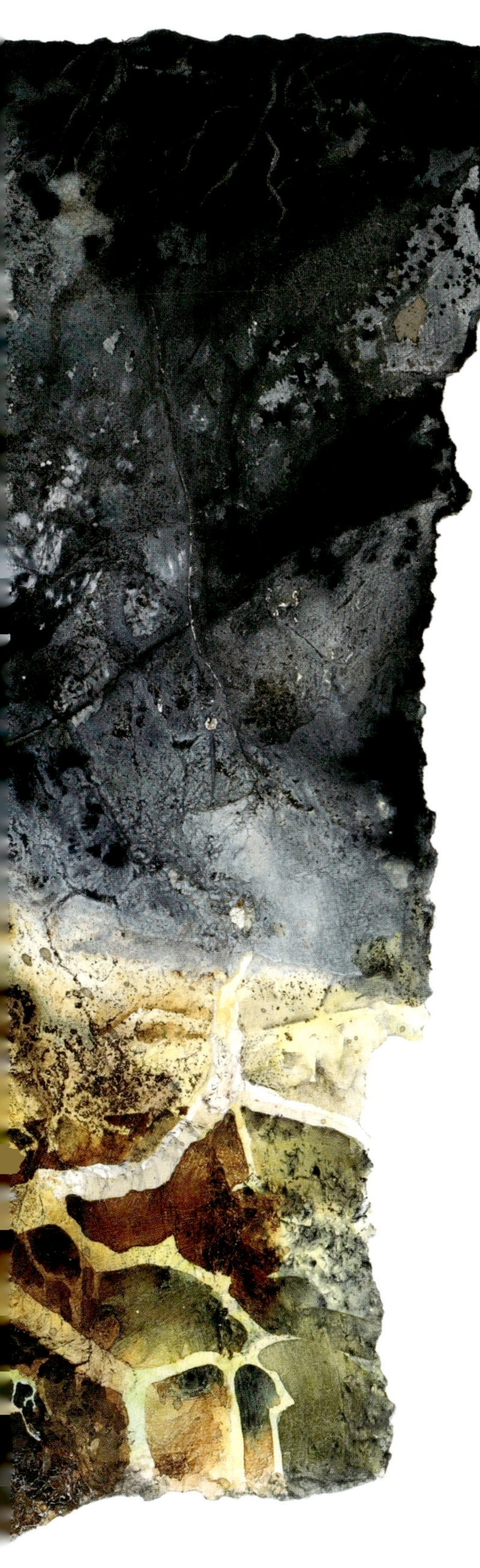

This winter the winds grew loud. Storms raged through our trees, upturning a shallow-rooted cherry and snapping branches off the dying ash. I felt so sad to see these great trees suffer from die-back disease and to know that they will need felling before they too fall over. But it was not long before my artist's eye moved into focus. Then I saw the amazing linear patterns the branches made and how tall trunks, usually seen upright, take on different forms in landscape pose. To emphasize the theme of breakage, I assembled pieces from an old watercolour made on paper into a new, irregular shape which I covered with gesso, embedding torn and shredded fabric pieces into this surface. It was my tiny tribute to the trees to make full use of the paper that it provides and recycle when possible and appropriate. Paint, ink and granulation medium were slashed on, allowing them to dribble and move, making earthy trails through the paint. The fallen tree was left bleached and pale, like a ghostly premonition for those still standing.

Left: Storm Tree

We compost and shred our garden waste as far as possible to avoid pollution, but in our neglected property, we have had to have some bonfires and I must confess I find them therapeutic. One evening, we lit a fire in our woodland clearing well away from the trees and sat to watch the flickers of light and wreaths of smoke curl into the air, weaving stories through the dark sky. I painted a series of pictures but, in spite of the poetry of the scene, the results were prosaic and overly detailed. My paintings were illustrations, too 'real' and far removed from the raw acrid smells, stinging eyes and burnt fingers of the experience. I tried loosening them with stubs of burnt, charcoaled sticks rescued from the fire, but the marks just looked dirty. I realized that the manufactured watercolour paper I had used was too bland for this job and instead located a textured piece of paper that I had made myself a long time ago. The paint fell into its irregular surface to create a shimmering backdrop around a small area of fire. I added a gouache trail of smoke and burnt around the edges – just because it felt right and because I could.

Right: Bonfire in the Wood

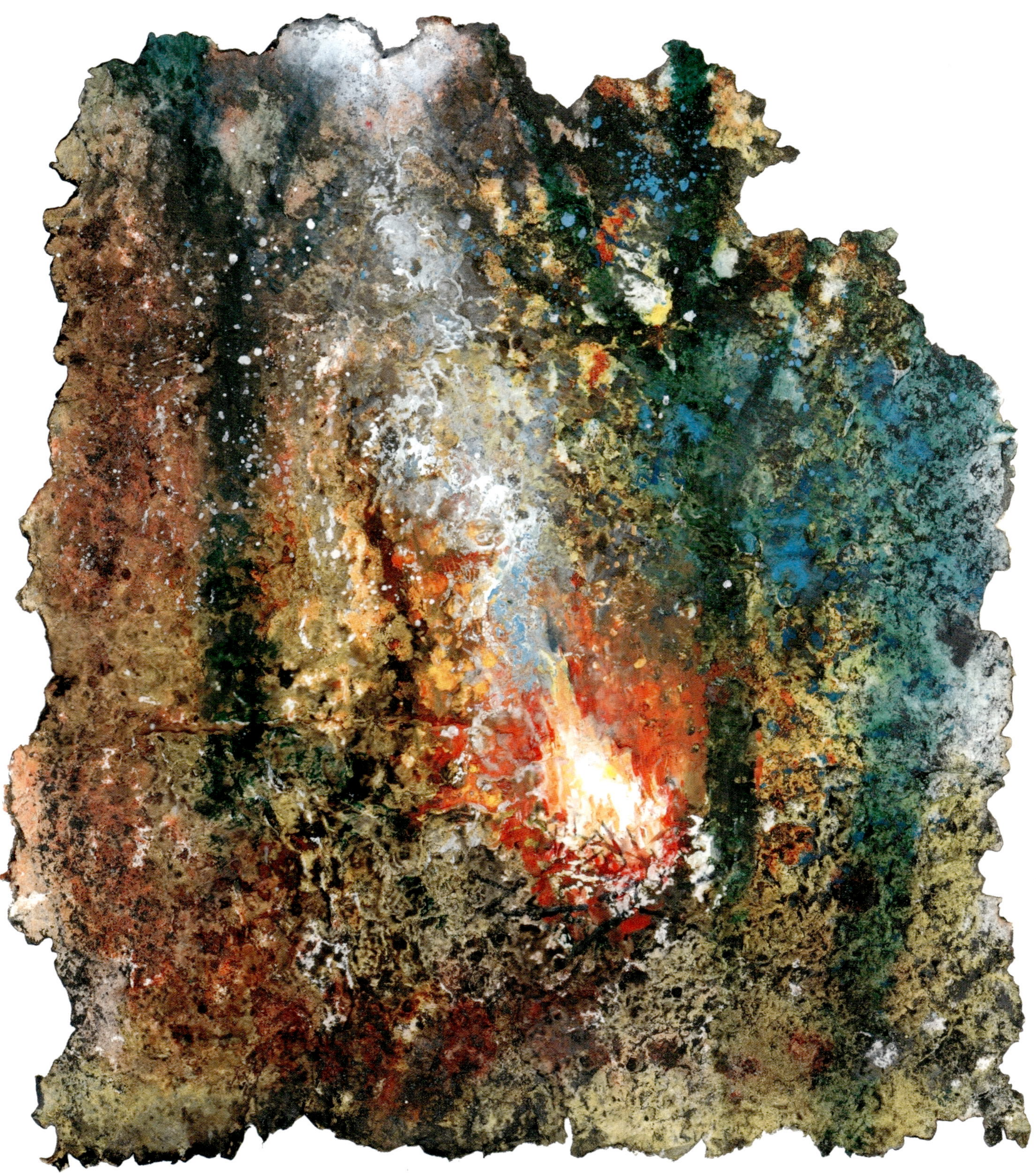

A great joy of my year has been a discovery of ceramics. This is something I had never considered doing, and if asked would dismiss the thought with, 'I don't work in three dimensions.' Following a neighbourly invitation to share a kiln and join a small untutored pottery group, I found myself in front of a lump of brown clay thinking, 'What on earth do I do with this?' I began to play, without pressure, expectation or fear, and found that I loved it! I decided to present my unsuspecting family with bowls of varied design for Christmas. It has taken me back to my childhood when I was continually 'making' in ways that were not labelled craft, art, textile or anything other than the simple pleasure of using materials to make gifts. I felt as if I had gone full circle. Eventually, I found myself carving out a bowl based on ivy leaves, similar in some ways to a paper version that I had collaged in my studio.

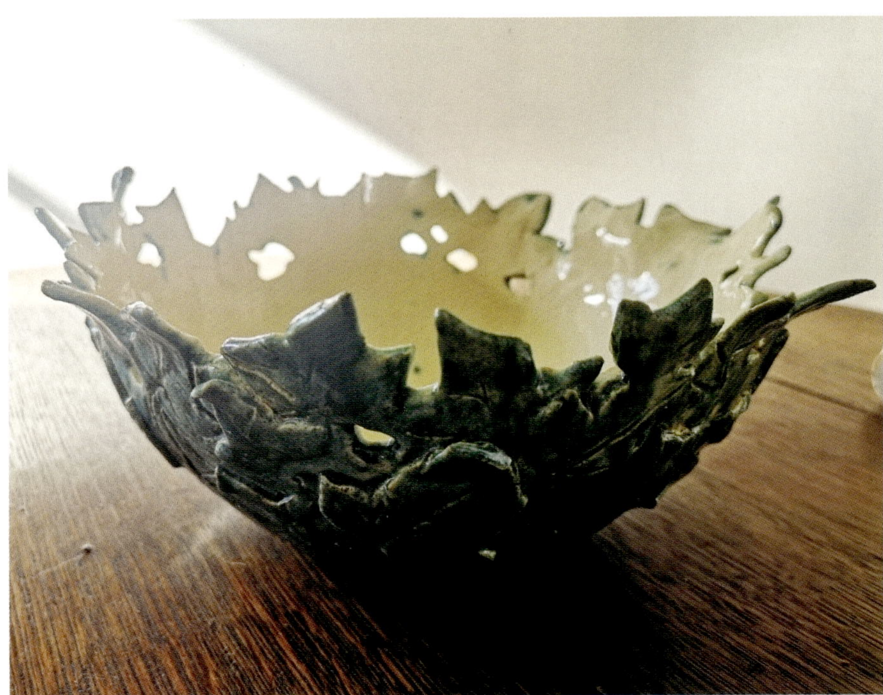

Left: Ivy bowl.

I found learning a totally new art form very difficult and frustrating. This and my new poetry writing sometimes felt like the struggle I was having in our woodland garden. Although full of beauty and delight, nature can also be unforgiving. Ivy that strangles the tree, brambles and nettles that fight, are an essential part of the ecosystem, just as being creative can be a battle. But you need to kick aside these limiting hurdles and rise to the challenge – grasp the nettle to reach that sunlit clearing in the wood.

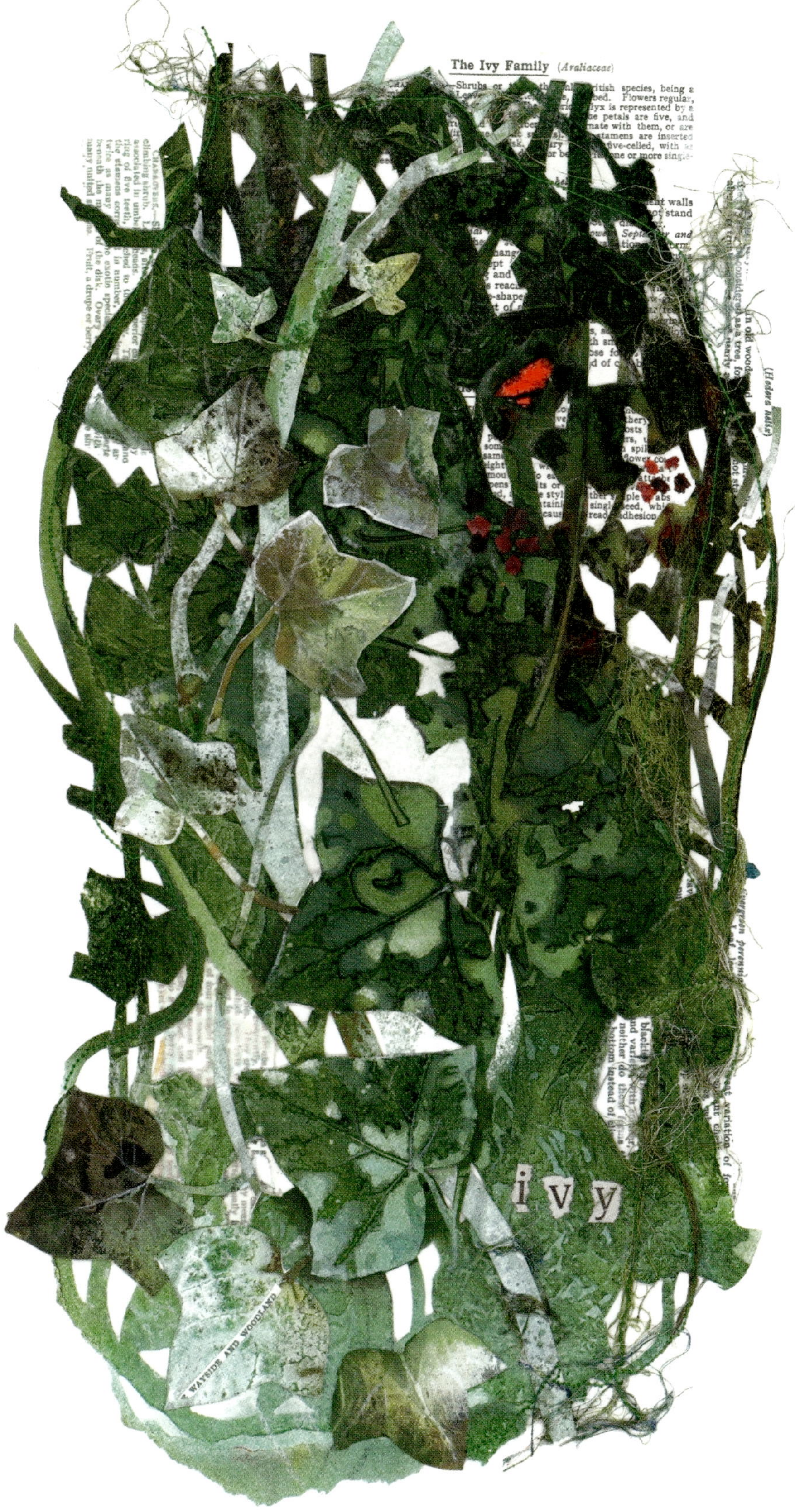

Right: Hedera Helix

Collage with cutwork watercolour, ivy prints and text.

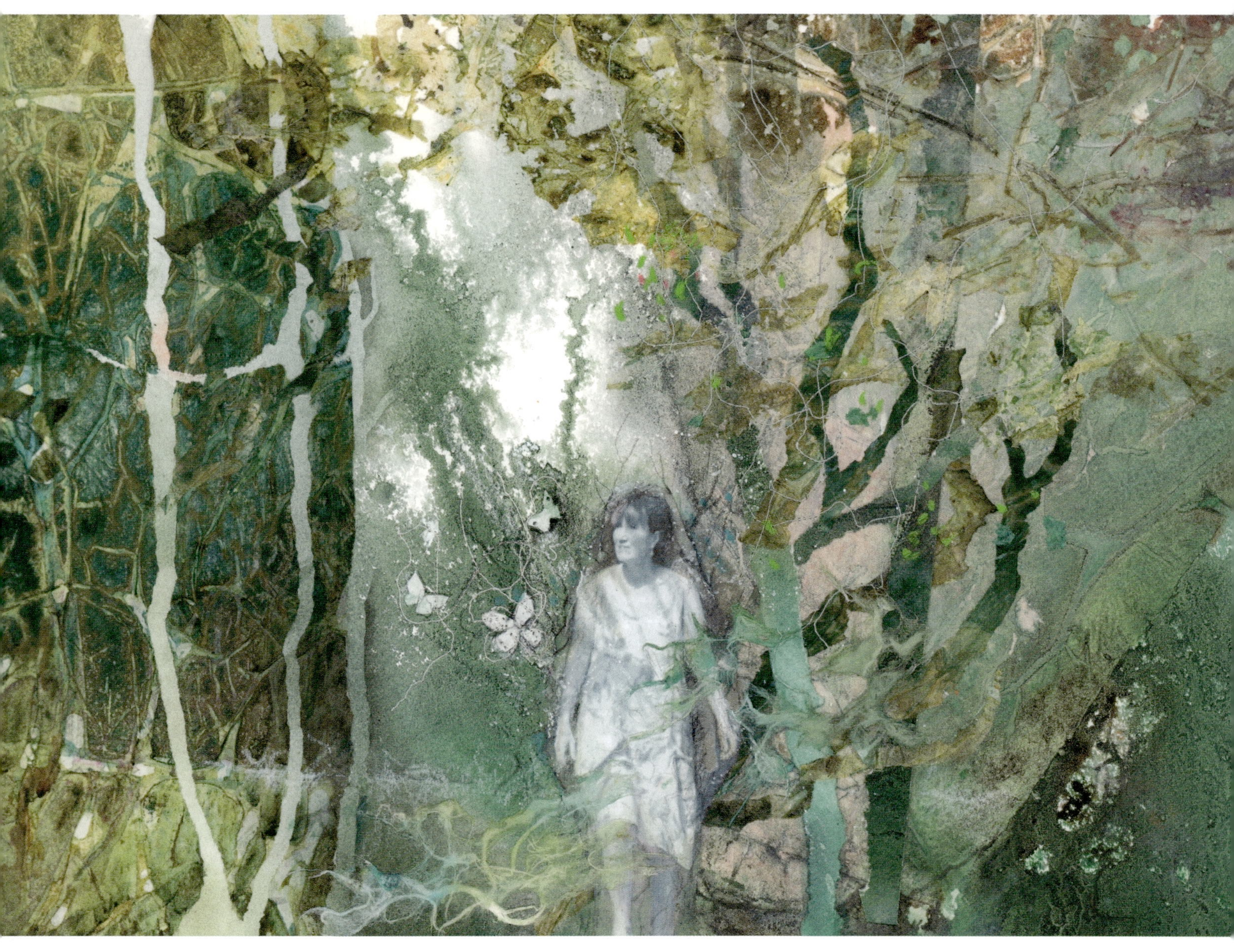

Above: As I Walked Out

Self-portrait in watercolour, photographic and assorted collage, and stitch.

Woodland Ballad

As I walked out one primrose dawn,
through campion and orchids bright,
between green trees, I thought I saw
a dreamlike ghostly sight.
I ran away from this nature queen
before she cast her woodland spell,
and I hid alone in my house of brick
in fear and without farewell.

But the faery gipsy of the wood
sang with the cuckoo calling,
as birds and butterflies took flight,
like cherry blossom falling.
She waltzed with moths from night 'til dawn
singing warning songs of sorrow,
'Be careful – or this verdant copse
will not be here tomorrow.'

A rusted fox began his prowl,
quintets of geese flew past grey cloud,
the wind's croon grew to plaintive howl,
whilst crows shrieked high and loud.
Autumnal salty mists swirled through
the smoky mystic wood.
Great oaks cast acorns from their bough
to where Mother Nature stood.

This lady of the wood she sighed
and shook her hair of leaves.
They drifted to the woodland floor
and began to curl and freeze.

She lay down on this oak leaf bed,
on frosted graphite ground,
and with icy stars above her head,
she waited to be found.

The charcoal smudge of winter spread.
The trees were bare and shivered,
but just as it felt the earth was dead,
brave silver snowdrops quivered.
As I walked out one primrose day
I saw a papery mound of leaves,
but these were quickly brushed aside
by a sudden eerie breeze.

And underneath the leaves I found
a muddy woodland maid of earth,
sleeping deeply without sound,
as spring began its birth.
Her hair was moss and grassy frond,
her limbs were bough and root.
And from her eyes two acorns grew –
new leaves began to shoot.

These saplings grew to great oaks tall.
They weathered pain and storm.
And the earthy mother smiled to know
that they were safe and warm.
As I walked out one primrose eve,
I stepped with mindful leisure,
to greet and hear; respect and see
each painted woodland treasure.

Afterword

There is another story behind my personal project. I decided to share it with you.

When the doctor told me not to make commitments for more than three months at a time, I was shocked. My world as an artist with its exhibitions and projects requires long-term planning. Instantly, I felt my life had been noosed into circles of rope that might shrink or grow at the drop of a pill. What was I to do? We had only just moved to begin a new life; to start our great adventure. I had dragged my husband, in the middle of a pandemic, to live in a house that needed rebuilding, with a neglected garden, and suddenly we were presented with a potentially short future. What was I to do next?

I swam around my goldfish bowl of misery, willing a creative glimmer to evolve from the swampy waters. I decided to discard the word 'next' and think in terms of 'now'. I could twist the consultant's cautious advice about limited time into a more motivating positive. Every three months is a new season. My paintings revolve around nature and the turning of the year. What if I began a project where I concentrated on each precious day, painting our wilderness of woodland garden with its trees, flowers and creatures? I could focus on how lucky we are to have all this. And by appreciating its magic, with a focus on 'today', I would count how many times I could navigate the moons of the year.

As soon as I made this decision the telephone rang. 'Ann – would you like to do an art book about trees or woodlands?' I explained the situation to my publisher, who agreed to support me by being flexible – that I could include my (still unwritten) poems and project. It was a synchronistic gift – permission to do whatever I wished. The book would be called *Poetic Woods* and as I write these words, statistics indicate that I will be here to celebrate its publication. None of us know how our lives will twist and turn but I do know that we need to grab and cherish every moment. So, don't wait for the phone to ring, or to be given permission – write poems, paint the woods, connect with your loved ones, dance and sing. Not next week, but now.

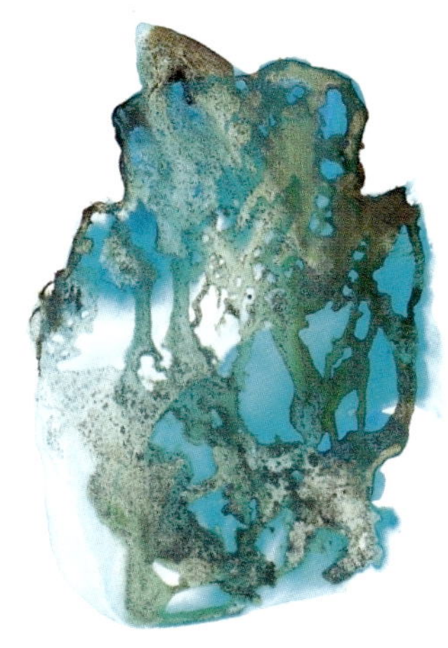

She said –
we cannot know when later is.
She said –
we do not know what is next.
But I know there is Now
in the apple blossom snow.
And that hope can seed
the meadow's
clock.

Index